SEMEIA 65

ORALITY AND TEXTUALITY IN EARLY CHRISTIAN LITERATURE

Editor: Joanna Dewey
Board Editor: Elizabeth Struthers Malbon

SEMEIA 65

Copyright © 1995 by the Society of Biblical Literature

All rights reserved. No part of this work may be reproduced or transmitted in any form or by any means, electronic or mechanical, including photocopying and recording, or by means of any information storage or retrieval system, except as may be expressly permitted by the 1976 Copyright Act or in writing from the publisher. Requests for permission should be addressed in writing to the Rights and Permissions Office, Society of Biblical Literature, 825 Houston Mill Road, Atlanta, GA 30329, USA.

ISSN 0095-571X
ISBN 1-58983-130-6

Printed in the United States of America
on acid-free paper

CONTENTS

Contributors to this Issue v

Introduction
    Joanna Dewey 1

I. CHRISTIANITY'S PLACE IN THE ANCIENT ORAL–LITERATE MEDIA WORLD: AN OVERVIEW

1. Jesus of Nazareth and the Watershed of Ancient Orality and Literacy
    Thomas E. Boomershine 7

2. Textuality in an Oral Culture: a Survey of the Pauline Traditions
    Joanna Dewey 37

3. Figuring Early Rabbinic Literary Culture: Thoughts Occasioned by Boomershine and J. Dewey
    Martin S. Jaffee 67

4. Oral, Rhetorical, and Literary Cultures: A Response
    Vernon K. Robbins 75

II. PAUL AND PERFORMANCE: SPECIFIC TEXTS

5. Pauline Voice and Presence as Strategic Communication
    Richard F. Ward 95

6. A Re–Hearing of Romans 10:1–15
    Arthur J. Dewey 109

7. Performance, Politics, and Power: A Response
    Antoinette Clark Wire 129

III. RECONSTRUCTING JESUS; UNDERSTANDING MEDIA: THEORETICAL ISSUES

8. Jesus and Tradition: Words in Time, Words in Space
   Werner H. Kelber 139

9. Words in Tradition, Words in Text: A Response
   John Miles Foley 169

10. Blowing in the Wind: A Response
    Bernard Brandon Scott 181

11. Modalities of Communication, Cognition, and Physiology of Perception: Orality, Rhetoric, and Scribality
    Werner H. Kelber 193

CONTRIBUTORS TO THIS ISSUE

Thomas E. Boomershine
   United Theological Seminary
   Dayton, OH 45406

Arthur J. Dewey
   Department of Theology
   Xavier University
   Cincinnati, OH 45207

Joanna Dewey
   Episcopal Divinity School
   Cambridge, MA 02138

John Miles Foley
   Center for Studies in Oral Tradition
   University of Missouri
   Columbia, MO 65211

Martin S. Jaffee
   Comparative Religion Program
   University of Washington
   Seattle, WA 98195

Werner H. Kelber
   Department of Religious Studies
   Rice University
   Houston, TX 77251

Vernon K. Robbins
   Department of Religion
   Emory University
   Atlanta, GA 30322

Bernard Brandon Scott
   Phillips Graduate Seminary
   Tulsa, OK 74104

Richard F. Ward
   Yale Divinity School
   New Haven, CT 06511

Antoinette Clark Wire
   San Francisco Theological
   Seminary
   San Anselmo, CA 94960

INTRODUCTION

Joanna Dewey

THIS VOLUME IS THE SECOND ISSUE of *Semeia* devoted to the work of the Bible in Ancient and Modern Media Group of the Society of Biblical Literature (see Silberman). All the authors and most of the respondents in the volume have been substantially involved in the meetings of this group. The two papers of Part II on Paul (Ward, A. Dewey) were first presented at a 1990 meeting of the Group. The papers and responses of Part III (Kelber, Foley, Scott) grew out of a 1991 session of the Group on *"The Oral and Written Gospel* Revisited," looking back on Kelber's seminal book. The essays of Part I, by the past and the present chairs of the Group, grew out of presentations in other settings (Boomershine's at a conference on "Jesus as Communicator" sponsored by the Gregorian University in Cavaletti, Italy, 1991; J. Dewey's at the 1992 annual meeting of the Catholic Biblical Association).

It is the conviction of the Bible in Ancient and Modern Media Group that the media system in which a work is created or used affects all aspects of the production and reception of the work. The manuscript media world of antiquity, with its high degrees of aurality and orality, functioned very differently from our modern print media system. In its work, the Group explores the implications of media systems for understanding early Christianity. Although building on ten years of work within the biblical field and much more in other disciplines, this investigation remains a difficult task for two reasons. First, our understandings and procedures based on our experience of print culture are so pervasive and so basic to us that they often function as unquestioned givens rather than as the culturally dependent and changing phenomena they are. It is difficult to escape our own print mentality. For example, even my reference above to a "work" as "created or used" suggests the understanding of a "work" as an original, singular document which is first created or produced and only then used or received. While such an understanding is a given in the print medium, it is highly problematic in a manuscript medium and entirely false in an oral medium. Second, the task is difficult because the ancient media world was as much a given for its contemporaries as ours is for us, so that our ancient texts assume rather than describe the impact of their media on their formation and use, and because, insofar as the ancient media world was oral, it has left us very few clues at all as to how it functioned. Nevertheless, the task of understanding Christianity in terms of its own media environment is worthwhile, indeed essential, for our interpretive enterprise.

The essays in this volume are divided into three parts. Part I contains two complementary overviews of the interaction of orality and literacy in early Christianity. These articles constitute a good introduction for those new to media studies. Thomas E. Boomershine describes the development of literacy and its incorporation into ancient communications systems; I give an overview of how literacy was used, who was literate, and the means of oral and literate communication. Boomershine shows development over time; I show a cross-section at one point of time. In addition, we present radically different hypotheses of Christianity's place in the ancient oral-literate media world. While we both understand first-century media as a complex interaction of oral and written communications, Boomershine stresses the literate side, arguing that "Jesus developed a mode of thought and communication that was a source for the distinctive ways in which early Christianity reshaped ancient Judaism in the culture of literacy." On the other hand, I stress the oral side, arguing that first-century Christianity "was an oral phenomenon in a predominately oral culture," using the Pauline traditions for illustration. The two responses in Part I both critique the two articles and extend the discussion based on each respondent's expertise. Martin S. Jaffee enriches the discussion out of his knowledge of early rabbinic culture, offering a critique of the Christian bias of Boomershine's and my work as well as a valuable discussion of the role of orality in early rabbinism. Working from his knowledge of ancient rhetorical culture, Vernon K. Robbins offers some helpful taxonomies of media cultures and of the interaction of orality and scribality in New Testament texts.

Part II applies our knowledge of the ancient media world to the understanding of specific Pauline texts, 2 Corinthians 10–13 and Romans 10:1–15. Richard F. Ward, a practitioner of performance studies rather than biblical studies, investigates the role of performance in the reception of Paul's letters. He argues that the *performance* of 2 Corinthians 10–13 to the Corinthian community established a powerful presence, supporting Paul's apostolic authority in the community. Arthur J. Dewey studies Paul's use of a written text (Deut 30:12–14) as part of an oral performance to the Roman church, contrasting it with Philo's use of the same text. Thus A. Dewey has begun the study of how New Testament writings employ both oral and written arguments in their attempts to persuade their audiences. Antoinette Clark Wire reviews Ward's and A. Dewey's arguments, suggests ways they might extend them, and urges us all to investigate "the extent to which different ways of recording affect how people think and act, the role of literacy in defining and intensifying differences in social power, and the continuing impact of traditional oral narratives in family and group identification." The essays in this section represent the beginnings of studies of particular texts in light of ancient media realities.

Part III is a more theoretical discussion of ancient media. In his first article, "Jesus and Tradition: Words in Time, Words in Space," Werner H. Kelber argues that our methods of reconstructing Jesus are based on Enlightenment logic and linear print modalities that seriously misrepresent the media realities of antiquity. Using the work of John Dominic Crossan as an example, Kelber argues that the concept of *ipsissimum verbum* is inappropriate to oral speech, which does not privilege any single original, and that the concept of *ipsissima structura* is characteristic of the stability of oral tradition and not of the creative originality of any individual. John Miles Foley views Kelber's work in the context of comparative studies in oral tradition, where it fits very well, and extends Kelber's argument with a discussion of linguistic register and metonymic referentiality (the part standing for the whole). In his response to Kelber, Bernard Brandon Scott asserts that Kelber's understanding of orality makes the quest for the historical Jesus impossible. Based on his work on the parables, Scott suggests some methods of working with texts that, he argues, enable us to "analyze the residue of orality (memory) from a literate perspective." In the final essay in this volume, Kelber argues that, in antiquity, modes of communication were understood as thoroughly "intertwined with cognitive and sensory perception." Citing an abundance of ancient authors and modern writers on media, Kelber seeks to understand the conventions of oral, rhetorical, and scribal communication and how each engages the senses of hearing and sight.

This volume discusses many aspects of the ancient media world. Before we can understand the New Testament more fully in terms of its own media world much work needs to be done, developing ideas presented here, applying them to New Testament texts, and investigating additional areas. In another ten years, these essays may well seem still too tied to the assumptions of print. Nonetheless, I believe this volume represents substantial progress in addressing early Christianity in the context of its own communication realities.

I would like to thank Joan Peabody Porter for her endowment of the Theological Writing Fund of the Episcopal Divinity School, which has contributed some support to this work.

WORKS CONSULTED

Crossan, John Dominic
    1991   *The Historical Jesus: The Life of a Mediterranean Jewish Peasant.* San Francisco: Harper San Francisco.

Kelber, Werner H.
    1983   *The Oral and the Written Gospel: The Hermeneutics of Speaking and Writing in the Synoptic Tradition, Mark, Paul, and Q.* Philadelphia: Fortress.

Silberman, Lou H., ed.
    1987   *Orality, Aurality and Biblical Narrative.* Semeia 39. Decatur, GA: Scholars.

I
CHRISTIANITY'S PLACE IN THE ANCIENT ORAL-LITERATE MEDIA WORLD: AN OVERVIEW

JESUS OF NAZARETH
AND THE WATERSHED OF ANCIENT ORALITY
AND LITERACY[1]

Thomas E. Boomershine
United Theological Seminary

ABSTRACT

As research sheds light on the relationship between communications technology and culture, (Thomas 1989, 1992; Havelock 1982; Patterson), the picture of the interaction between oral and written communications systems and the religious communities of Israel in antiquity is changing. Rather than a smooth, linear transition from orality to literacy, the formation of the communications system of writing and reading in antiquity was associated with a long, highly complex cultural revolution. The first task is, then, to sketch a more complex and, hopefully, more accurate picture of the watershed between orality and literacy in the ancient near East.

Since the dominant picture of Jesus was decisively shaped by nineteenth century assumptions about the transition from orality to literacy that now appear inaccurate, Jesus' role looks very different when seen from this new perspective. His role needs to be seen now in the context of the long struggle of Judaism with Hellenistic literate culture. Jesus' role in this cultural setting is clarified by comparison with the role of Socrates, who wrote nothing but developed a mode of thought and communication that was generative for the emerging literate culture. There are clear signs in the overall social context of Hellenistic Galilee and in the corpus of Jesus' parables that Jesus developed a mode of thought and communication that was a source for the distinctive ways in which early Christianity reshaped ancient Judaism in the culture of literacy.

COMMUNICATIONS RESEARCH AND
BIBLICAL METHODOLOGY

The field of communications research has emerged in the twentieth century in response to the need to understand the complex effects of electronic communications technology on contemporary culture (Carey;

---

[1] I am deeply grateful to Lawrence Welborn for his suggestions for the bibliographical resources, to Gilbert Bartholomew and Amelia Cooper for their suggestions for the editing of the text, and to the editor of this volume, Joanna Dewey, without whose toughminded encouragement this article would not have been completed.

Czitrom; Delia: 20–98; Fiske; Lowery and DeFleur). Contemporary communications research has developed a more comprehensive and nuanced awareness of the complex interactions between communications systems and cultural formation. The foundational conclusion of this research has been that changes in communications systems are related to profound shifts in modes of perception and thought, patterns of cultural formation, and religious values.

The most widely recognized figure in communications research has been Marshall McLuhan. From the foundations laid by Harold Innis (1951, 1972), McLuhan popularized communications research in his book *Understanding Media*, which contained the now famous cliché, "the medium is the message." McLuhan argued that communications media are, rather than neutral transmitters of meaning, the major factor in the formation of culture.[2] In the past three decades, the basic presuppositions of communications research have been applied to the history of orality and literacy, above all by Walter Ong. Building on the work of McLuhan, Milmann Perry, Albert Lord, and Eric Havelock, Ong has traced the impact of changes in communications technology throughout the history of human civilization (Farrell: 25–43).

The methodological presuppositions of form criticism were based on the communications theories of the nineteenth–century. The assumption was that oral and literary communications were relatively neutral means for the transmission of tradition. In light of Ong's work, Werner Kelber recognized the formative role of this presupposition in the work of Bultmann and Gerhardsson. Kelber accurately identifies Bultmann's underlying assumption:

> What strengthened Bultmann's model of an effortlessly evolutionary transition from the pre-gospel stream of tradition to the written gospel was his insistence on the irrelevance of a distinction between orality and literacy. In most cases it was considered "immaterial" (*nebensachlich*) whether the oral or the written tradition has been responsible; there exists no difference in principle (6).

This nineteenth–century picture of the orality/literacy transition in antiquity was a basic presupposition of form criticism. The key to understanding the history of tradition was the identification of the earlier oral forms of the sayings and stories. This picture generated a relatively narrow focus in historical critical study of the Gospels on the tradition history of individual pericopes. While form criticism theoretically

---

[2] While McLuhan's work has been appropriately criticized as media determinism, his descriptions of the pervasive influence of communications systems have been highly generative; see, for example, the reflections upon McLuhan's work by Eco: 135–44.

included the critical analysis of the differences between oral and written tradition,[3] it primarily treated oral tradition as a causal factor in the formation of the written tradition and saw no need to interpret the Gospel tradition in the context of the shift from orality to literacy in the broader culture.[4] As a result of recent orality/literacy research, however, we now know that changes in communications systems are complex, pervasive, and conflictual, rather than smooth and easy. Furthermore, if these inaccurate assumptions have shaped our picture of the New Testament tradition, they also have affected our picture of Jesus.

THE PUZZLE OF OUR PRESENT PICTURE OF JESUS

When seen from the perspective of communications systems, our present picture of Jesus is profoundly enigmatic. The problem is the apparent discontinuity between Jesus' life and the movement that developed from his life and work. The radical distinction between the so-called historical Jesus and the Christ of faith may have been discredited, but remnants of that distinction remain very much in place.[5] One of those remnants is our picture of Jesus' relationship to the watershed of oral and written communications systems in antiquity.

Jesus was largely seen as an oral communicator within a Palestinian Jewish environment that was significantly separated from the more literate Hellenistic world.[6] His ministry was mainly to Jews (Sanders 1985; Senior and Stuhlmueller; cf. Hahn 1974:26–41). The assumption is that he spoke Aramaic (Fitzmyer: 6–10), though a few scholars suggest Greek as well (Argyle; Sevenster). The historical Jesus was then a relatively insignificant oral teacher who formed one of the several proto–messianic

---

[3] The point was grasped by Overbeck in 1882. The systemic differences between oral and written communication were more fully appreciated in the school of form criticism that descends from Martin Dibelius to Philip Vielhauer and Gerd Theissen.

[4] This criticism applies mainly to Bultmann's use of form criticism in his history of the synoptic tradition. A further problem in historical criticism has been the assumption that, once the tradition had been written down, the communications system of antiquity was the same as that of the later periods of print culture. As a result, the role of the communications system of the Enlightenment in the formation of historical criticism has been almost wholly unrecognized. Throughout this period, for example, scholars have continued to refer to "the reader" as if ancient receptors were generally readers reading manuscripts alone in silence rather than audiences listening to public readings (Achtemeier).

[5] While Martin Kähler is the source of the classic articulation of the distinction, the ghost is still abroad in a work such as that of Burton Mack.

[6] While this picture of Jesus dominated the last century, it is largely absent from recent scholarship, though it still lingers in textbooks. Among recent scholars, E. P. Sanders argues that Jesus' Galilee was not greatly influenced by Greek and Roman culture.

movements in first-century Judaism (so Horsley). According to this construction, Paul was the great innovator who formed the Hellenistic Gentile church as a distinctive development that went far beyond the intentions of Jesus (Harnack 1924). In Bultmann's *Theology of the New Testament*, for example, Jesus is identified with the Jewish sources and the beginnings of New Testament theology are identified with Paul (Bultmann 1951:3–26; see also Braun). Paul formed a literate communications system that, in turn, established a new form of Judaism in the midst of Hellenistic culture (Hartman: 137–46). Thus, Jesus operated in the communications world of orality while Paul moved aggressively into the communications world of literacy. In this process, Jesus became the Christ whose death and resurrection were the decisive events in the history of salvation but whose actual life and teaching were of relative insignificance (Heitmüller 1972:308–19; Wrede: 53).

The movement Jesus established within Judaism had some impact for a time. The history of Jewish Christianity is a sign of this ongoing movement; the opposition of the rabbis of the post-70 CE period confirms its existence (Simon 1948:145–325; Daniélou; Schoeps 1949). The Jewish mission was, nevertheless, only minimally successful (Strecker: 241–85; Simon 1972:37–54; Lüdemann: 161–73, 245–54). It was within the urban Greek-speaking world that Christianity flourished and became a religion that far exceeded its ethnic, oral roots. From this perspective, Paul was the central figure in the transformation of the movement of Jesus into a religion in which Jesus Christ was the central figure.

This understanding of Jesus' role is related to our picture of the communications situation in the first-century of the common era: Jesus was an oral communicator who wrote virtually nothing, the only recorded instance being whatever he wrote—a symbol, doodlings, a word, or a picture—to a woman accused of adultery (John 8:2–11). Early Christianity was significantly based on the composition and distribution of documents (Barnett; see also Harnack). From a communications perspective, our present picture paints Jesus as the oral precursor for the more literary movement that rapidly developed around his memory. Furthermore, Kelber's picture of orality and literacy in early Christianity (1983) widens the chasm between the communicators of the oral gospel— Jesus and his nonliterate followers, particularly Peter—and the more literate authors of the written gospel, such as Mark. Thus, the watershed between oral and written communications systems is presently located between Jesus and the traditions of the church.

Yet this conclusion is itself a puzzle. Is it probable that there would be such radical discontinuity between the founder of a movement and the movement itself?[7] Was Paul such a charismatic figure that he was able to turn the Jesus movement in a radically different direction from that initiated by Jesus himself?[8] Furthermore, if Jesus lived more or less exclusively on the oral side of the great divide between the systems of orality and literacy, is it likely that he would have founded a movement that was structurally related to the world of literacy?

A needed step in a reexamination of these questions is to clarify the roles of oral and written communications in the first century. Just as we used to assume that Judaism and Hellenism were radically distinct until it became clear that Hellenism had thoroughly permeated Palestine (Hengel 1974; Momigliano: 74–122; Batey), so also the interaction of oral and written communications systems may have been far more complex than we have previously assumed. The formation of early Christianity and the documents of the New Testament need to be seen in the context of the history of communications systems in antiquity and in the religion of Israel.

Orality and Literacy in Antiquity

A comprehensive picture of the transition from orality to literacy in antiquity can only be drawn in its broadest outlines here. The extension of literacy in the ancient world was a slow process. The earliest evidence now available places the invention of writing in both Mesopotamia and Egypt near the end of the fourth millenium BCE (ca. 3200–3000 BCE)(Baines: 334). The extensive tablets discovered in Elba reflect the uses of writing that were dominant until the later centuries of the second millennium BCE: records of business transactions and military victories. Throughout the next two and a half millenia (3200–700 BCE), writing was the province of a professional group of scribes and was limited in its overall cultural impact. This is reflected in the political roles of the scribes: they were subordinants to illiterate kings who used scribes but exercised power by oral decree. Thus, the communications system of literacy was developed in service of oral communication.

The first period in which writing appears to become a dominant factor in the formation of culture begins around 500 BCE. Though the same processes may have been happening elsewhere in the ancient world, the

---

[7] The use of the criterion of dissimilarity, while methodologically necessary for purposes of historical verifiability, accentuates the disjunction between Jesus and Christianity. For a critique, R. S. Barbour: 5–20. On the question in general, see Bultmann 1967:445–69; Hahn 1974:11– 77; Käsemann: 23–65.

[8] This was the position of the "history of religions" school in general: see the critique by Schoeps 1961:53. This view of the radical disjunction between Jesus and Paul has recently been revived by Hyam Maccoby.

most extensive evidence for the formation of an early literate culture is in Athens. There a critical mass of early philosophers, scientists, and historians developed the characteristic institutions and modes of thought of literate culture. The Hellenistic empire of Alexander and his successors was the preeminent promoter of literate culture in the ancient world (Tarn; Hadas; Hengel 1974:58–106). In the Hellenistic empire, writing and its modes of communication were organized around the Greek language, and the disciplines of philosophy and rhetoric gradually became important factors in the shaping of communication and culture (Hengel 1979:94–115, 126–43). Particularly in urban centers, writing became the preeminent system of communication and culture as the literate minority controlled the instrumentalities of power (Jones: 285). This process continued through the early centuries of the Roman empire (MacMullen: 1–56; Rostovtzeff 1957:255–78, 344–52).

The watershed between orality and literacy in antiquity is probably most accurately drawn in the Hellenistic era of the fourth to the third centuries BCE. The transition from archives to libraries is one sign of that watershed. The earliest archives of written materials, such as Ashurbanipal's (668–627 BCE) collection of some 25,000 tablets, essentially functioned as museums for the preservation of written monuments. The first libraries of manuscripts designed to facilitate reading and study appear in classical Athens during the fourth century. The most famous collection was founded by Aristotle and became the model for the great library at Alexandria, which was built by Ptolemy II Philadelphus in the third century (308–246 BCE) (Francis: 856–57).

While the basic elements of the communications system of literacy were formed during the Hellenistic era, the ability to read and write remained relatively rare in the general population. Estimates of the levels of literacy in the ancient world are steadily being revised downwards as the documentary evidence is being assessed. Thus, William Harris, in a recent work, *Ancient Literacy*, concludes that the overall rate of literacy in Attica is not likely to have risen above 10–15% by the end of the fourth century (328). Literacy was largely confined to the ruling classes, hoplites and above (Thomas 1992; Harvey: 585–635; Harris). In the period of the Hellenistic empire, literacy levels in regions other than Greece gradually increased to levels closer to that of classical Athens (Hengel 1974:58–59). Furthermore, Harris's conclusions are that the great majority of the populations of the Roman Empire, including Rome itself, remained nonliterate. He estimates that the combined literacy level in Rome in the period before 100 BC is unlikely to have much exceeded 10% (329). Literacy was largely confined to free men, although at least some slaves and women in the Roman world became literate (see also Youtie 1966:

127–43; 1971a:161–76; 1971b:239–61; Beard). While the levels of literacy may have been relatively low, the cultures of the Hellenistic world were nevertheless dominated by the culture of literacy. Power and prestige in every area of life were connected with literacy (Jüthner: 25–26, 34; Marrou: 95– 100, 150; Hengel 1976:106; Youtie 1975).

However, while the literate culture became increasingly dominant, the marks of oral culture were always present and remained central for the majority of persons. Harris's conclusion about literacy in the world of antiquity is appropriately nuanced:

> there occurred a transition away from oral culture. This was, however, a transition not to written culture (in the sense in which modern cultures are written cultures) but to an intermediate condition, neither primitive nor modern. In this world, after the archaic period, the entire elite relied heavily on writing, and the entirety of the rest of the population was affected by it. But some of the marks of an oral culture always remain visible, most notably a widespread reliance on, and cultivation of, the faculty of memory (327).

Thus, the overall picture of communications in the ancient world is constituted by the new mix composed of the growing power of writing in the midst of a changing though always present oral culture. The communications systems of literacy were inextricably connected with the emergence and power of the great empires of the era. It is no coincidence that the centers of literacy—Babylonia, Persia, Egypt, Greece, Rome—were also the centers of military, economic, and political power that successively subjugated Israel. As Claude Lévi-Strauss has provocatively observed about the role of literacy in human civilization, "The primary function of written communication is to facilitate slavery" (299).[9]

ORAL AND LITERATE COMMUNICATIONS SYSTEMS IN ISRAEL

The appropriation of literacy in ancient Israel was an extremely complex process. Three stages can be identified in this process: initial signs of writing, the formation of literate systems of communications, and the development of sustainable communication systems for the preservation and extension of the religion in the culture of literacy. The signs of formation of a literate communications system are the integration of reading and writing into the structural patterns of religious and political life. The integration of literacy into the life of Israel was a response to the emergence of literate culture in the empires of the ancient

---

[9] In his discussion of slavery, Lévi-Strauss clearly is referring to political, cultural, and economic domination rather than chattel slavery. His discussion is of particular importance because of the tendency of scholars and other high literates to idealize literacy in comparison to both oral and electronic communications systems.

Near East. Israel's experience of the culture of literacy was inextricably connected with political and economic domination by the literate centers of power: Babylonia, Persia, Egypt, Greece, and finally, Rome. Israel was, however, also a distinctive participant in the development of the culture of literacy.

Initial Signs

The first references to writing in Israel are to Moses, who writes the covenant (Exod 24) and reads his song and the law (Deut 31). Descriptions of reading and writing without further editorial comment refer to Joshua (Josh 1:8; 24:26), Samuel (1 Sam 10:25), David (2 Sam 11:14), Jezebel (1 Kgs 21:8–9), Jehu (2 Kgs 10), and Hezekiah (2 Kgs 19) (Millard: 388). The first accounts of the reading of major literary compositions with relatively specific historical dates in the history of Israelite religion are the reading of the Deuteronomy scroll (2 Kgs 22—approximately 621 BCE) and the reading of Jeremiah's scroll (Jer 36—approximately 605 BCE).

Epigraphic evidence, particularly from the seventh to the early sixth century BCE, corroborates the biblical signs of an emerging literate communications system in Israel (Millard: 338). Furthermore, the synagogue as a community where literacy was required for the reading of sacred writings was probably established during the exile (Schürer: 447; Hengel 1974:82–83). And it was probably during the period of the exile that the Pentateuch and the classical prophets were codified. That is, the first substantial signs of more extensive literary activity, and the initial formation of a literate culture and institutions based on reading and writing, appear in the seventh and sixth centuries BCE.

Formation of a Literary Communications System

The first accounts in biblical literature in which the marks of a literary communications system appear are the descriptions of the restoration under Ezra and Nehemiah. In the accounts of the covenant renewal in 444 BCE, the authors of Ezra and Nehemiah fully integrated reading and writing into the narrative fabric of Israel's religious life. Ezra, as the leader of the religious community, is named as a scribe. He is presented as the first fully literate person in the history of Israel to have significant political power. The introductions of Ezra emphasize his literate credentials: "He was a scribe skilled in the law of Moses that the Lord the God of Israel had given . . ." (Ezra 7:6); "For Ezra had set his heart to study the law of the Lord, and to do it, and to teach the statutes and ordinances in Israel" (7:10); "This is a copy of the letter that King Artaxerxes gave to the priest Ezra, the scribe, a scholar of the text of the commandments of the Lord and his statutes for Israel . . ." (7:11). This last reference suggests a connection between Ezra's literacy and his authorization by King Artaxerxes of Persia.

As described in Nehemiah 8, the foundational act in the covenant renewal ceremony is a new communications event: a combination of the written and the oral Torah. While Ezra read the book of the law of Moses, the Levites, thirteen of whom are listed (8:7), provided an oral interpretation of the Law, "so that the people understood the reading" (8:8). During the celebration of the Feast of Booths that followed, Ezra is described as reading from the book of the law of God each of the seven days (8:18), and on the twenty-fourth day the people made confession to God after hearing a reading from the book of the law for "a fourth part of the day" (9:1–3). This story is the first sign in the tradition of the characteristic pattern of the dual torah: written texts combined with oral commentary on those texts. A further dimension of the integration of reading and writing into the account of the covenant renewal is the signing of the written covenant (Nehemiah 10). Apparently the scribes wrote a new covenant and representatives of the people—officials, Levites, and priests—signed it. The names of those who signed the covenant are listed in Nehemiah 10:1-27.

The composition of Ezra and Nehemiah is now dated between 400 and 300 BCE (Klein: 732). Thus, the first descriptions of the systematic integration of reading and writing into the religious life of Israel appear in the early second temple period. The identification of this time period as the watershed between orality and literacy in Israel is supported by additional literary records. It was during this period that the literature that formed the balance of the Scriptures was written. The later canonical writings, the Apocrypha, and the Pseudepigrapha are the records of extensive literary movements that developed in Israel during the Hellenistic and Roman eras. These movements were based on the composition of documents by authors who apparently wrote them for distribution to communities of literate Jews. This was also the period of the Septuagint translation (third century BCE to early first century BCE). Furthermore, the discovery of the literary legacy of the community at Qumran has given us a picture of a Jewish religious community in the late second temple period that had thoroughly appropriated reading and writing into its internal life. And, not surprisingly, all of this literary activity took place in the same period as the emergence of literate systems in the wider Hellenistic culture. From the perspective of communications systems, therefore, these developments in the literature of Israel are further signs of the emergence of a full system of literary communications.

As the reform of Ezra and Nehemiah indicates, however, the political impetus in Israel for the development of a system of communications based on writing was the desire to protect Israel from corruption by the culture of Hellenism. This desire was, however, in tension with the inevitable need to adapt to the new cultural system and, in a variety of ways, to adopt Hellenistic ways. As Martin Hengel has shown in his richly nuanced studies (1974, 1976), the adoption of Hellenistic civilization by ancient Judaism and the conflict which resulted was a highly complex development that involved many levels of extreme tension. The issue for Judaism throughout the second temple period was how to deal with the powerful cultural forces of Hellenism, an integral aspect of which was the power of reading and writing.

The Emergence of Sustainable Communications Systems

The next major development in communications systems in the history of ancient Judaism was, from the point of view of media history, in many ways the most remarkable. In the aftermath of the Jewish war and the destruction of the temple, two significantly different communications systems emerged, the systems that shaped the basic character of what have become Judaism and Christianity.

The formation of rabbinic Judaism was associated with the development of the communications system that produced the writings and symbolic system of the dual Torah. As a result of the historical critical analysis of the canonical writings of rabbinic Judaism, most characteristically the Mishnah and the Talmud, we now have a much clearer picture of the distinctive character of this system. As Jacob Neusner has shown in his multi-faceted analyses and comparisons with other literatures, the Judaism of the dual Torah was a fully literate system based on the formation of textual communities.[10] The formation of the mind of rabbinic Judaism was based on highly sophisticated textual logics that interpreted the written texts in relation to the realities of Jewish life in the new cultural setting created by the loss of the temple.

The distinctiveness of the Mishnah and Talmud was in part the result of the particular combination of oral composition and transmission in a fully textual environment. Thus, for example, the students of the Rabbis memorized their oral sayings,[11] thereby approximating the accuracy of

---

[10] Neusner, on the one hand, rejects the significance of the differences between orality and literacy as "vastly overstated, especially for the culture of the Jews in antiquity;" (1988:14). On the other hand, at other points in his work he utilizes, in a fully acknowledged manner, both the categories and concepts that have grown out of the investigation of orality and literacy (1987:8–19).

[11] See Jacob Neusner (1984:28; also 1985:112).

written transmission in oral tradition. In the manner of oral tradition, nothing was written for decades or even centuries, but the modes of oral transmission were rigorous. The entire cultural communications system on which rabbinic Judaism was thereafter established had its foundations in the systematic oral interpretation of written Scripture.

The complexity and importance of the relationship between the development of Judaism and modes of communication can be seen in a fact that is initially surprising. The formation of rabbinic Judaism in the aftermath of the destruction of the temple was based on the more or less exclusive development of the communications system of the dual Torah (Vermes: 79–95). Eventually the literary tradition of the second temple period virtually disappeared from the transmitted Jewish tradition. Samuel Sandmel writes:

> By the strangest quirk of fate respecting literature that I know of, large numbers of writings by Jews were completely lost from the transmitted Jewish heritage. These documents stem roughly from 200 B.C. to A.D. 200. Not only the so-called Pseudepigrapha, but even such important and extensive writings as those by Philo and Josephus have not been part of the Jewish inheritance from its past; these were preserved and transmitted by Christians (xi).

This disassociation of rabbinic Judaism from the literary traditions of the second temple period did not happen immediately. The contents of the two volumes of Charlesworth's *Old Testament Pseudepigrapha* provide clear evidence that Jews continued to write apocalyptic, testaments, wisdom, and even philosophy in the second – fourth centuries of the common era. Furthermore, these literary traditions may have been preserved in some rabbinic circles in the tannaitic and amoraic periods. Nevertheless, the new system that the rabbis established in the late first century CE *eventually* resulted in the characteristic patterns of Judaism that Sandmel has described.

In light of the recognition of the radical character of shifts in communications systems, we can speculate that the exclusion of whole categories of Jewish writings was more or less intentional, analogous to Plato's exclusion of the poets from the Republic, rather than a quirk of fate or a puzzling forgetfulness. It may be that the rabbis recognized instinctively that the only way to maintain a community of purity in the midst of Gentile culture was to form a distinctive communications system and to cut the explicit links of the religion to Hellenistic literary culture. Regardless of the reasons for its formation, however, the system of the dual Torah was a highly creative and distinctive innovation in communications systems that sustained rabbinic Judaism throughout the ages of the dominance of literate communications systems in the West.

The other new development in communications systems among ancient Jews was the formation of the system of the Jewish sectarians who accepted Jesus of Nazareth as Messiah. The early Christian church developed a communications system that was another new synthesis of oral and written tradition. The composition of the New Testament writings in the first – second century CE established a tradition that generated the writings of first the Apologists and then the ante–Nicene fathers. The development of theology was, from the perspective of communications, a radically new post–biblical development within early Christianity. In the patristic period, Christian writers produced a veritable flood of new literary forms and traditions—the rhetorical traditions of homiletics, liturgical writings, hymns, letters, dogmatic writings, and early canon law—as well as the more traditional literary forms—Gospels, Acts, Apocalypses, and Epistles—now collected in the so–called New Testament Apocrypha.

Christians established a network of textual communities that produced and distributed a widely diversified literary tradition. Christians were aggressive in the appropriation of the communications technology of literacy. For example, among the earliest archeological discoveries of the codex rather than the scroll, as a means of producing and distributing written works, are fragments of Christian books from the second century CE. The development of a new communications system was foundational to the expansion of what began as a small Jewish sect into what became, in the fourth century, the dominant religion of the Roman Empire.

If there is a significant positive correlation between the emergence of new religious traditions and the development of new communications systems, then the split between Judaism and Christianity may have been, in addition to the various doctrinal, organizational, and ethnic differences, a consequence of different directions in their communications systems. The rabbis of the Mishnaic tradition maintained the role of texts as the recording of long–established oral traditions and poured their energy into the development of the oral Torah. This system defended the culture and religion of Israel from corruption by the culture of Hellenism and appropriated literacy as a communications system in strict subordination to orality.

In contrast, early Christians developed an extensive contemporary literary tradition in continuity with other aspects of the literary communications system that was formed in the period of the second temple (Alexander: 221–47; Roberts). This literature was either composed in writing, dictated to a secretary, or composed orally and written down after a relatively short period of oral transmission. It was then more or less immediately distributed in manuscripts for public reading. Christianity was then the Jewish sectarian group in the post-70 CE period that continued and further developed these characteristics of the literate communications system of the second temple period. In this context, Christian preservation of the literary traditions of the Pseudepigrapha and other writings of the second temple period was a natural and consistent development. In the internal struggle within Judaism about the uses of writing, the Christian sect continued the approach to literate communications developed by the more Hellenistic Jewish writers of the second temple period. In contrast to the communications system of rabbinic Judaism, which preserved and defended the community's cultic purity, the communications system formed by early Christianity extended the knowledge of God in Hellenistic culture and transformed the impact of literacy on religious and political life.

When seen in relation to the transition from oral to literate communications systems in antiquity, however, both of these new systems were efforts to enable the religion of Israel to survive and to maintain faithfulness in a new cultural environment. Both rabbinic Judaism and Christianity formed new systems of literate communications that have continued to be viable in the literate cultures of the West. It is within these broad parameters that new light may be shed on the puzzle of the relationship between Jesus of Nazareth and the formation of Christianity.

ORALITY AND LITERACY IN JESUS' GALILEAN MINISTRY

Clear evidence about the extent of literacy in Galilee is sparse, but the general situation can be discerned in broad outlines from the available data. It is generally assumed that there was a close association between the extension of literacy and the extension of Hellenism. The assumption may not be fully valid since there were persons who were literate in Hebrew who may not have known Greek. Nevertheless, it is probable that in the overall cultural world of the first centuries BCE/CE, there was a general correlation between Hellenistic culture and literacy. Wherever there is evidence of Hellenistic culture and the use of Greek, there are also signs of the extension of literacy.

One of the more surprising results of recent archeological work has been the evidence of the wide use of Greek in Galilee (Batey: 56, 80, passim). There is an overall consensus in the current discussion that Aramaic was the primary language of Palestine. Evidence, however, continues to grow that Greek was also an important language of social intercourse and perhaps even family life. The most striking signs of the use of Greek that have surfaced are the ossuary inscriptions. More than two-thirds of those discovered in Palestine are in Greek. As Meyers and Strange summarize the data, "From a corpus of 194 inscribed ossuaries, 26 percent are inscribed in Hebrew or Aramaic, 9 percent are in Greek and a Semitic language, and 64 percent are inscribed in Greek alone" (65). In the excavation of Beth Shearim, a second century town in Galilee, 33 of the 37 inscriptions discovered in catacombs 12 and 13 were in Greek and only 4 in Hebrew and Aramaic, with an additional 4 Hebrew inscriptions in catacomb 14 (Schwabe: 249). This evidence indicates that Greek was widely used even in the highly private context of family burials.

A further surprising indication of the prevalence of Greek is the third letter of the Bar-Kokhba corespondence. This letter, written from within the fortress in the last year of the revolt (135 CE), asks for palm branches and citrons for "the camp of the Jews" and then states, "the letter is written in Greek as we have no one who knows Hebrew [or Aramaic]" (Yadin: 130). This is, if anything, even more striking in relation to the prevalence of Greek since speaking Greek was regarded by many conservative Jews as a sign of defection to the Hellenists. The explanation is clearly in response to conservative sensibilities.

These archeological data are the most striking of the widespread attestations of Greek material in Palestine in the time of Jesus. Furthermore, the evidence in regard to Galilee indicates that, with the exception of Jerusalem itself, Greek was used more widely in "Galilee of the Gentiles" than elsewhere in Palestine. This makes sense since Galilee was on the boundary between Palestine and the northern and eastern countries dominated by Greek culture. Finally, the extensive use of Greek is a sign of the degree to which Hellenistic culture had permeated Galilee in this period (see also Downing 1987, 1988; Mack: 65–66; Crossan: 19–324; Kee: 15).

Jesus' Language

Both this general evidence and specific episodes in the records of Jesus' life indicate that he may have spoken Greek as a second or third language after Aramaic and Hebrew. There are reports of Jesus' conversations with Gentiles in the Gospels: the centurion (Matt 8:5–13; Luke 7:6–10); the Syro-Phoenician woman, whom Mark calls "a Greek" (Mark 7:24–30; Matt 15:21– 28); and Pilate (Matt 27:11–14; Mark 15:2–5; Luke 23:3; John 18:33–19:11). It is highly unlikely that any of these persons would have known Aramaic or Hebrew. In the absence of any translators, these conversations were only possible if Jesus spoke Greek. There are, however, significant historical questions in relation to these reports. In Luke's version of the centurion story, Jesus never speaks with the centurion directly but only through mediators who could have also been translators. Whether the version of Luke or Matthew, in which Jesus speaks directly to the centurion, is more historically accurate is difficult to determine. In the Pilate trial narratives, only in John does Jesus say more than two words in Greek to Pilate. The Syro–Phoenician woman episode is only recorded in Mark and Matthew and may have been generated by Mark's interest in including Gentiles in Jesus' mission.

Thus, while the evidence from the Gospels at most indicates a probability that Jesus spoke some Greek, the emerging picture of language use in Galilee makes it more likely. John Meier's conclusion seems accurate: "Jesus regularly and perhaps exclusively taught in Aramaic, his Greek being of a practical, business type, and perhaps rudimentary to boot" (268). In light of the growing evidence of the prevalence of Greek in Palestine among Jews, however, it is possible to suggest that he did teach in Greek as well as in Aramaic to some Greek-speaking groups of Jews.

This heterodox language situation in Galilee is also reflected in the names of Jesus' disciples. Andrew, Philip, and Bartholomew are familiar Greek names; Simon can be derived from the Hebrew Simeon, but was also a widely-attested Greek name; likewise Thomas can be derived from the Aramaic for "twin," but was also a widely attested Greek name. Thus, Jesus' disciples reflected a wide range of definitions of what it meant to be Jewish, including having a Greek name.

The question of Jesus' ability to read is in some ways more difficult. The rates of literacy in Galilee during this period can only be inferred on the basis of comparative data. On the basis of Harris' data, it would be difficult to think of literacy rates higher than ten percent in Galilee. Meier rightly observes that Judaism in this period had generated written Scriptures, which fostered high respect for literacy. And while it was fully possible to be a Jew who was unable to read, the practice of the religion was increasingly organized around reading and discussing sacred texts (Meier: 258–59). That is, there was a growing Jewish literate culture in the first century.

The only credible evidence in the Gospels that Jesus may have been literate is his conversations with scribes and Pharisees about the interpretation of the Scriptures. The specific stories in the Gospels that present Jesus as literate are historically ambiguous. Luke's story of Jesus reading in the Nazareth synagogue, not present in Matthew and Mark, is the most explicit account of Jesus' literacy. The distinctiveness of Luke's version, the composite character of the Isaiah text, and the presence of Lukan motifs are, however, signs of Lukan composition (see Fitzmyer 1981:526–28). The Lukan narrative is, therefore, an uncertain source of historical information since it is an integral part of the editor's portrayal of Jesus as a literate teacher. The story in John 8:6 of Jesus drawing on the ground proves nothing about his ability to write, even if it is a historically reliable tradition, since nothing is specified about what he drew. However, the question of the Jerusalem skeptics in John 7:15—"How does this fellow know his letters [know how to read: γράμματα οἶδεν] when he has not studied?"—has no obvious redactional motive. It reflects the overall picture of Jesus in the Gospels as a person with a solid knowledge of Scripture and skill in interpretation that was frequently tested. In the absence of other figures in Judaism in this period who had this reputation and were illiterate, the most probable explanation is that this text reflects a tradition of Jesus as literate.

John Meier has investigated the question of Jesus' literacy, first in relation to these texts and then in relation to the broader context of Jewish education in the period. While the state of Jewish education in the first century is unclear, there is no doubt that there was an extensive community of scriptural debate in Palestinian Judaism in which virtually all streams of Gospel tradition show Jesus as a skilled participant. While it was possible to know the Scriptures from hearing them read in the synagogue, the range of knowledge and distinctiveness of interpretation reflected in the conflict stories is most naturally explained by Jesus having the ability to read the texts himself. Meier concludes as follows:

> . . . general considerations about first-century Palestinian Judaism, plus the consistent witness of many different streams of Gospel tradition about Jesus' teaching activity, plus the indirect evidence from John 7:15 make it likely that Jesus could both read the Hebrew Scriptures and engage in disputes about their meaning (278).

Thus, it is probable that Jesus was literate.

The literacy of the disciples is doubtful. In Acts 4, Peter and John are described as ἀγράμματοί, which characterizes them as at least unable to write but probably as illiterate. There are no explicit signs that any of the disciples were literate, although the possibility is that Levi, the tax collector, was at least able to handle written records. It is highly unlikely, however, that literacy was a requirement for discipleship. Unlike the rabbinic schools of the post-70 period, which were located in a place and could have books, Jesus taught his disciples on the move; there are no indications that they carried scrolls with them.

Finally, John Dominic Crossan's recent study of the historical Jesus pursues a radically different methodology for the quest, which has yielded surprising results. When the available data about Jesus of Nazareth is compared with the various movements in the world of the period, the highest degree of congruence both in lifestyle and modes of thought is with the Cynics. Crossan distinguishes between upper–class, urban, literate Cynics and the lower–class, peasant variety whose literacy is improbable (84–88), in which class Jesus presumably falls. It is not necessarily valid, however, to extend these broad generalizations about Cynic lifestyles to a particular Jewish teacher. In my view, the overall picture is that Jesus adopted aspects of the ways of the Cynics in a highly distinctive Jewish way that in no way excludes literacy. This congruence between Jesus and a broad philosophical movement in the Greco–Roman world is another indication of the degree to which Jesus of Nazareth can be seen within the overall framework of the Galilean Hellenistic literate culture.

Thus, Jesus' ministry was far more complex than that of a simple Galilean peasant who taught Aramaic parables to other Jewish peasants. The world of Jesus' day was going through a major shift in communications and culture. There is abundant evidence that this shift was happening in Galilee, as well as elsewhere in the Hellenistic world. In that cultural world, Jesus was a teacher who was probably literate, who spoke Aramaic, some Greek, and probably also Hebrew. His level of literacy was probably relatively low and did not include the ability to write. His ability to read was probably largely centered on reading the already orally familiar Scriptures. For example, he probably did not read Greek philosophical literature of the period. Whether he had read Jewish works written in Greek, such as Enoch, appears initially unlikely, but the influence of apocalyptic on Jesus' teaching leaves open the possibility.

JESUS AS TEACHER

The Socratic Analogy

Even if Jesus was literate to some degree, spoke Greek, and was in dialogue with Hellenistic culture, how could he have been the seminal figure in the establishment of a movement that participated so rapidly and thoroughly in the culture of literacy when he himself wrote nothing? The search for a clue to the puzzle of Jesus' role in relation to orality and literacy leads to Socrates. Socrates' role in the formation of the literate culture of Athens was seminal. He accomplished the essential task of enabling his students to think constructively in the patterns and forms of the emerging culture of literacy. In order to do this, he did not need to write but rather used oral speech in a new way. The similarities between these two pivotal figures in antiquity are striking. Socrates, like Jesus, was an oral teacher who did not write but who trained followers who did write. In the writings of Plato, Socrates is the main character of the dialogues, just as Jesus is the main character of, for example, Matthew's

Gospel. Socrates anticipated a radically new age for which he prepared his students by the establishment of a new community, the Academy. He did this by forming their minds to think about ideas objectively in the manner of the age of literacy. And, like Jesus of Nazareth, Socrates was martyred for his role in initiating radical cultural and religious change.

Socrates' dialogues laid the foundations for the ways of knowing associated with literacy. In *Preface to Plato*, Eric Havelock argued that Plato banished the poets from the Republic because he wanted to break the ways of knowing that were characteristic of oral culture. Plato identifies Socrates as the person who established a new way of knowing. In Plato's writings, Socrates is steadily seeking to needle his dialogue partners into reflection on ideas, instead of continuing to identify uncritically with the heroes of the great poetic epics. Socrates' questions were a steady invitation to step back from the immediacy of experience and to reflect critically on the presuppositions and ideas that were implicit in the conversation. What Havelock calls the "separation of the knower from the known," in which the known can be examined as an object, is the essential turn of mind that makes it possible to participate in the world of literacy (Havelock 1963:197–233). Socrates and his student, Plato, invited persons to stand back from experience and to think objectively about ideas.

Furthermore, Plato's theory of forms shifts the definition of reality from the world of sense experience to the world of a priori ideas present in the mind. For Plato, the enemy was the centuries long practice of self-identification with oral tradition. As Havelock writes, "The net effect . . . of the theory of forms is to dramatize the split between the image-thinking of poetry and the abstract thinking of philosophy" (Havelock: 266). This Platonic move established the foundations for the communications culture of literacy over against the culture of orality (Szlezák).

Thus, prior to Jesus, at an earlier stage in the extension of literacy in Hellenistic culture, Socrates was another seminal figure who was fully literate but did not write. In a radically different context, Socrates established the foundations for the development of literate culture and its ways of knowing.

The Parabolic Teaching of Jesus

Did Jesus in any analogous manner develop a way of knowing that was seminal in the establishment of a movement within Judaism that became rapidly literate? As with Socrates, there is no evidence that Jesus wrote. Furthermore, the teachings of both men were composed for oral transmission. The form of Socrates' oral teaching, the dialogue, is the most visible sign of the new epistemology of the culture of literacy. The characteristic form of Jesus' teaching was the parable.

Bernard Brandon Scott's recent comprehensive study of the parables has clarified the distinctiveness of Jesus' parables. Against the background of the Hebrew Bible, the parables are related to the *mashal*, any saying that is "proverblike." The *mashal* utilizes connotative language, is memorable through the use of metaphors and vivid images, and is typical and representative rather than context-specific (Scott: 13). In Jesus' usage, however, the parable is, to use Scott's definition, "a *mashal* that employs a short narrative fiction . . ." (8). While Nathan's warning to David and Ezekiel's tale of the eagle are developments toward parable, Scott rightly concludes: "no *mashal* in the Hebrew Bible directly parallels parable as a short narrative" (13).

Furthermore, Jesus' use of the form of parable is distinctive when compared with the traditions that can be reasonably identified with the Pharisees of the pre-70 CE period. Jacob Neusner's survey of pre-70 Pharisaic traditions finds wisdom sentences in the tradition, but not parables: "As to other sorts of Wisdom literature, such as riddles, parables, fables of animals or trees, and allegories, we find nothing comparable in the materials before us" (1972: 360). The parable is used extensively as a form of scriptural exegesis in the Palestinian (400 CE) and Babylonian (600 CE) Talmuds and occurs in the Tosephta (twelve instances) and the Mishnah (one parable). This use of parable is both later than and distinct from that found in the Jesus tradition (Scott: 13–18). Thus, when seen as a whole, the traditions of Jesus are distinctive in the centrality and uniqueness of the form of parable.

Recent literary–critical research on the parables from a variety of perspectives has come to a surprisingly wide consensus about the overall effect of Jesus' characteristic form of teaching. From Jeremias's traditions history reconstruction to Scott's recent literary critical study, a common theme is that the parables are shocking and profoundly paradoxical. The question is whether this shock can be seen as a new epistemology that is in any way structural to Jesus' parables.

Two characteristic elements in the structure of Jesus' parables that have emerged in recent study are the reversal of expectation and hyperbole. Sometimes only one of these elements occurs, as in the hyperbolic celebration of the shepherd in the parable of the lost sheep or the reversal of expectations in the parable of the Pharisee and the publican. Frequently, however, both reversal and hyperbole are present, as in the celebration of the younger son's return in the prodigal son or in the punishment of the "one-talent" servant. What, then, is the epistemological effect of these two characteristic elements in Jesus' parables?

An analysis of the parable of the rich fool (Luke 12:16-21) reveals a dynamic structure that is characterized by what can be called epistemological shock. The parable begins by leading the audience into the rich man's dilemma—"What am I going to do?"—and decision—"I know what I'll do."[12] The function of an extensive inside view is to invite involvement:

> What will I do, since I have nowhere to store my crops? I know what I'll do: I will pull down my barns, and build larger ones; and there I will store all my grain and my goods. And I will say to my soul, "Soul, you have ample goods laid up for many years; take your ease, eat, drink, and be merry!" (Luke 12:17-19).

Jesus' listeners were invited to enter into the rich man's problem and his joyful anticipation of being free from any anxiety about the necessities of life. In its oral performance, this section of the parable probably moved from the rich man's quiet meditation on his problem to the boisterous celebration of his plan. The structure of the internal dialogue inside the rich man's mind—question, answer, and address to his soul—is an appeal to the listener to enter into the mind of the rich man and to experience his dilemma, his solution, and his celebration of freedom from anxiety. It is from this place inside the rich man's mind that the listener hears God's judgment: "But God said to him, Fool! This night your soul is required of you; and the things you have prepared, whose will they be?" (Luke 12:20). In the oral reading or telling of the parable, God's speech is experienced as being addressed directly to each listener.

The parable is structured as a highly-charged shock to the listeners. The combination of hyperbolic judgment in the sentence of death and the reversal of expectations from a long life of ease to sudden death is psychologically and linguistically wrenching. Insofar as Jesus' listeners identified with the rich man, they experienced the possibility of instant and total reversal of fortune in the moment of hearing the word of God: "Fool!" The impact of this parable is far more than a point such as: "It is not wise to build up money as a strategy for abundant life in the future Kingdom of God" or "It is not wise to mismanage the miracle of God's abundant harvest by appropriating it for one's own self-interest." The

---

[12] The inside views of the shrewd steward's dilemma (Luke 16:4) and the prodigal son's meditation (Luke 15:17-19) have introductory formulas similar to the inside view of the rich man. Furthermore, the structure of the rich man's speech (12:17-18) is the same as the shrewd steward's (16:3-4): "What am I going to do . . . I know what I'll do . . ." These verbal and structural similarities in each case invite listener involvement with the character's dilemma.

parable shocks the listeners into reflection on their relationship to God and their attitudes about wealth. The reversal forces the listeners to stand back suddenly from preoccupation with the "real world" and to think from a radically different perspective.

The effect of the parable, then, is what could be called an alienation effect: it creates a high degree of separation or mental distance between the listener and everyday experience. The ones who are seeking knowledge about the Reign of God are suddenly distanced from the object seeking to be known and are forced to think and reflect about their own assumptions. I would propose that this effect, this sudden shock, is the same epistemological move that Socrates made in asking questions of his interlocutors. In place of sympathetic identification with the people of Israel escaping from Egypt and entering the promised land as a way of knowing the Reign of God, the experience of hearing Jesus' parable was a sudden reversal of expectations that created psychological distance and demanded reflection. Jesus' parable makes the same basic epistemological move in knowing the Reign of God as Socrates' dialogues in knowing the world of the forms. It is the foundational epistemological move of the literate culture of Hellenism: the turn of mind away from the experiential ways of knowing associated with oral culture to the reflective ways of knowing associated with literacy.

Is this alienation effect characteristic of Jesus' parables? A similar dynamic structure can be found in a number of parables in which there is an appeal for identification with characters who are sympathetic or gifted at the beginning and who are radically criticized or condemned at the end: the parable of the vineyard/wicked tenants (Mark 12:1-11/Matt 21:33-44/Luke 20:9-18/Thomas 65); the unmerciful servant (Matt 18:23-35); the workers in the vineyard (Matt 20:1-16); the great banquet and the guest without a wedding garment (Matt 22:1-14/Luke 14:16-24/Thomas 64); the faithful/unfaithful servant (Matt 24:45-51/Luke 12:42-46); the ten virgins (Matt 25:1-13); the talents (Matt 25:14-30/Luke 19:12-27); the last judgment (Matt 25:31-46); the prodigal son, in which the climactic emphasis is on the elder son (Luke 15:11-32); and the rich man and Lazarus (Luke 16:19-31). Variations on this structure occur in the parable of the dishonest steward (Luke 16:1-9), in which a character with whom the listener is invited to identify is first condemned and then surprisingly praised, and the parable of the good Samaritan (Luke 10:30-35), in which there is a primary reversal of audience expectations in the actions of the priest/Levite and the Samaritan.

The effect or impact of these parables is the same as that of the parable of the rich fool. The parable invites the listeners to enter into a situation in which a character is initially presented positively but is condemned in the parable's final turn. The distinctiveness of these short narrative fictions is that the puzzle or paradox of the reversal is necessarily connected with the audience's understanding of the Reign of God. Jesus' parables have the same effect as Socrates' questions: they require the audience to reflect from a position of psychological distance.

The question then is whether the new epistemology implicit in the parables can be traced back to Jesus. Undoubtedly, many of the parables have been shaped by subsequent redactors. The dynamic structure is, however, so pervasive in the parables that it is highly improbable that the redactors created it. The higher probability is that this was a pattern of oral teaching that Jesus established and that the redactors preserved to varying degrees. Thus, what can be identified here is the deep structure of a distinctive way of teaching about God.

In a seminal essay, Ernst Käsemann proposed that the origins of theology are to be found in apocalyptic: "Apocalyptic was the mother of all Christian theology - since we cannot really class the preaching of Jesus as theology" (Käsemann: 102). What Käsemann calls "apocalyptic" is essentially cosmic, holistic thinking. In apocalyptic the key question is: "to whom does the sovereignty of the world belong?" Thus, one might rephrase Käsemann: reflection on cosmic questions was the beginning of Christian theology.

As a result of his rejection of the authenticity of the third person Son of Man sayings, and indeed all of the apocalyptic sayings of Jesus, as creations of the early church, Käsemann sees the beginnings of theology only in the writings of Paul. The primary evidence of apocalyptic modes of thought in the teachings of Jesus is not, however, in the apocalyptic sayings, but in the parables. The structure of epistemological shock identified above is directly related to the cosmic modes of apocalyptic thought. The essential characteristic of the parables is thinking back from the end of time into the present. The parable of the last judgment is the most explicit in its cosmic, apocalyptic content, but each of the parables listed above has this holistic perspective. The shocking reversals of the parables communicate a new understanding of the character of God's sovereignty in cosmic time.

Jesus' development of the dynamic structures of the parable was, therefore, directly related to the epistemological sources of theology. Just as Socrates developed styles of argumentation in his dialogues, which led to the full emergence of philosophy, so Jesus developed a style of oral discourse in his parables that led to the development of theology. Jesus' oral discourse was characterized by a dynamic structure that shocked listeners into reflection and an implicit demand for thought that was cosmic in scale. Jesus developed a way of interpreting the tradition of

Israel's religion that was both congruent with the tradition and viable in the emerging literate culture. The clearest sign of its viability in literate culture is the impact of Jesus' parables in the two millenia of Western civilization. Whether his teaching was faithful to the traditions of Israel is an ongoing debate.

DIRECTIONS

When seen against the background of the communications systems of the Hellenistic world and the religion of Israel in the second temple period, the teachings of Jesus of Nazareth can be interpreted as moving toward a literate religious culture. Obviously, this inquiry is only an initial exploration of a certain direction in research. The initial results suggest that a clearer picture of the broad developments of the communications systems of orality and literacy in the ancient world may modify our understanding of Jesus' relationship to the formation of Christianity. If, for example, Jesus established the epistemological foundations for a form of Judaism that was viable in Hellenistic literate culture and in a literate communications system, there may be deeper lines of continuity between Jesus and Paul than were previously recognized. From this perspective, Paul simply developed what Jesus had already initiated.

Furthermore, a clearer picture of the history of religious communications systems may help to clarify the conflicts between Jesus and the Pharisees as the predecessors of the nascent movements that became Judaism and Christianity in the post-70 CE period. Both of the Jewish sectarian movements that survived the war developed new and viable ways of maintaining faithfulness to the God of Israel in the midst of literate Hellenistic culture. The study of communications systems may shed new light on the common problem they faced and the different approaches they developed. Thus, the decision of the rabbis to disassociate rabbinic Judaism from most of the literary heritage of the second temple period made sense as an effort to control the impact of the new habits of mind and the patterns of communication associated with Hellenistic literate culture that were changing Israel's tradition. Likewise, the decision of early Christian Jews to develop further the literary traditions of the second temple period in a manner that would invite the Hellenistic literate world to participate in the monotheism of the religion of Israel also makes sense.

When the interaction of oral and written communications in antiquity is seen as the interaction of communications systems instead of simply as a neutral stage in the formation, transmission, and meaning of individual literary works, the outline of a different picture of Jesus of Nazareth emerges. The image is somewhat more literate and is set against a more thoroughly Greek background. The picture also reveals more lines of connection with Paul and the early church than have appeared in the past. These lines appear because the basic transition from orality and literacy in the culture of antiquity happened *before* rather than *between* them. The Jewish sects that survived in the literate culture of the future did so because they formed new systems of thought and communication. In this picture, Jesus and Paul were both working on the same task. Furthermore, when this image of Jesus is seen against the background of the watershed of orality and literacy in antiquity, it can be seen that he established a distinctive style of communication that made a form of Judaism viable in the emerging culture of literacy.

WORKS CONSULTED

Achtemeier, Paul
    1990   "*Omnes verbum sonat*: The New Testament and the Oral Environment of Late Western Antiquity." *JBL* 109:3–27.

Alexander, Lovejoy
    1990   "The Living Voice: Scepticism Towards the Written Word in Early Christian and in Graeco–Roman Texts." Pp. 221–47 in *The Bible in Three Dimensions*. JSOT, Sup 87. Ed. D. J. A. Clines. Sheffield: JSOT.

Argyle, Aubrey W.
    1955   "Did Jesus Speak Greek?" *Exp Tim* 67:91–93.

Baines, John
    1992   "Literacy (ANE)." Pp. 333–37 in *The Anchor Bible Dictionary*, vol. 4. New York: Doubleday.

Barbour, R. S.
    1972   *Traditio–Historical Criticism of the Gospels*. London: SPCK.

Batey, Richard
    1991   *Jesus and the Forgotten City: New Light on Sepphoris and the Urban World of Jesus*. Grand Rapids: Eerdmans.

Braun, Herbert
    1979   *Jesus of Nazareth: The Man and His Time*. Philadelphia: Fortress.

Bultmann, Rudolph
    1951   *Theology of the New Testament*. New York: Scribner's.
    1963   *The History of the Synoptic Tradition*. New York: Harper & Row.

1967 "Das Verhältnis der urchristlichen Christusbotschaft zum historischen Jesus." Pp. 445–69 in *Exegetica*. Ed. E. Dinkler. Tübingen: J. C. B. Mohr.

Carey, James W.
1989 *Communication as Culture: Essays on Media and Society*. Boston: Unwin Hyman.

Charlesworth, James H., Ed.
1983 *The Old Testament Pseudepigrapha*. Garden City, NY: Doubleday.

Crossan, John Dominic
1991 *The Historical Jesus: The Life of a Mediterranean Jewish Peasant*. San Francisco: Harper San Francisco.

Czitrom, Daniel J.
1982 *Media and the American Mind: From Morse to McLuhan*. Chapel Hill: University of North Carolina Press.

Daniélou, Jean
1965 *The Theology of Jewish Christianity*. Philadelphia: Westminster.

Delia, J.
1987 "Communication Research: A History." Pp. 20–98 in *Handbook of Communication Science*. Ed. Charles R. Berger and Steven H. Chaffee. Newbury Park, CA: Sage.

Downing, F. Gerald
1987 *Jesus and the Threat of Freedom*. London: SCM.
1988 *The Christ and the Cynics*. Sheffield: JSOT.

Eco, Umberto
1986 *Travels in Hyperreality*. New York: Harcourt Brace Jovanovich.

Farrell, Thomas J.
1991 "An Overview of Walter J. Ong's Work." Pp. 25–43 in *Media, Consciousness, and Culture: Explorations of Walter Ong's Thought*. Ed. Bruce E. Gronbeck, Thomas J. Farrell, Paul A. Soukup. Newbury Park, CA: Sage.

Fiske, John
1982 *Introduction to Communications Studies*. New York: Methuen.

Fitzmyer, Joseph A.
1979 *A Wandering Aramean: Collected Aramaic Essays*. Missoula: Scholars.
1981 *The Gospel according to Luke I–IX*. Garden City, N.Y.: Doubleday.

Francis, Sir Frank C.
1980 "Library." Pp. 856–67 in *Encyclopaedia Britannica*, vol. 10. London: Helen Hemingway Benton.

Hadas, Moses
1972 *Hellenistic Culture: Fusion and Diffusion*. New York: Norton.

Hahn, Ferdinand
1965 *Mission in the New Testament*. Naperville, IL: Allenson.

1974 "Methodische Überlegungen zur Rückfrage nach Jesus." Pp. 11–77 in *Rückfrage nach Jesus*. Ed. K. Kertelge. Munich: Kaiser.

Harnack, Adolf von
1924 *Die Mission und Ausbreitung des Christentums in den ersten drei Jahrhunderten*. 4th ed. Leipzig: Hinrichs.
1926 *Die Briefsammlung des Apostel Paulus*. Leipzig: Hinrichs.

Harris, William V.
1989 *Ancient Literacy*. Cambridge: Harvard University Press.

Hartman, Lars
1986 "On Reading Others' Letters." Pp. 137–46 in *Christians Among Jews and Gentiles: Essays in Honor of Krister Stendahl*. Ed. G. W. E. Nickelsburg and G. W. MacRae. Philadelphia: Fortress.

Harvey, F. D.
1966 "Literacy in the Athenian Democracy." *Revue des études Greques* 79:585–635.

Havelock, Eric A.
1963 *Preface to Plato*. Cambridge: Harvard University Press.
1982 *The Literate Revolution in Greece and Its Cultural Consequences*. Princeton: Princeton University Press.

Heitmüller, Wilhelm
1912 "Zum Problem Paulus und Jesus." *ZNW* 13:320–327.
1972 "Hellenistic Christianity Before Paul." Pp. 308–19 in *The Writings of St. Paul*. Ed. Wayne Meeks. New York: Norton.

Hengel, Martin
1974 *Judaism and Hellenism: Studies in Their Encounter in Palestine during the Hellenistic Period*. Philadelphia: Fortress.
1976 "Hellenisierung als literarisches, philosophisches, sprachliches und religiöses Problem" and "Die Übernahme griechischer Sprache und Bildung durch die jüdische Diaspora im ptolemäischen Ägypten." Pp. 94–115 and 126–44 in *Juden, Griechen und Barbaren: Aspekte der Hellenisierung des Judentums in vorchristlicher Zeit*. SBS 76. Stuttgart: Katholisches Bibelwerk.

Horsley, Richard A.
1987 *Jesus and the Spiral of Violence: Popular Jewish Resistance in Roman Palestine*. New York: Harper & Row.

Humphrey, J. H., ed.
1991 *Literacy in the Roman World*. Journal of Roman Archaeology, Supplementary Series 3. Ann Arbor, MI.

Innis, Harold.
1951 *The Bias of Communication*. Toronto: University of Toronto Press.
1972 *Empire and Communications*. Toronto: University of Toronto Press.

Jones, A. H. M.
1940 *The Greek City from Alexander to Justinian*. Oxford: Clarendon.

Jüthner, Julius
    1923   *Hellenen und Barbaren*. Leipzig: Teubner.

Kähler, Martin
    1964   *The So–Called Historical Jesus and the Biblical Christ of Faith*. Philadelphia: Fortress.

Käsemann, Ernst
    1969   *New Testament Questions of Today*. Philadelphia: Fortress.

Kee, Howard Clark
    1992   "Early Christianity in the Galilee: Reassessing the Evidence from the Gospels." Pp. 3–22 in *The Galilee in Late Antiquity*. Ed. Lee Levine. New York and Jerusalem: Jewish Theological Seminary.

Kelber, Werner
    1983   *The Oral and the Written Gospel: The Hermeneutics of Speaking and Writing in the Synoptic Tradition, Mark, Paul and Q*. Philadelphia: Fortress.

Klein, Ralph W.
    1992   "Books of Ezra–Nehemiah." Pp. 731–42 in *The Anchor Bible Dictionary*, vol. 2. New York: Doubleday.

Lévi-Strauss, Claude
    1973   *Tristes Tropiques*. Trans. John & Doreen Weightman. New York: Atheneum.

Lord, Albert B.
    1978   *The Singer of Tales*. New York: Atheneum.

Lowery, Shearon A. and Melvin L. DeFleur
    1983   *Milestones in Mass Communications Research: Media Effects*. New York: Longman.

Lüdemann, Gerd
    1980   "The Successors of Pre–70 Jerusalem Christianity." Pp. 161–73, 245–54 in *Jewish and Christian Self–Definition, vol. 1: The Shaping of Christianity in the Second and Third Centuries*. Ed. E. P. Sanders. Philadelphia: Fortress.

Mack, Burton L.
    1988   *A Myth of Innocence: Mark and Christian Origins*. Philadelphia: Fortress.

MacMullen, Ramsay
    1974   *Roman Social Relations 50 B.C.–A.D. 284*. New Haven: Yale University Press.

Maccoby, Hyam
    1986   *The Myth–maker: Paul and the Invention of Christianity*. New York: Harper & Row.

Marrou, Henri Irenee
    1982   *A History of Education in Antiquity*. Madison: University of Wisconsin Press.

McLuhan, Marshall
    1964   *Understanding Media: The Extensions of Man.* New York: McGraw–Hill.

Meier, John P.
    1991   *A Marginal Jew: Rethinking the Historical Jesus.* New York: Doubleday.

Meyers, Eric and James F. Strange
    1981   *Archeology, the Rabbis, and Early Christianity.* Nashville: Abingdon.

Millard, A. R.
    1992   "Literacy (Israel)." Pp. 337–40 in *The Anchor Bible Dictionary*, vol. 4. New York: Doubleday.

Momigliano, Arnaldo
    1975   *Alien Wisdom: The Limits of Hellenization.* Cambridge: Cambridge University Press.

Neusner, Jacob
    1972   "Types and Forms in Ancient Jewish Literature: Some Comparisons." *HR* 11:354–90.
    1978   "Comparing Judaisms: Essay–Review of *Paul and Palestinian Judaism* by E. P. Sanders," *HR* 18:177–91.
    1984   *Invitation to the Talmud.* 2nd ed. San Francisco: Harper and Row
    1985   *The Memorized Torah: The Mnemonic Sytem of the Torah.* Chico, CA: Scholars.
    1987   *The Making of the Mind of Judaism.* Atlanta: Scholars.
    1988   *The Formation of the Jewish Intellect.* Atlanta: Scholars.

Ong, Walter J.
    1967   *The Presence of the Word.* New Haven: Yale University Press.
    1982   *Orality and Literacy.* New York: Methuen.
    1986   "Text as Interpretation: Mark and After." Pp. 147–169 in *Oral Tradition in Literature: Interpretation in Context.* Ed. John Miles Foley. Columbia: University of Missouri Press.

Overbeck, Franz
    1882   "Über die Anfänge der patristischen Literatur." *Historische Zeitschrift* 12:417–72.

Pattison, Robert
    1982   *On Literacy: The Politics of the Word from Homer to the Age of Rock.* Oxford: Oxford University Press.

Roberts, Colin Henderson
    1979   *Manuscript, Society and Belief in Early Christian Egypt.* Oxford: Oxford University Press.

Rostovtzeff, Mikail Ivanovich
    1957   *The Social and Economic History of the Roman Empire.* 2nd ed. Oxford: Oxford University Press.

Sanders, E. P.
    1985   *Jesus and Judaism.* Philadelphia: Fortress.
    1992   *Judaism: Practice and Belief, 63 BCE–66CE.* Philadelphia: Trinity.

1993 "Jesus in Historical Context." *T Today* 50:429–48.

Sandmel, Samuel
1983 "Foreword for Jews." Pp. xi–xiii in *The Pseudepigrapha of the Old Testament*, vol. I. Ed. James H. Charlesworth. Garden City, N.Y.: Doubleday.

Schoeps, Hans–Joachim
1949 *Theologie und Geschichte des Judenchristentums*. Tübingen: Mohrlsiebeck.
1961 *Paul: The Theology of the Apostle in the Light of Jewish Religious History*. Philadelphia: Westminster.

Schürer, Emil
1979 *The History of the Jewish People in the Age of Jesus Christ*, vol. II. Rev. and ed. by G. Vermes, et al. Edinburgh: T. & T. Clark.

Schwabe, M.
"Greek Inscriptions Found at Beth Shearim in the Fifth Excavation Season, 1953." *IEJ* 4:249–261.

Scott, Bernard Brandon
1989 *Hear Then the Parable*. Minneapolis: Fortress.

Senior, Donald and Carroll Stuhlmueller
1983 *The Biblical Foundations for Mission*. Maryknoll, NY: Orbis.

Sevenster, J. N.
1968 *Do You Know Greek? How Much Greek Could the First Jewish Christians Have Known?* NovTSup 19. Leiden: Brill.

Simon, Marcel
1948 *Verus Israel: Étude sur les relations entre chrétiens et juifs dans l'empire romain*. Paris: Boccard.
1972 "La Migration à Pella: Légende ou réalité?" in *Judéo–Christianisme: volume offert au Cardinal Jean Daniélou*. RSR 60:37–54.

Strecker, Georg
1971 "On the Problem of Jewish Christianity" Pp. 241–85 in *Orthodoxy and Heresy in Earliest Christianity*. Ed. Walter Bauer. Philadelphia: Westminster.

Szlezák, Thomas Alexander
1985 *Platon und die Schriftlichkeit der Philosophie*. Berlin: de Gruyter.

Tarn, William Woodthrope
1956 *Alexander the Great*. Boston: Beacon.

Theissen, Gerd
1974 *Urchristliche Wundergeschichte: Ein Beitrag zur formgeschichtlichen Erforschung der synoptischen Evangelien*. Gütersloh: Mohn.

Thomas, Rosalind
1989 *Oral Tradition and Written Record in Classical Athens*. Cambridge: Cambridge University Press.

1992 *Literacy and Orality in Ancient Greece*. Cambridge: Cambridge University Press.

Vermes, Geza
1986 "Scripture and Oral Tradition in Judaism: Written and Oral Torah." Pp. 79–95 in *The Written Word: Literacy in Transition*. Ed. G. Baumann. Oxford: Oxford University Press.

Vielhauer, Philipp
1975 *Geschichte der urchristlichen Literatur*. Berlin: De Gruyter.

Wrede, William.
1907 *Paulus*. Göttingen: Vandenhoeck & Ruprecht.

Yadin, Yigael
1971 *Bar–Kokhba*. London: Weidenfeld and Nicolson.

Youtie, H. C.
1966 "Pétaus, fils de Pétaus, ou le scribe qui ne savait pas écrire." *Chronique d' Egypte* 41:127–43.
1971 "*Agrammatos*: An Aspect of Greek Society in Egypt," *Harvard Studies in Classical Philology* 75:161–76.
1971 "*Bradeos graphoth*: Between Literacy and Illiteracy," *GRBS* 12:239–61.
1975 "*Hypographeus*: The Social Impact of Illiteracy in Graeco–Roman Egypt," *Zeitschrift für Papyrologie und Epigraphik* 17:201–21.

TEXTUALITY IN AN ORAL CULTURE:
A SURVEY OF THE PAULINE TRADITIONS

Joanna Dewey
Episcopal Divinity School

ABSTRACT

This article begins to explore the hypothesis that, for its first century of existence, Christianity was an oral phenomenon in a predominately oral culture. Part I looks at literacy and oral communication media in the first-century Mediterranean world. Literacy in Greco-Roman antiquity was limited both in the ways it was used and in the percentage of the population who were literate. People lived in a oral culture. Even the most literate would have made little use of reading or writing for either business or pleasure. On the other hand, writing was essential for the creation and maintenance of the Roman Empire. It was both an instrument of power and a symbol of power. Part II investigates the roles of literacy, textuality, and orality in the extant texts related to Paul. Paul and his congregations lived in a largely oral media world, with minimal use of written texts or appeal to manuscript authority. Although Paul produced texts for long-distance correspondence, which later became authoritative texts, Christians did not yet view texts as central. 2 Thessalonians, Colossians, and Ephesians provide evidence of a developing literary tradition; however, the Pastorals and the canonical and Apocryphal Acts seem to derive from the oral memory of Paul rather than from his letters. The letters are not yet important in forming the churches' views of Paul. Part III suggests some implications that recognition of the relative unimportance of textuality among early Christians has for our reconstruction of early Christian history. Early Christian texts are not necessarily representative of early Christianity as a whole, but rather of the views of the small, educated male minority, the only group that was literate. Recognition of the chiefly oral media world of early Christianity makes the task of historical reconstruction more difficult, but it also opens possibilities for richer understanding.

INTRODUCTION

In studying the development of early Christianity, scholars have on the whole assumed that the first-century media world functioned much as our modern print media world does, giving priority to logical linear thinking and to written texts. Since the early days of form criticism, we have acknowledged that there was an oral stage prior to the written gospels. We have, however, assumed that the progression from oral performance to written text was a continuous linear development, with writing rapidly becoming the primary medium for Christians, and with written texts supplanting oral tradition as soon as they were composed. We have tended to equate Christianity with written documents, whether extant texts or our own hypothetical reconstructions. We have yet to grasp fully the implications the ancient oral/aural media world have for understanding the formation of early Christianity.

It is true that scholars have become more aware of ancient orality since the publication of Werner Kelber's *The Oral and the Written Gospel: The Hermeneutics of Speaking and Writing in the Synoptic Tradition, Mark, Paul, and Q* in 1983 and since the formation of the "Bible in Ancient and Modern Media Group" of the Society of Biblical Literature by Thomas Boomershine in the same year (Kelber; Silberman). As a result, it is no longer unusual to find biblical scholars who have read the work of Walter Ong and who stress that early Christians heard rather than read the gospels. Nonetheless, we are still a long way from understanding the high degree of orality in ancient Mediterranean cultures and the ways orality and literacy interacted, working together and working against each other. We have only begun to investigate how literates and nonliterates shared the same culture and, at the same time, participated in quite different cultural worlds. We do not yet have an overview of how orality and literacy affected the development of the early churches and the formation of the New Testament canon. We have yet to consider fully how Christianity itself participated in orality and literacy. We are just beginning to develop a sense of the first-century media world and how Christianity fits within it.

Stated provocatively, my guiding hypothesis is that Christianity began as an oral phenomenon in a predominately oral culture within which the dominant elite were literate and made extensive use of writing to maintain hegemony and control. Only gradually did Christianity come to depend upon the written word. The growing number of Christian texts and of literate Christians[1] in the second and following centuries helped facilitate the shift to manuscript-based authority and to the hegemony and control of Christian churches by a small educated male elite.[2] Our tendency to equate Christianity with written texts and to see these texts as typical of all of early Christianity, leads us to construct a distorted and one-sided view of the nature and spirit of the early churches. This article represents an exploratory step toward investigating the hypothesis by

---

[1] In sheer numbers, not necessarily in the percentage of Christians who were literate.

[2] There were of course other sociological forces at work contributing to this change. The importance of the media shift to textuality, however, has not yet been sufficiently recognized.

studying the roles of literacy, textuality, and orality in the Pauline traditions. In order to do so, we need some grasp of the extent and uses of literacy in antiquity. Therefore, Part I looks at literacy and to a lesser extent at oral communication media in the first-century Mediterranean world. Part II is an investigation of the role of literacy and orality in the extant texts related to Paul: the undisputed letters, the deutero-Pauline letters, the canonical Acts of the Apostles, and the apocryphal Acts of Paul. I have chosen to focus on the Pauline materials for two reasons: first, we have sufficient materials to make such a study possible; and second, the Christian churches based in urban Mediterranean cities were likely the most literate of the early Christian groups. These two factors, of course, are not unrelated. In Part III, I shall suggest some implications that recognition of the relative unimportance of textuality among early Christians has for our reconstruction of early Christian history.

PART I
LITERACY AND ORALITY IN THE ANCIENT MEDITERRANEAN

The first-century media world was a manuscript culture with high residual orality (Ong: 158). But to define it that way is to define it from the perspective of the elite, those few who could read and write, and who ruled the Empire. Most people living during the first century were not literate: occasionally for specific very limited purposes they made use of writing, but that writing was done by someone else. Furthermore, writing and reading were not silent, individual activities. They were closely allied to the oral world, to speech. Botha writes, "Greco-Roman literacy—the little that existed—remained a kind of imitation talking" (1992a:206).

It is still not unusual to read scholarly estimates of widespread literacy in ancient cities. Recently, however, we have become aware that these estimates are gross overestimates. Scholars investigating cross-cultural agrarian and advanced agrarian societies estimate that only between two and four percent of ancient Mediterranean people were literate (Malina and Rohrbaugh: 3; Rohrbaugh 1993:115; Bar-Ilan: 56). It is generally agreed that literacy rates were much lower among women than among men and much lower in rural than in urban areas. William V. Harris' recent massive work, *Ancient Literacy*, attempts to summarize all the ancient evidence on literacy, and the following discussion draws heavily on his work.[3] He gives somewhat higher estimates than the social scientists do, suggesting 15 percent or less for males in Italian cities (267)

---

[3] For reviews of his work, see Humphrey; Keenan. While many have argued about specifics of Harris's description, as Humphrey (5) notes, few question his basic thesis of low literacy rates.

and similar or lower levels for males in the eastern Mediterranean. What constituted literacy is also not clear. Reading and writing were distinct skills in antiquity; literacy could mean anything from the simple ability to write one's own name to fluency in both reading and writing. Harris tends to use a minimal definition of literacy. But whatever definition one chooses, it seems safe to conclude that literacy was not widespread in antiquity. For the purposes of this paper, nonliterates were those who neither read nor wrote. And in the first-century, most people were nonliterate.

That literacy rates were low should not surprise us. A very small educated elite, plus a few literate slaves and freedpeople, could handle the writing needed to maintain an empire and to conduct long distance trade, about the only activities in antiquity that absolutely depended on writing. Most people had little or no use for reading and writing skills. In the following sections, I shall describe first the typical uses of literacy, second the portion of the population who was literate, and third, the means of literate and oral communication.

Uses of Literacy

Among the ruling elite, the top two-to-five per cent of the population,[4] literacy was used for the arts. There was considerable production and consumption of literature. All literary works seem to have been written for this small group. Even the Greek romance was not the first-century equivalent of the mass market paperback: rather than appealing to a wider audience, it was the light reading of the very limited reading public "possessing a real degree of education" (Harris: 227-28). "[L]iterature was a symbol of social status (and conversely, a point of access to the upper class, a way of making contact with the elite), and remained the preserve of the aristocracy" (Botha 1992a:206). This literature, however, was usually experienced aurally (Yaghjian). Readings and performances were common at the gatherings of the elite. "Texts were produced to be read out loud in a communal setting" (Cartlidge: 406, n.37; cf. Knox; Slusser).

The primary practical use of writing in antiquity was the ruling of the empire (Botha 1992a:208). The administrative letter was the essential tool for regulating the empire's business. "In the context of the Roman imperial administration, correspondence was the most important

---

[4] Percentages as always are elusive. The governing classes rarely exceed two percent of the population in an agrarian society (Lenski: 219; Duling and Perrin: 56; Rohrbaugh 1993:17). Since some of the higher status merchants and retainers may have participated in the elite culture, a somewhat higher percentage is perhaps an appropriate guess.

instrument with which the affairs of the vast and often distant provinces could be regulated and adjudicated" (Koester 1991:355). Writing was a practical necessity for the empire. In addition to administrative correspondence, the government used writing for inscriptions of laws posted in public places. These inscriptions were not the normal way for officials to communicate with the public: this was done orally by means of public criers. Thus, the public inscriptions may have been more to convey the prestige and power of the law than to communicate the content to the ruled. They were symbols of the power and authority of Rome (Botha 1992a:197). Perhaps precisely because it could be read by so few, writing carried a sense of authority and stature. "Virtually every culture that has mastered the art of writing, or even only come into direct contact with scribal or chirographic culture, has assigned immense importance and prestige to the written word" (Graham: 12). The empire both used writing and also made use of the status of writing as a means to rule.

Long-distance trade, which was by definition in luxury items, also required writing. In addition, personal letters to kin living at a distance were common. Nonliterates, and frequently also literates, would employ scribes for writing letters. Writing, whether for government, business, or personal matters, was primarily a tool that enabled communication at a distance, when oral communication was not possible.

Little use of reading and writing was necessary to get along in everyday life, either personally or economically, and the little necessary could be done by professional scribes. By the first-century, wills and marriage and divorce agreements were frequently written.[5] It was easy to have such documents drawn up by scribes even if one was not literate. In the economic sphere, there is extensive documentary evidence of contracts and apprenticeship agreements made on behalf of nonliterates. Most business transactions, however, would not require writing at all. Trading was usually face-to-face and oral. Tradespeople and artisans did not need writing to conduct their small businesses; only contracts for large sums of money were normally put in writing. One could live and conduct business without being literate. This would be true even for an elite man with extensive estates. For him it would be a social shame more than a practical inconvenience not to be literate, for his slaves or freedpeople could do the work for him (Harris: 248–51).

One final area for consideration is religion. Religions made some use of the written word for prophecies and inscriptions. The use of writing gave the content special power or solemnity:

---

[5] Written wills and formal marriage and divorce agreements presuppose at least minimal property and thus were probably not needed by many in the population. Legal marriage (with written documentation) was the exception rather than the rule.

> [T]he written word itself exercised religious power: it was sometimes believed (or simply felt) to have some special and profound quality that caused or allowed people to bring about extraordinary results. One need only remember the Sibylline Books. . . . There are also the magical papyri and Jewish attitudes to writing the name of God (Botha 1992a:209).

This public use may be akin to the public posting of civil laws. Nonetheless, participation in religious ceremonies or looking after a household altar did not require literacy. Religious propaganda addressed to the general public was oral. Letter-writing was not a typical means of religious propaganda, although writing to communicate at a distance was occasionally used for religious purposes. Jews and Epicureans seem to have used letters to connect geographically-separated groups (Harris: 220); Paul certainly wrote to his churches to communicate at a distance.[6] Textuality was perhaps more central to Judaism since the Jews had created written texts—Scripture—as an integral part of their religion, and some among them engaged in oral interpretation of these written texts—developing the Oral Torah. To be a good Jew, however, did not require the ability to read the sacred texts.

In addition to the very limited need for writing for the large majority of the population, two other factors militated against the spread of literacy. First, writing materials were inconvenient and expensive (Harris: 193–96). The writing materials used for practical purposes were small potsherds or wax-covered tablets. The tablets, gathered in codexes of ten, could hold about fifty words on a side. These were inexpensive and easy to reuse, but inconvenient, bulky, and useless for texts of any great length. Papyrus and parchment, used extensively by the elite, would have been prohibitively expensive for most people. In Egypt, about 45 CE, when skilled laborers earned six obols a day, and unskilled three a day, a single sheet of papyrus sold for two obols (Harris: 194); prices were likely higher outside of Egypt. Writing materials for texts of any length, such as most of Paul's letters or a gospel, were beyond the means of most of the population.

Second, given the limited use of literacy, there was virtually no public support for mass education. Schooling seems to have declined in the Eastern Mediterranean with the advent of Roman power (Harris: 281). Insofar as the Roman Empire needed literate clerks, it trained slaves rather than the free population. Schooling, while relatively cheap compared to the price of papyrus, had to be paid for by the family, and there was little economic advantage to be gained by teaching one's sons or daughters to read and write. Schooling in elementary letters was

---

[6] Koester (1991) suggests that Christians used the letter as the empire used the administrative letter—to create unity.

uncommon even in the cities (Harris: 235–46; Botha 1992a:202–4). Unlike the situation in early modern Europe, there were neither economic nor religious forces fostering literacy.

Who Was Literate?

From a grasp of the uses of literacy in antiquity, it is relatively easy to describe who was and was not literate. Literacy was nearly universal among the politically and socially elite men of the Empire (Harris: 248–52). Harris writes, "Within the elites of the established Graeco–Roman world a degree of written culture was a social necessity, and an illiterate male would have been regarded as bizarre" (248). However, even within this stratum of society, a person would not need to do much if any reading or writing. In addition to the elite themselves, a variety of functionaries of the elite—the males of the retainer class—were likely to have a fairly high literacy rate.[7] In the army, legionaries could sometimes read, and literacy did provide some chance for advancement. Not surprisingly literacy correlated with military rank. In addition, there were literate slaves and freedmen who carried out much of the clerical work of the empire, but they would constitute only a very small proportion of all slaves and freedpersons.

Outside of the social–political elite and their retainers, literacy was quite restricted (Harris: 253–281). Merchants in international trade might well be literate—or employ literates. Practitioners of a few crafts tended to be literate. In classical Greece, doctors,[8] engineers, surveyors, and rhapsodes were generally literate (Harris: 82). Some, such as doctors, were also often slaves, at least by the time of the Empire (Meeks: 57). There is little evidence that the number of crafts requiring literacy increased in Hellenistic or Roman times. In addition to those in specific occupations, wealthy business people were also often literate. However, we know of historical and fictional wealthy businessmen who were not literate themselves (Harris: 197–98). Ownership of a prosperous business increased the likelihood that a person was literate, but did not require it. The newly wealthy in particular often lacked education (Harris: 251).

Two groups require special consideration: women and Jews. At every social level, women's literacy rate was lower than men's. The difference would be least among the elite. Within this group, women may have been nearly as literate as men (so Harris: 252), or considerably less literate (so Veyne: 20). Literacy skills would have been useful to these women as

---

[7] The size of the retainer class is difficult to ascertain from historical records. Lenski estimates it to be about five times the size of the governing class (245).

[8] Midwives, however, were sometimes exhorted to be literate, suggesting that many of them were not (Harris: 203).

managers of large households. There were ancient women authors of considerable literary artistry, particularly in the genres of lyric and elegiac poetry (Snyder; see also Kraemer; Lefkowitz). Outside of the elite, women's literacy was rare, but it did occur, generally associated with wealth or with a particular occupation (see Pomeroy 1977; Pomeroy 1981:309–16; Cole). There is considerable evidence of families in which the men were literate and the women not, and little evidence of the opposite (Harris: 279).

The question must be raised as to whether the Jews were more literate than other nationalities in the Roman Empire, since the importance of Scripture in their religion may have functioned to encourage literacy. Little evidence is available. On the basis of cross-cultural analysis and rabbinic references, Bar-Ilan (56) suggests a literacy rate of less than three percent in the lands of Israel—about the same as others estimate for the empire as a whole (Malina and Rohrbaugh: 3; contra Townsend: 154–57). Harris also suggests that widespread Jewish literacy was very unlikely (281). Literacy rates among Jews most likely correlated with their social status. Many of the chief priests, elders, and Pharisees were probably literate—and literate in more than one language. The chief priests and elders were the wealthy landowners, part of the generally literate governing elite. The Pharisees were retainers, bureaucrats for whom scribal skills were useful (Saldarini; Horsley: 73–75). The Pharisees' literacy could be and was used for religious purposes in reading and interpretation of Scripture. However, the Pharisaic emphasis upon the writings probably had not yet resulted in any increase in literacy beyond the retainer class.

In summary, literacy in Graeco-Roman antiquity was quite limited both in the percentage of the population who were literate and in the ways literacy was used. It is virtually impossible for modern academics to realize how unimportant writing and reading were for the conduct of daily life. Although nonliterates would be familiar with the existence of written documents and might make use of writing through an intermediary a few times in their lives, they could nevertheless live nonliterate lives without shame or inconvenience. And likewise, even those who were most literate would have made very little use of reading or writing for either business or pleasure. On the other hand, writing was essential for the creation and maintenance of the Roman Empire. It affected everyone's lives through written laws, administrative correspondence, and debt records. In a world in which most were nonliterate, writing was both an instrument of power and a symbol of power. So although few could read or write, reading and writing were fundamental in structuring relations in the ancient world. At least a partial analogy can perhaps be made to nuclear weapons. Few of us know how to make them; even fewer control their use. Yet a nation's possession or lack of nuclear weapons is important in determining its status and power, and all of us are affected by our knowledge of the power of such weapons.

Means of Literate and Oral Communication

By the standards of modern industrialized society with its print and electronic communication systems, mass communication in the ancient world was extremely limited and usually oral. Literacy was essential to the formation and communication of the dominant culture. Among elite males, the formal rhetorical education with its attendant literacy created a shared and relatively homogenous culture and value system (Sjoberg: 119, 290). "And the homogeneity of the ruling elite has had the major consequence of permitting the expansion of empires" (290). This homogeneity facilitated control and hegemony by the governing elite (Botha 1992a:208).

Yet even the elite were dependent upon word–of–mouth for most communication (Sjoberg: 286). For them—as well as for less literate groups—literacy was used to enhance and facilitate orality. David Cartlidge writes, "The evidence from late antiquity is that oral operations (presentation and hearing) and literary operations (reading and writing) were (1) inescapably interlocked, and (2) they were communal activities. Chirographs were created for and by the community and in the service of orality" (407). This was true not only of literature. Letters were not read silently by individuals; they would be read aloud; letters to groups would be performed orally. "[O]ne must reckon with the letter as having been prepared for a careful performance, and [with the fact] that eventually the letter was delivered like a proper speech" (Botha 1992b:24). Textuality, when it existed, existed as an aid to oral presentation.

As noted earlier, official communication to the population at large was by means of public criers ($\kappa\eta\rho\nu\kappa\epsilon s$, *praecones*). They were numerous and attached to government officials at all levels (Harris: 208). But probably even more influential in diffusing knowledge among the nonliterates were the street entertainers, storytellers, actors, and musicians (Sjorberg: 287). When we think of oral performers in antiquity, we tend to think first of the rhapsodes who performed Homer and other ancient literature both at gatherings of the wealthy and in public theater performance. But the rhapsodes were literate and provided entertainment primarily for the elite. The street performers were normally nonliterates entertaining the nonliterate. Only a little information is available, because such people were scorned by the class that composed the written texts

(Sjorberg: 287–89; Scobie). Those who earned their living by storytelling were among the many itinerant street artists of antiquity; they eked out a living telling stories in the company of musicians, dancing girls, astrologers, cynic street-preachers, sword-swallowers, and the rest. A second group consisted of official religious storytellers, associated with temples, who told of the miracles accomplished by the particular god or goddess of the place. The temple storytellers would both amuse their listeners and teach them. This group had greater status than the street performers who were usually outcasts; their social status was similar to that of the temple priests (Scobie: 241).

In addition, there were many storytellers who did not make their living from performing, but who would be known in their village, town or region as good tellers of tales. They would entertain and teach in the work places, to their neighbors in the evening, or while travelling. Storytelling was also particularly associated with women and children. There are numerous references to nursemaids, servants or slaves in the houses of the elite, who told stories to frighten the children in their charge into obedience, or to lull them to sleep (Scobie: 244–51).

It is through the stories of these popular storytellers that nonliterates would become familiar with the dominant tradition. "A prominent part of the repertoires of the story-tellers are [sic] selections from the society's most revered literature: the religious writings, the sagas of traditional heroes, and the great poets" (Sjorberg: 287). It is probably through such storytellers that most Jews gained their familiarity with Scripture. Storytellers were important not only in diffusing the dominant tradition but also in "distorting it" (Sjorberg: 136–37; 289). Sjorberg suggests that distortion is due partly to lack of literacy, that is, reliance on memory, and partly to "their efforts to dramatize a story to gain more listeners and thereby increase their earnings" (289). I would argue that distortion, i.e. change, is *also* due to the shift in social location of both the storyteller and the audience. The storytellers would reinforce values of the dominant culture contained in the stories, but they would also alter the stories to reflect popular values and popular resentments against the elite that they shared with their audiences (Ong; James C. Scott). In addition, there would generally be local stories known to particular sub-groups but not to the elite (Vansina: 154). It was probably with good reason that the elite distrusted entertainers as "potential purveyors of ideas that threaten the authority structure" (Sjorberg: 136). Even the women's stories to children were suspect. Plato wrote in the *Republic* IIC:

> We must begin, then, it seems, by a censorship over our storymakers, and what they do well we must pass and what not, reject. And the stories on the accepted list we will induce nurses and mothers to tell to the children and so

shape their souls by these stories far rather than their bodies by their hands. But most of the stories they now tell we must reject (177).

Contact between literates and nonliterates was probably rather limited. While governing elites and nonliterates would have little if any direct contact in ancient society, some of the retainer class and successful merchants probably would interact with urban nonliterates (Sjorberg: 108-44; Rohrbaugh, 1991). Within a city, outside of the elite area, people tended to live in ethnic and occupational groupings, often organized into guilds. Within these groupings, there might be some literates who interacted often with nonliterates. Certainly in many families in which there was any literacy, the man had some degree of literacy and the woman had none. Nonliterates would honor reading and writing as symbols of culture and status; they would also fear them as instruments of social and political oppression. It is in this milieu, largely nonliterate, mostly dependent on criers and storytellers for knowledge and communication, but with some connection to literates, that urban Christianity took shape.9

PART II
LITERACY AND ORALITY IN THE PAULINE TRADITION

It is difficult to determine the extent and functions of literacy in Graeco-Roman antiquity. Given our lack of knowledge about the precise makeup of early Christian communities, it is even more difficult to estimate the degree of literacy among Christians. Furthermore, how much literacy and of what sort becomes an important question. It would require a high degree of reading literacy to read aloud a Pauline letter if one were not already thoroughly familiar with its content. It would require only minimal literacy to present the letter orally to a congregation, if one had heard it and had been prepared to deliver it to a group. Even the degree of literacy needed to compose and dictate letters such as Paul's is open to question. Nonetheless, it is possible to approach the issue with greater precision than heretofore and thus gain a better picture of the importance of literacy in the Pauline churches. I shall look first at the authentic letters of Paul for what we can learn about who was literate and how literacy was used in the early churches. Then I shall look at the deutero- and related Pauline material for what we can tell about both the development of a literate tradition and the continuing importance of orality.

---

9 Rural Christianity would have had even less connection with literates (Oakman; Rohrbaugh 1993).

Literacy and Textuality in Paul's Letters

Who Was Literate. Probably the best and most extensive discussion of social location in early urban Christianity remains Wayne Meeks' study of the Pauline communities (1983). Meeks' analysis supports the consensus that the early churches contained a cross-section of the social scale, excluding at the top the ruling elite, and at the bottom, the most destitute (51–53, 73). The exclusion of the extreme top, however, means the exclusion of the only group for whom fluent literacy was the norm. To state this in another way, there may have been *no* Christians in the mid-first century who had received the education of the governing elites. Thus, for those early Christians who were to some degree literate, writing would have been a particular achievement, not something taken for granted as part of their social milieu.

According to Meeks, the typical member of a Pauline church was a free artisan or small trader (63–72), the person who worked for a living and could contribute to the Jerusalem collection only bit by bit (1 Cor 16:1–2). Harris' evidence suggests that people in this group were generally not literate, for, as we have seen, there would be no need for literacy for the conduct of business or craft. If this group indeed made up the large majority of Paul's churches, then the literacy rate among early urban Christians was low, probably even in comparison to what was customary in ancient cities. The Pauline congregations included both slaves and slave owners. Those slaves who were clerks would have been literate; thus it is possible that a higher proportion of the slaves than of the free artisans and tradespeople were literate. However, most would not be literate, as slaves generally were not literate.

The writing of letters to and from the churches suggests, though it does not require, that some people in the communities were literate. Meeks discusses in detail the social location of all those named in Paul's letters about whom we can determine anything. Those who were prominent enough for the names to be mentioned were usually high-ranking in some aspect of status—although not part of the ruling elite. It is members of this group who were most likely to have some skills of reading or writing. Looking at Meeks' data, it is possible to make some observations about the literacy of this group.

First of all, Paul himself was literate. Furnish describes him as "apparently trained in the subjects that constituted the lower and middle levels of Hellenistic education" (11). Paul may have been literate because of his social class—he spoke of his craft labor as if it were choice rather than economic necessity—and/or because of his training as a Pharisee. Given our own literate biases, however, we may overestimate the degree of Paul's literacy and his reliance on writing. Like other literates, he often dictated rather than wrote himself (Rom 16:22; see also 1 Cor 16:21; Gal 6:11; Phil 19). We cannot really determine the extent of Paul's education. His letters are certainly not written in a high style, but letters often were not composed in a high style. Scholars have increasingly recognized Paul's rhetorical skill and sophistication.[10] Yet rhetoric was pervasive in the ancient world, permeating the nonliterate oral culture as well as the literate culture. It is fully possible that Paul was more of a street or popular rhetorician than someone the elite would have recognized as a polished rhetorician. What we can say with certainty is that Paul (or Paul and his co-authors) had enough rhetorical skill to invent lengthy letters.

Even Paul's literacy, however, can be called into question. Most recently, P. J. J. Botha has put forward this possibility (1992b: 22–23). He suggests that Paul's statement about writing in large letters in Gal 6:11 is actually a reference to his inability to write:

> An interesting side issue is the very strong probability that Paul was *agrammatos*. Strictly speaking, Paul probably relied on scribes because he could not write Greek. A perusal of comments on Galatians 6:11 bears out that though the similarity to the illiteracy formula is well known, no-one wants to accept the implication of this similarity! (23).

Whether or not one wishes to pursue Botha's thought this far, Botha is certainly correct that literacy is much less necessary for the creation and reception of Paul's letters than we instinctively assume. Botha writes:

> Paul's letter was not written by him as an individual, sitting at a desk and dropping a note to some friends. We must become aware of a much more complex event: some persons combined their efforts to deliberate and "perform" a letter; there was someone involved in the creation and transportation of it, finally "recreating" for others a presentation/ performance of the "message" intended for sharing (22).

Some of the other traveling missionaries probably were also literate. The "superapostles" of 2 Corinthians apparently claimed great rhetorical skill, which implies education.[11] Apollos is described in Acts 18:24 as "an eloquent man, well versed in the scriptures," again implying education (if Luke can be trusted, given his bias for wealthy Christians). But traveling missionaries need not have been literate; Peter and John are described in Acts 4:13 as unlettered.[12] Literacy was not necessary for missionary work:

---

[10] For references on Paul and rhetoric, see Furnish: 11, n. 21.

[11] The debate about wisdom in 1 Cor 1–4 is cast in terms of speaking; it is unlikely that writing was involved (so also Kelber: 173–75). Indeed, how much the contest between Paul and the superapostles in 2 Cor involved rhetoric as understood by the literate elite is open to doubt.

[12] In ancient usage, the term ἀγραμματοι could mean nonliterate, or more generally, uneducated, in which case the person could have received the first stages of

preaching was oral, and new cults were normally propagated by word of mouth (Harris: 220). Insofar as the missionaries were itinerant charismatics, writing would have been no particular advantage and not a likely skill.

The people who carried Paul's letters to the Christian communities may well have possessed some literacy, for that would assist them in using the letter as the basis for their recitation to the congregation. If Phoebe not only carried Paul's letter to Rome but was also Paul's representative in performing the letter to Roman Christians, which is the natural inference, then she was probably literate. Of individuals named in Paul's letters (see Meeks: 57–62), the only ones of whose literacy we can be reasonably sure on the basis of their occupations are Luke as a physician (Phlm 24; cf. Col 4:14) and Erastus as a city official, a keeper of accounts, whether slave or free (Rom 16:23). Lydia, engaged in an international luxury trade, would either be literate or the employer of literate slaves.[13] Judging from their occupation as tentmakers, Prisca and Aquila would not have been literate. If Acts 18:8 is correct that Crispus, whom Paul mentions in 1 Cor 1:14, was the ruler (patron?) of a synagogue, then he may well have been literate, in light of the synagogue's respect for written Scriptures.

The Christian churches clearly contained members wealthy enough to offer their houses for the lodging of Paul and others and for gatherings of the community. To what extent this wealth implies literacy is not evident. Such wealthy patrons were not part of the governing class; however, the extent of their wealth suggests use of writing, whether by themselves, by slaves, or by freedpeople in their employ. On the one hand, their status inconsistency of possessing greater wealth than social standing could have functioned as an incentive to better themselves socially through education. (Yet, their choice to join a despised and shameful religion does not suggest social climbing.) On the other hand, it is precisely this group, wealthy merchants and business people, whom the elite often scorned as not literate and not educated. All that we can say is that literacy is a possibility but not a necessity for them. Even if literacy was high among this group, the overall literacy of Pauline congregations would remain low.

Uses of Literacy in Paul's Churches. Literacy comes into play in Paul's churches in four respects: the production of letters, the reception of the letters, the possible use of Scripture in worship, and the use of Scripture in

---

education, learning the letters, but little further education (Harris: 5).

[13] She is mentioned only in Acts (16:14, 40). If Schottroff is correct that Lydia is lower class, in a profession despised because of its foul odor (65), then Lydia is not likely literate.

debate. The primary use of literacy was for letters traveling a long distance: Paul's letters, at least one letter from Corinthian Christians to Paul (1 Cor 5:9), and letters of recommendation (2 Cor 3:1-2). Here letters are a substitute for personal presence, not the preferred means of communication (Funk: 81-102), although Paul may have upon occasion deliberately chosen to write rather than to go himself, as the more effective means of influencing a community (Mitchell). Furthermore, as noted above, oral preparation seems to be an integral part of the creation of the written texts. Here, literacy seems definitely in the service of oral communication. While texts were produced that later became very important within Christianity *as texts*, these texts began as aids to orality, and seemingly had little importance in themselves.

Literacy is also less crucial to the reception of the letters than we are likely to assume. In the first place, given the nature of manuscripts, one needed to be quite familiar with a text in order to read it aloud, a familiarity that was perhaps more likely to have been gained by hearing it orally than by prior reading. "At the most basic level, the oral text was the 'base text', if only because reading a manuscript text virtually demanded prior knowledge of the text" (Graham: 36). The text was likely orally dictated and orally performed. In the initial instance the letter is likely to have been read—or performed—by the person carrying it.[14] Doty writes:

> I wonder if the Pauline letters may not be seen as the essential part of the messages Paul had to convey, pressed into brief compass as a basis for elaboration by the carriers. The subsequent reading of the letters in the primitive Christian communities would then have been the occasions for full exposition and expansion of the sketch of material in the letters (45-46).

Performance of the letter to a congregation probably involved a complex of literate and oral activities—and need not have involved literacy at all.

Later repeated use of Paul's letters in the communities to which they were originally sent and the exchange of his letters among Christian communities would require literacy. The fact that the letters were written documents gave them a permanence that oral discourse never has, and thus constituted a first step towards a developing literate tradition, a tradition that eventuated in the Christian canon. Although Paul's letters themselves were in the service of orality, they provided, if you will, both the raw material for and the impetus towards a communication system based on textuality.

Among Jews, Scripture, i.e. the writings, had already come to play a central role.[15] Yet Scripture seems not to have played a role in worship in

---

[14] On the letters as performance, see Ward's article in this volume.
[15] See Boomershine's article in this volume. That written texts were integral to

Paul's communities. Reading and interpretation of Scripture are not mentioned either in lists of gifts for church leaders or in instructions for orderly conduct of worship. When Paul lists gifts for church leadership, there is no reference to the Scripture at all (Rom 12:6–8; 1 Cor 12:27–31). Both lists do refer to teaching and/or teachers, but there is no indication that teaching consists of Scripture, or of readings of any sort. The Christian gospel proclaimed orally, or some aspect thereof, is the more likely content. The list of activities in worship (1 Cor 14:26) likewise refers to someone having a teaching (διδαχὴν ἔχει) but it seems to have in mind someone standing up and speaking spontaneously during worship, rather than a reader of the writings.

In his discussion of order in worship (1 Cor 12; 14), Paul wants to limit the number prophesying and speaking in tongues, and to have only one person speak at a time. He shows no concern, however, for order or silence while Scripture was being read. Interpretation refers not to interpretation of readings but of spoken prophecy or tongues. Thus, there is no evidence that Scripture readings were important in the worship of Paul's communities and it seems unlikely that they occurred at all. There is also no indication in Paul's letters that these mostly gentile Christians participated in synagogue worship and thus heard Scripture read or performed there. The picture of Paul preaching in the synagogues comes from Acts, which was written at a later time, and that picture does not seem very probable on the basis of Paul's letters. Indeed Scripture-reading in Christian worship is not mentioned until the early second century (1 Tim 4:13), and the regular use of Scripture-reading in services is first attested by Justin Martyr (1 Apol 67:3) around the middle of the second century (Aune 1992:977, 983; Graham: 123). The only reading done during worship in Paul's churches was the reading—or rather performance—of Paul's letters.

Although Hebrew Scripture does not appear to be part of worship, it certainly informs Paul's basic view of God, history, and salvation. Such an understanding does not require extensive participation in manuscript culture. It could be, and for most Jews was, acquired orally through participation in the popular culture, through storytelling rather than manuscript reading. Paul, however, quotes and alludes to specific scriptural passages in his letters—which indicates participation in manuscript culture at some point in his history.[16] He is able to quote extensively from memory—since as a missionary for Christ he is unlikely

---

the religion of the Jewish elite (both the ruling and retainer classes) seems indisputable. To what extent popular Jewish practice drew on written texts is an area in need of investigation.

[16] On Paul's use of Scripture, see e.g. Hays; James M. Scott.

to have had access to Bible scrolls. The question then becomes, how central is Paul's textual use of Scripture? Is Scripture *as written text* central for Paul?

I would argue that it is not. In most of Paul's letters (1 Thes, 1 Cor, 2 Cor, Phil, Phlm), if scriptural quotations appear at all, scriptural arguments are secondary, providing additional supporting evidence for positions already taken. It is only in Galatians and Romans that argumentation on the basis of Scripture is central. In Galatians, the necessity to argue from Scripture seems to have been forced upon Paul by his opponents. In a mixed oral/written media culture there is prestige attached to appealing to an ancient powerful written tradition and the opponents in Galatia seem to have made this appeal. Paul responds, using Scripture often against its traditional meaning, arguing that Christians already have the Spirit—the written word would confine them (see A. Dewey; Kelber: 140–83). The opposition to Paul on the part of some Jewish Christians is the reason for the focus on Scripture in Romans; Paul must show that his understanding of the place of the Law is in accord with Scripture. Paul's more primary appeal, I believe, is an appeal to experience, his own and his churches' experience. The picture of Paul arguing on the basis of Scripture to prove Christianity is, of course, based on Acts, not Paul.

A contrast with Jewish use of Scripture is perhaps helpful at this point. The Pharisees were developing the Oral Torah, the oral interpretation of written texts, as a dominant mode of discourse. While the interpretation was oral, it was quite precisely interpretation of a written (and probably memorized) text. The manuscript—the text itself—was foundational and central for the oral interpretation. In contrast to this, for Paul, Christ is central. While Paul is clearly influenced by Jewish understandings of God, history, and apocalyptic, he seems little concerned with the text as text. Paul can and does appeal to Scripture when it is helpful to support his argument, but it does not appear to be the foundation for his understanding or the constant reference point. On the other hand, the way Paul uses Scripture as part of a larger rational theological argument about, say, the nature of justification, points ahead to later Christian debates focusing on what constitutes correct doctrine or belief, debates carried out in the manuscript medium, debates for which literacy was essential.

Summary. Paul and his congregations lived in a largely oral media world, with minimal use of written texts or appeal to manuscript authority. Writing was used for long-distance correspondence (often with the adjunct of personal emissaries), but otherwise Christian life was oral, without even much reliance on Jewish Scripture. Paul's churches were not unique in their reliance on orality. As Antoinette Wire argues, the positions and activities of the Corinthian women oral prophets were characteristic of Hellenistic Christian communities prior to Paul. Christian worship and Christian mission could be and were carried on independent of writing. Christians were not yet a "people of the book." The hermeneutics of these churches were oral hermeneutics; authority was not yet vested in manuscripts. Yet Paul produced texts that later became authoritative texts; he began a way of arguing that was later developed extensively in Christian writings. The seeds of manuscript-based Christianity are found in Paul; they are not, however, dominant in Paul. Orality remained the dominant medium for Christianity for some time to come.

Literary Continuations of Paul's Letters

In a world as oral as the first century was, intertextuality, the use of one text by the author of another text, need not mean actual copying (literary dependence), but may mean using oral memory of written texts to create new written texts. Paul's letters clearly constitute the beginning of an intertextual literary tradition that likely involves both memory and copying. The author of 2 Thessalonians made use of 1 Thessalonians. Ephesians is a classic case of intertextuality with its heavy use of Colossians and frequent allusions to most of Paul's letters. The author's use of several letters also suggests the beginning of a collection of Paul's letters. Furthermore, a Christian letter-writing tradition has begun: in due course, we have the Catholic Epistles, Clement of Rome writing to the Corinthian Christians, and St. Ignatius writing to everyone. With Paul's creation of Christian texts, letters written to substitute for his personal presence, he begins a written textual tradition that rapidly develops a life of its own. This textual tradition continues not just in the letter genre but in other genres in the writings of both heterodox and orthodox Christians from the time of Irenaeus onward (Babcock). Paul may have preferred the Spirit to the letter; yet his letters and arguments began a literate tradition.

Continuing Oral Understandings of Paul

Paul may have begun a literate tradition; however, it was a long while before this literate tradition became the dominant one. The content of Paul's letters appears to be largely irrelevant to the understanding of Paul in the first and second centuries. While Paul's method of communicating at a distance is imitated, his thought is largely ignored. The oral memory of Paul seems to be far more central to Christian debate and life than what he or his successors wrote. If we consider the canonical Acts of the

Apostles, the traditions of the Apocryphal Acts of Paul, and the Pastoral Epistles, we have three different and competing interpretations of Paul in the early second-century, *none* of which has anything to do with either the texts of the Pauline letters as texts or with the content of Paul's theology found in those letters.[17]

These differences in images of Paul are common knowledge among New Testament scholars and expounded in New Testament introductions (e.g. Duling and Perrin: 223-59; 365-400; 484-93). I shall focus rather on the absence of references to the textual tradition of Paul's genuine letters in these writings. In neither the Acts of the Apostles nor the Pastorals is there any reference to Paul as letter-writer. In none of these writings is there any quotation or allusion to Paul's letters, although there are quotations and allusions to the Septuagint and occasionally to the gospels.[18] In all these writings we see not the textual Paul of the letters but the oral Paul of Christian memory. Even the Pastorals, which use the device of the pseudonymous letter, neither view Paul as a letter-writer nor appeal to his written authority. 2 Tim 1:11 reads, "I [Paul] was appointed a preacher and apostle and teacher." 2 Tim 4:13 instructs Timothy to bring the books (τὰ βιβλία) and the parchments (τὰς μεμβράνας). It is not clear what these refer to, but given the absence of any quotations or allusions to Paul's writings, parts of the Septuagint and gospels would seem more probable than letters of the apostle.[19] MacDonald (1990) argues that the various Acts present a different Paul from the Paul found in his own letters because of their narrative genre based on the gospel genre. Certainly narrative does dictate a different content emphasis; but the Pastorals, which are not narrative, equally ignore the letters of Paul.

The Paul of the late first- and early second-century texts is not the Paul we know from the letters.[20] I want to suggest that a major reason the letters were ignored was that Christianity still relied on oral memory and oral authority. Since the rhetoric of the letters, unlike narrative, is not easily remembered, the letters never became as well known among Christians. They did not become part of Christian oral "literature." Even

---

[17] The same lack of reference to the content of the letters seems to be true of the writings of the Apostolic Fathers (see de Boer; cf. Lindemann).

[18] The only possible exception is Deut 25:4, "not to muzzle an ox that is treading grain," which is quoted both in 1 Cor 9:9 and 1 Tim 5:18. The passage in 1 Tim hardly seems a reference to the Corinthian letter.

[19] Given the reference to the reading of Scripture in 1 Tim 4:13, and the reference to books, the Pastorals have moved in the direction of manuscript-based authority. The Pastoral epistles, however, do not yet appeal to Paul's own letters.

[20] The letters of Paul are used from the mid-to-late second century on, both by the heterodox (Marcionites and Gnostics) and also by the orthodox (see Babcock).

the more highly literate and textually oriented of the New Testament writers such as Luke and the author of the Pastorals ignore Paul's letters. Only as the more literate Christian leaders turned away from oral memory and oral authority to manuscripts, does the Paul of the letters begin to creep into Christian discourse. This shift to the centrality of manuscripts may perhaps be dated around the middle of the second century when we first see exact quotations from the gospels rather than paraphrases from memory (Koester, 1957). Indeed, to leap through the centuries with a sweeping generalization, it was the invention of print and the spread of literacy to a broader segment of the population that ultimately created the context within which the thinking of Paul as encountered in the canonical letters could be central for the Protestant reformation.

PART III
SOME IMPLICATIONS

In spite of the fact that Paul composed written letters and quoted passages from written texts in those letters, Paul and his churches were fundamentally dependent on the oral medium and oral authority. Only gradually did the Christian churches shift to reliance on manuscripts, Christian texts. The endurance of the oral perspective can be seen in the textual treatments of Paul in the early second-century. But by the mid-second-century, both orthodox and a variety of heterodox Christian leaders are appealing to manuscripts rather than to oral tradition and authority.[21] The oral hermeneutics of the Pauline congregations were becoming the textual hermeneutics of the church fathers. This shift was facilitated by the emergence of an hierarchical, male, educated—thus literate—church leadership and then reinforced by such leaders' use of the manuscript medium. But for the first century or so of its existence, Christianity remained predominantly an oral phenomenon, relying on oral hermeneutics and appealing to oral authority. The Paul of this church was the Paul whose life and work could be recalled to memory, not yet the Paul chiefly apprehended through the letters.

The shift from oral hermeneutics and authority to manuscript hermeneutics and authority is *not* a neutral matter.[22] A full exploration of the consequences of the shift to manuscript media exceeds the scope of

---

[21] For centuries to come, the huge majority of Christians of course remained nonliterate. However, their relationship to the churches changed as the leadership came to rely on the written medium, from which they were excluded.

[22] In addition to the articles in this volume, see Kelber; Ong; Havelock; Boomershine.

this article. In brief, writing affects both what content is included and how that content is presented (J. Dewey 1994b). How content is interpreted depends in part on whether it is read or performed orally (J. Dewey 1994a). Furthermore, reliance on manuscript media drastically restricts access to leadership positions. Our reconstruction of early Christianity has been largely based on manuscript (and print) understandings. We need much more research on orality and literacy and their interaction in the first centuries of the common era in general and in early Christianity in particular. As our knowledge grows, our reconstructions of the early church will increasingly need to be revised as we recognize how much difference it makes when we interpret texts in the context of a predominately oral culture. The following is a list of some consequences and methodological implications we need to consider if we are to begin to take seriously the importance of the oral communication medium in the early churches.

1) Narrative can be remembered easily orally; therefore it was more central for early Christian development.[23] The stories about Paul were more formative for first- and early second-century Christians than Paul's written letters. This was true even for the literate, more elite Christians—Luke and the author of the Pastorals. It presumably was even more true for the nonliterate majority. The Paul of his own letters, our canonical Paul, was not very important in the first decades of Christianity, because the content of the letters could not be easily remembered. Just because a text was written and later became part of the New Testament canon does not mean that it was important to early Christians or influential to early Christian development.

2) Methodologically, we need to distinguish between two stages: first, the Christian use of writing in the service of orality, e.g. Paul's letters, and second, the Christian creation,[24] use of, and eventual reliance on writings as writings.[25] The first use of Paul's letters to communicate at a distance does not seem to be a major rupture in the fundamentally oral context. The reuse and collection of those letters for continued use in the church in situations quite independent of their original context is a move toward the primacy of manuscripts over orality, of fixed texts over contexts. Similarly

---

[23] This has interesting implications for our understanding of the synoptic tradition: it suggests that the miracles and the parables may have been more important than the isolated sayings tradition—even if that material was written down earlier.

[24] Aune (1987:205) has suggested that the Pastorals were initially composed to be part of a codex of Christian writings in order to supplement or correct other *writings* in the codex, rather than being addressed to particular individuals at all.

[25] In regard to the use of Jewish or Christian writings, we also need to pay attention to whether early Christians were actually using manuscripts or whether they were drawing on oral knowledge of scriptural traditions.

the composition of Mark's gospel may still have been in the service of orality, as a script for storytelling (J. Dewey 1994a). Later, when authorized readings had to be taken from a collection of written gospels, then manuscripts had become primary. In our reconstructions of Christian history, we have tended to conflate these two stages, assuming that the reliance on the text was present from the moment of the text's initial composition. These are two separate events, separated by decades or more, and they need to be treated separately in our historical reconstructions.

3) In order to understand both Judaism and Christianity, it is helpful to compare how they used oral and manuscript media. Pharisaic Judaism seems to have taken the step to reliance on manuscripts earlier than Christianity. Boomershine describes Pharisaic Judaism as follows:

> [It] adopted writing as an integral part of biblical interpretation. But in that new paradigm the oral law remained primary. The oral tradition which produced the Mishnah and the Talmud was organized around memorization of oral law, the interpretation of the written law in relation to the living of individual and communal life, and the maintenance of face to face community (146).

Boomershine describes here a very typical way that literates in antiquity made use of texts in the service of orality. The oral law was a means of interpreting and using the written law. Precisely speaking, it was a use of specific written Scriptures. The Pharisees who engaged in this oral disputation were mainly relatively elite educated literate males. Pharisaic Judaism was much more textually grounded than Pauline Christianity, which, in Paul's own words, was based on the life of the Spirit rather than the letter of the law (see Kelber: 140–83).

It is perhaps reasonable to suggest, then, that where the influence of synagogues and Jewish teachers (either by Jews or by Christian Jews) on Christianity was greater, the importance of literacy, the emphasis on reading and interpreting texts, would also be greater. It is in Paul's letters to the Galatian and Roman Christians, where issues of relationship to Jews and Jewish Christians are at issue, that Paul makes greatest use of arguments from Scripture. The Torah seems more important in the more Jewish Gospel of Matthew than it does in the other synoptic gospels.[26] Christianity's later interaction with rabbinic Judaism may have pushed the early Christian groups towards greater reliance on the manuscript medium.

Eventually, from the late second century and after, Christian writers carried manuscript hermeneutics further than rabbinic Judaism did.

---

[26] Mark is probably also addressed to a Jewish Christian audience—but to a peasant, nonliterate audience (Rohrbaugh, 1993).

Judaism retained a mixed oral–written hermeneutic in its development of the Oral Law. Christianity, on the other hand, moved away from oral understandings into abstract theological thought, making issues of doctrine and belief central (so Boomershine: 147–48). This is a later Christian development, however, and should not be read back into the New Testament period.

4) The fact that our access to early Christianity is only through written texts means that our knowledge is biased in favor of the views of those of higher social status, the only ones who were literate. As noted earlier, literacy is an instrument of power and control in a society in which most people are not literate. In *Tristes Tropiques*, Lévi–Strauss writes:

> The only phenomenon with which writing has always been concomitant is the creation of cities and empires, that is the integration of large numbers of individuals into a political system, and their grading into castes or classes ... it seems to have favoured the exploitation of human beings rather than their enlightenment ... My hypothesis, if correct, would oblige us to recognize the fact that the primary function of written communication is to facilitate slavery (quoted in Harris: 38).[27]

While Lévi–Strauss' view may be extreme, it is certainly true of Christianity that the shift to manuscript hermeneutics and manuscript-based authority coincided with the shift to a hierarchal male leadership that upheld the patriarchal empire and family. As long as Christianity was based on oral authority, as it was in the early urban churches, full participation and leadership were open to all regardless of class and gender. Slaves, freedpeople and women of all classes were able to become leaders; lack of literacy did not exclude one from leadership. As Christianity increasingly appealed to the authority of manuscripts in the second and following centuries, leadership became increasingly restricted to those with education, that is, to a small male elite who were free men and heads of households.

The shift from spirit–led oral leadership open to all regardless of status or education to hierarchical authority is most easily demonstrated with regard to gender. The shift from a more egalitarian "discipleship of equals" to a hierarchal structure in which obedience and fear were the proper behavior of subordinates including all women has been well documented by Elisabeth Schüssler Fiorenza (160–204, 243–315) and others. The connection with literacy is perhaps as easily seen. The active role of women in the oral church is obvious in the early period, as can be seen in 1 Corinthians and Romans 16 (Wire; Schüssler Fiorenza). Women's continued oral leadership is evident from the stories of the

---

[27] In Galatians 3 Paul certainly interprets the written law as facilitating slavery.

Apocryphal Acts and from the effort of relatively elite men to silence women's storytelling: "Have nothing to do with godless tales of old women" (1 Tim 4:7). Indeed a major aim of the Pastorals seems to have been to restrict the roles and authority of Christian women (MacDonald, 1983; J. Dewey, 1992). Of course at the time they were written, the Pastorals did not represent general church practice. Rather, they were prescriptive statements, evidence of how the author would like to see Christian women behave, and thus evidence that the opposite behavior was occurring. Women without husbands to maintain authority over them were gathering in houses and travelling from house to house teaching. Their teaching was oral, however, while the prescriptions of the Pastorals were in writing. As Christianity became manuscript-based and developed its own canon, the writings of the literate male leaders restricting women's behavior became canonical and the oral-based teaching of Christian women was gradually lost and suppressed. Our New Testament writings are not fully representative of the world of early Christianity but are distorted in the interests of the relatively few who were literate.

In summary, I would suggest that early Christianity was an oral phenomenon in a predominately oral culture; the culture of the dominant elite, however, was a manuscript culture. This first-century oral Christianity was a diversified, non-hierarchical, and relatively egalitarian movement. Some early Christian communications were committed to writing, if they needed to travel a long distance, possibly if they were needed to aid memory, and if they accorded with the interests of those of higher status among Christians, the only ones who could write. Thus, early Christian texts are not necessarily representative or typical of early Christianity as a whole. As Christianity gradually shifted from oral-based authority to manuscript-based authority in the second through the fourth centuries, these selective and biased writings gained authority to determine what was or was not Christian.

The restriction of power within Christianity to a small educated male elite was greatly facilitated by their literacy in a society and church in which most were not literate. Media changes, in this case from orality to writing, affect not only hermeneutics, i.e. ways of thinking and deriving meaning, but, perhaps more importantly, relationships of power, i.e. patterns of dominance and submission. A religion that began with the claim, "There is neither Jew nor Greek, there is neither slave nor free, there is 'no male and female'" (Gal 3:28) became a religion justifying the power structure of the dominant (literate) culture of the Roman Empire. In reconstructing early Christian history we need to address these biases as best we can, as we strive for a fuller view of what early Christianity was like. Recognition of the chiefly oral perspective of early Christianity makes our task of reconstruction more difficult, but it also opens possibilities for richer understanding.

WORKS CONSULTED

Aune, David E.
1987   *The New Testament in Its Literary Environment*. Philadelphia: Westminster.
1992   "Worship, Early Christian." Pp. 973–89 in *The Anchor Bible Dictionary*, vol 6. Ed. David Noel Freedman. New York: Doubleday.

Babcock, William S., ed.
1990   *Paul and the Legacies of Paul*. Dallas: Southern Methodist University Press.

Bar-Ilan, Meir
1992   "Illiteracy in the Land of Israel in the First Centuries c.e." Pp. 46–61 in *Essays in the Social Scientific Study of Judaism and Jewish Society*, vol 2. Ed. Simcha Fishbane and Stuart Schoenfeld with Alain Goldshläger. Hoboken, NJ: KTAV.

Boomershine, Thomas E.
1987   "Biblical Megatrends: Towards a Paradigm for the Interpretation of the Bible in Electronic Media." Pp. 144–57 in *SBLASP*. Ed. Kent Harold Richards. Atlanta: Scholars.

Botha, P. J. J.
1992a   "Greco-Roman Literacy as Setting for New Testament Writings." *Neot* 26:195–215.
1992b   "Letter Writing and Oral Communication in Antiquity: Suggested Implications for the Interpretation of Paul's Letter to the Galatians." *Scriptura* 42:17–34.

Cartlidge, David R.
1990   "Combien d'unités avez-vous de trois à quatre?: What Do We Mean by Intertextuality in Early Church Studies?" Pp. 400–11 in *SBLASP*. Ed. David J. Lull. Atlanta: Scholars.

Cole, Susan Guettel
1981   "Could Greek Women Read and Write?" Pp. 219–45 in *Reflections of Women in Antiquity*. Ed. Helene P. Foley. New York: Gordon & Breach Science.

Crossan, John Dominic
1991   *The Historical Jesus: The Life of a Mediterranean Jewish Peasant*. San Francisco: Harper San Francisco.

de Boer, Martinus C.
1990 "Which Paul?" Pp. 45–54 in *Paul and the Legacies of Paul*. Ed. William S. Babcock. Dallas: Southern Methodist University Press.

Dewey, Arthur J.
1982 "Spirit and Letter in Paul." Harvard University Th.D. Dissertation. Forthcoming from Edwin Mellen.

Dewey, Joanna
1992 "1 Timothy," "2 Timothy," "Titus." Pp. 353–61 in *The Women's Bible Commentary*. Ed. Carol A. Newsom and Sharon H. Ringe. Louisville: Westminster/John Knox and London: SPCK.
1994a "The Gospel of Mark as Oral/Aural Event: Implications for Interpretation." Pp. 145–63 in *The New Literary Criticism and the New Testament*. Eds. Elizabeth Struthers Malbon and Edgar V. McKnight. Sheffield: Sheffield University Press.
1994b "Jesus' Healings of Women: Conformity and Non–Conformity to Dominant Cultural Values as Clues for Historical Reconstruction." *BTB* 24:122–131.

Doty, William G.
1973 *Letters in Primitive Christianity*. Philadelphia: Fortress.

Duling, Dennis C. and Norman Perrin
1994 *The New Testament: Proclamation and Parenesis, Myth and History*. Fort Worth: Harcourt Brace.

Funk, Robert
1982 *Parables and Presence: Forms of the New Testament Tradition*. Philadelphia: Fortress.

Furnish, Victor Paul
1994 "On Putting Paul in His Place." *JBL* 113:3–17.

Graham, William A.
1987 *Beyond the Written Word: Oral Aspects of Scripture in the History of Religion*. Cambridge: Cambridge University Press.

Harris, William V.
1989 *Ancient Literacy*. Cambridge, MA and London: Harvard University Press.

Havelock, Eric A.
1963 *Preface to Plato*. Cambridge: Belknap of Harvard University Press.

Hays, Richard B.
1989 *Echoes of Scripture in the Letters of Paul*. New Haven/London: Yale University Press.

Horsley, Richard A.
1987 *Jesus and the Spiral of Violence: Popular Jewish Resistance in Roman Palestine*. San Francisco: Harper & Row.

Humphrey, J. H., ed.
  1991   Literacy in the Roman World. *Journal of Roman Archaeology*, Supplementary Series No. 3. Ann Arbor, MI.

Keenan, James G.
  1991   "Review of William V. Harris, *Ancient Literacy*." *Ancient History Bulletin*, 5:101–6.

Kelber, Werner H.
  1983   *The Oral and the Written Gospel: The Hermeneutics of Speaking and Writing in the Synoptic Tradition, Mark, Paul, and Q*. Philadelphia: Fortress.

Knox, Bernard M. W.
  1968   "Silent Reading in Antiquity." *Greek, Roman and Byzantine Studies.* 9:421–35.

Koester, Helmut
  1957   *Synoptische Überlieferung bei den Apostolischen Vätern*. Berlin: Akademie-Verlag.
  1991   "Writings and the Spirit: Authority and Politics in Ancient Christianity." *HTR* 84: 353–72.

Kraemer, Ross S.
  1991   "Women's Authorship of Jewish and Christian Literature in the Greco-Roman Period." Pp. 221–42 in *"Women Like This": New Perspectives on Jewish Women in the Greco-Roman World*. Ed. Amy-Jill Levine. Atlanta: Scholars.

Lefkowitz, Mary R.
  1991   "Did Ancient Women Write Novels?" Pp. 199–219 in *"Women Like This": New Perspectives on Jewish Women in the Greco-Roman World*. Ed. Amy-Jill Levine. Atlanta: Scholars.

Lenski, Gerhard E.
  1966   *Power and Privilege: A Theory of Social Stratification*. New York: McGraw-Hill.

Lindemann, Andreas
  1990   "Paul in the Writings of the Apostolic Fathers." Pp. 25–45 in *Paul and the Legacies of Paul*. Ed. William S. Babcock. Dallas: Southern Methodist University Press.

MacDonald, Dennis Ronald
  1983   *The Legend and the Apostle: The Battle for Paul in Story and Canon*. Philadelphia: Westminster.
  1990   "Apocryphal and Canonical Narratives about Paul." Pp. 55–70 in *Paul and the Legacies of Paul*. Ed. William S. Babcock. Dallas: Southern Methodist University Press.

Malina, Bruce J. and Richard L. Rohrbaugh
  1992   *Social–Science Commentary on the Synoptic Gospels*. Minneapolis: Fortress.

Meeks, Wayne
1983   *The First Urban Christians: The Social World of the Apostle Paul.* New Haven/London: Yale University Press.

Mitchell, Margaret M.
1992   "New Testament Envoys in the Context of Greco–Roman Diplomatic and Epistolary Conventions: The Example of Timothy and Titus." *JBL* 111:641–62.

Oakman, Douglas E.
1991   "The Countryside in Luke–Acts." Pp. 151–79 in *The Social World of Luke–Acts: Models for Interpretation.* Ed. Jerome H. Neyrey. Peabody, MA: Hendrickson.

Ong, Walter J.
1982   *Orality and Literacy: The Technologizing of the Word.* London/New York: Methuen.

Plato
1953   *The Republic.* LCL. Tr. Paul Shorey. Cambridge: Harvard University Press.

Pomeroy, Sarah B.
1977   "*Technikai kai Mousikai*: The Education of Women in the Fourth Century and in the Hellenistic Period." *American Journal of Ancient History* 2:51–68.
1981   "Women in Roman Egypt: A Preliminary Study Based on Papyri." Pp. 303–22 in *Reflections of Women in Antiquity.* Ed. Helene P. Foley. New York: Gordon & Breach Science.

Rohrbaugh, Richard L.
1991   "The Pre–Industrial City in Luke–Acts: Urban Social Relations." Pp. 125–49 in *The Social World of Luke–Acts: Models for Interpretation.* Ed. Jerome H. Neyrey. Peabody, MA: Hendrickson.
1993   "The Social Location of the Marcan Audience." *BTB* 23:114–27.

Saldarini, Anthony J.
1988   *Pharisees, Scribes, and Sadducees in Palestinian Society.* Wilmington: Glazier.

Schottroff, Luise
1993   *Let the Oppressed Go Free: Feminist Perspectives on the New Testament.* Tr. Annemarie S. Kidder. Louisville: Westminster/John Knox.

Schüssler Fiorenza, Elisabeth
1983   *In Memory of Her: A Feminist Theological Reconstruction of Christian Origins.* New York: Crossroad.

Scobie, Alex
1979   "Storytellers, Storytelling, and the Novel in Graeco–Roman Antiquity." *Rheinisches Museum für Philologie* 122:229–59.

Scott, James C.
1990   *Domination and the Arts of Resistance: Hidden Transcripts.* New Haven/London: Yale University Press.

Scott, James M.
1993   "Paul's Use of Deuteronomic Tradition." *JBL* 112:645–65.

Silberman, Lou H., ed.
1987   *Orality, Aurality and Biblical Narrative.* Semeia 39. Decatur, GA: Scholars.

Sjoberg, Gideon
1960   *The Preindustrial City: Past and Present.* New York: Free Press, MacMillan.

Slusser, Michael
1992   "Reading Silently in Antiquity." *JBL* 111:499.

Snyder, Jane McIntosh
1989   *The Woman and the Lyre: Women Writers in Classical Greece and Rome.* Bristol: Bristol Classical.

Townsend, John T.
1971   "Ancient Education in the Time of the Early Roman Empire." Pp. 139–63 in *The Catacombs and the Colosseum: The Roman Empire as the Setting of Primitive Christianity.* Valley Forge: Judson.

Vansina, Jan
1985   *Oral Traditions as History.* Madison: University of Wisconsin Press.

Veyne, Paul
1987   "The Roman Empire." Pp. 5–233 in *A History of Private Life.* Ed. Paul Veyne. Cambridge: Belknap of Harvard University Press.

Wire, Antoinette Clark
1990   *The Corinthian Women Prophets: A Reconstruction through Paul's Rhetoric.* Minneapolis: Fortress.

Yaghjian, Lucretia B.
1994   "'Do You Understand What You Are Reading?' Defining and Refining Reading in its New Testament Context." Presented at the New England Region SBL/CBA Meeting, March 25, 1994.

FIGURING EARLY RABBINIC LITERARY CULTURE: THOUGHTS OCCASIONED BY BOOMERSHINE AND J. DEWEY

Martin S. Jaffee
University of Washington

A rabbinic oral tradition—omitted, unfortunately, from manuscript redactions of the Babylonian Talmud's encyclopedia of eschatological signs (Sanh. 90a–99a)—teaches that Messiah will come when the scribal descendants of Jacob and Esau reach consensus about a common cultural model for interpreting the origins of rabbinism and the early church. Thomas Boomershine and Joanna Dewey, it appears, have inched us a moment closer to the reign of the King. We at least know what to talk about until the End— may we not live to see it.

The conversation, in fact, has been developing for some time. Gerhardsson's influential study of 1961 pushed the discussion in a fruitful direction, drawing attention to the epistemological significance of oral tradition as a cultural medium in early rabbinic and Christian literary circles. But, as Neusner's corrective studies of the 1970's and 1980's demonstrated, Gerhardsson's confidence in the capacity of rabbinic traditions to illumine the first–century Palestinian milieu was ill-warranted. This brief space, of course, offers no possibility of doing justice to Neusner's framing of the problem of rabbinic oral tradition (e.g. Neusner 1980, 1987).

It is enough to point out that the hermeneutical situation among students of rabbinic literature has moved beyond Neusner's original interests in the historical reliability of rabbinic tradition or the rhetoric of early rabbinic texts. His passing acknowledgement of Lord's work has been supplemented in the past decade by scholars who have tried to incorporate into their work what they learned about literacy and orality from Ong, Goody, Finnegan, Foley, Stock, Carruthers and many others. Few recent students of rabbinic oral tradition, therefore, assume an evolutionary model of tradition that posits an inevitable march from "orality" to "literacy." Similarly, there is an increasing appreciation of the interpenetration of both cultural registers at all levels of the compositional and transmissional processes (e.g., Shinan; Green; Fraade; Strack and Stemberger: 35–49; Alexander; Jaffee 1992, 1994; Elman; Swartz). But the overall assessment of orality in the cultural life of early rabbinism is still in its infancy.

This is the setting in which I would like to engage the essays by Boomershine and Dewey. Each has thoroughly absorbed the implications of recent scholarship on Greco-Roman literacy for imagining the oral matrix in which the earliest Christian literary compositions emerge. Each is fully alert to the hermeneutical implications of this matrix. Each—and I speak here as an outsider to early Christian studies—has enriched my own appreciation of the what it might mean to locate the figures of Jesus and Paul concretely in such a matrix.

Each, as well, attempts to place the oral culture of early Christianity in the surrounding setting of the oral culture of early Judaism. To that degree, Boomershine and Dewey continue the academic tradition of understanding the early church against the "Jewish background" and in adducing rabbinic material as illustrative of that background. This has its dangers, as Neusner's work has shown. I am not sure that either Boomershine or Dewey has avoided all of them. But both at least exhibit due caution.

What is fundamentally new is their attempt to identify as the point of comparison a cultural process—the transition to wide-scale literacy—which, precisely because it infused the cultures of all peoples and communities in the Greco-Roman world, promises a theologically neutral framework of interpretation. Accordingly, I mark as my point of entry into the discussion the ways in which representations of early rabbinic tradition serve as a comparative figure in the service of understanding the Christian settings. At issue is whether the rhetorical construction of rabbinic tradition in the essays before us aids us in thinking only in a single direction—the illumination of early Christianity—at the expense of the obscuring of rabbinism. In what follows I focus on two such figurings: Boomershine's representation of the rabbinic Oral Torah tradition as a mode of resistance to the hegemonic literary culture of Hellenism, and Dewey's representation of the rabbinic oral tradition as a scripturally-grounded tradition of a literate male elite.

Boomershine has developed, to my knowledge, a fundamentally fresh model within which to draw comparative observations between early Judaism and early Christianity. This is the notion that rabbinic disciple groups and the early community surrounding Jesus can be viewed as the creators not of religions but of "communications systems" constructed to negotiate the transmission of Judaic tradition within a culture increasingly penetrated by the textual culture of Hellenism. In Boomershine's view, the emergent rabbinic communications system responds to its environment by cultivating an oral tradition—Oral Torah—which "defended the culture and religion of Israel from corruption by the culture of Hellenism and appropriated literacy as a communications system in strict subordination to orality." The cost was the obliteration of the earlier extra-canonical Judaic literary tradition. The gain was the fertile legal and narrative worlds of rabbinism.

By contrast, early Christian communities employed a rather different strategy. Where rabbinism used orality to create a new cultural space as a defense against Hellenistic literary culture, early Christian groups moved in precisely the opposite direction, developing "an extensive contemporary literary tradition in continuity with other aspects of the literary communications systems that formed the literary traditions of Judaism in the period of the second temple." The gain of this strategy was the Christian tradition's capacity to retain the literary heritage of Hellenistic Judaism as part of its canonical and extra-canonical heritage, even while developing a new literary culture fully able to appropriate—and transform—Hellenistic philosophical culture in particular. It is not clear what the loss was.

It depends, one supposes, on the degree to which one claims, with Boomershine, that Christianity indeed "enable(d) the religion of Israel to survive and to maintain faithfulness in a new cultural environment." The judgment that Christianity in some sense preserved the religion of Israel requires clarification. I, for one, would be more comfortable pointing out that, whatever (and whenever) "the religion of Israel" was, it became something else in rabbinism and in Christianity. But this is a quibble.

Others will perhaps want to probe with greater insistence Boomershine's portrayal of Jesus as the prescient creator, through the art of parable, of a cultural system that would facilitate the transition to literary culture, thus ensuring the survival of the religion of Israel. I only point out here that Boomershine's discussion of the unique rhetoric of Jesus' parables would have benefitted from attention, by way of comparison, to David Stern's recent study of Jewish and rabbinic parables from late antiquity (e.g. Stern: 185–206).

But let us consider Boomershine's figuring of rabbinic oral tradition. Opting, apparently, for Gerhardsson's model over Neusner's, Boomershine portrays early rabbinic tradents as "word-for-word" memorizers of "systematic oral interpretation(s) of written Scripture" in a cultural setting in which "nothing was written for decades or even centuries." There has by now been enough work on early rabbinic literary culture to avoid such an un-nuanced construction of the role of texts in rabbinism. Over the past fifteen years or so a number of scholars (see Works Consulted) have presented models of rabbinic literary culture as one in which written and oral texts were in constant mutual penetration. Moreover, by "written texts" such scholars have not always meant "Scripture."

The rabbinic deployment of scriptural verses for a variety of rhetorical purposes reveals a total oral mastery of the written text. The primary difference—from the perspective of media analyses—between scriptural texts and rabbinic texts is that only the former were ever treated as ritual objects or declaimed from written copies in ceremonial settings (see Green: 153–65). As a cultural tradition, Scripture was at least as "oral" a phenomenon among the Sages as a "written" one. In the same measure, "oral" tradition included texts available in some form of writing—from Scripture to the various redactions of the Fasting Scroll, Mishnah, Tosefta, and other tannaitic materials that served as reflections of or bases for rabbinic oral performance (see especially, Fraade: 1–23; Elman: 71–111; Jaffee 1994).

From this perspective, Boomershine's estimate of the rabbinic media achievement might need some modification. I would argue that the rabbinic suppression of Second Temple Jewish literature may have much to do with deciding what is going to be called "Scripture"—that is, what text will be read in liturgical settings. Thus, the matter of creating a purely oral cultural space protected from Hellenistic literary imperialism must be evaluated in a somewhat richer ideological setting. Sages knew their traditions in written and oral form—but what they insisted upon was that *only* knowledge transmitted by *Sages* was Torah, whether it was in writing or not. From this perspective the difference between early rabbinic and early Christian literary culture is not as stark as Boomershine would have it. If Philo or Enoch became texts read only by Christians, factors beside media–culture must be considered as explanations.

This last point is crucial as well in evaluating Dewey's contribution. Her construction of the textual situation of the Pauline letters has many more salient parallels to later rabbinic literary culture than she allows. For one thing she, like Boomershine, misconstrues, in my judgment, the cultural role of the written scriptural text in Rabbinism. In rabbinic culture, she asserts, "the manuscript—the text itself—was foundational and central for the oral interpretation." This is the rabbinic foil for constructing Paul. "While Paul is clearly influenced by Jewish understandings of God, history, and apocalyptic, he seems little concerned with the text as text."

True, there is nothing in Paul vaguely reminiscent of the rabbinic phenomenology of the scriptural text characteristic of the mature *massorah*. Rabbinic scribalism is foreign to Paul. But as soon as one moves from the scriptural text as written object to the text as a discursive system, there is a good deal more similarity than difference. Paul seems no less capable of deploying an apt scriptural quotation than any Sage, nor of making his own points through adept scriptural citations and allusions.

And Sages' scriptural quotations are, no less than Paul's, quotations from memory in service of more ambitious rhetorical constructions. I fail to see what significant difference one can find between Pauline and rabbinic oral mastery of Scripture. Paul knew his Greek text as thoroughly as Sages knew their Hebrew version. I assume he learned it by both hearing it and reading it, just as they did theirs. But, having mastered it, the written text was useful as a mnemonic aid, not a crutch. Neither Paul nor the Sages had writings before them as they composed their discourses. That the Sages surely regarded the Torah scroll as a cultic object while Paul probably did not, is essentially irrelevant to interpreting the literary culture of Pauline and rabbinic communities.

Indeed, I find in Dewey's essay one singularly helpful point which students of rabbinic literary culture might wish to explore. Adducing Graham and Doty, she suggests that the real "content" of the Pauline letter was not in the written text but in the public oration in which the text's message was delivered and made present to the community. "The fact," she continues, "that the letters were written documents gave them a permanence oral discourse never has, and thus they constituted the first step towards a literate intertextual tradition .... Although Paul's letters themselves were in the service of orality, they provided ... both the raw material for and the impetus towards a communications system based on textuality." This is precisely the sort of interpenetration of the oral and written registers that, it seems to me, needs further exploration by students of rabbinic literary culture. It is of special relevance for imagining the social role of the earliest compilations of rabbinic lemmata into coherent compositions, e.g., mishnaic tractates, midrashic collections.

Finally, let me attend to an aspect of Dewey's argument that, at first glance, suggests the power of an "oral" theory genuinely to illumine the Christian setting. This is her gender- and class-analysis of what must be seen as the "fall" of the early Church from an egalitarian society, characterized by orality, to one in which "leadership became increasingly restricted to those with education, that is a small male elite, free men, heads of households." This is a very astute observation. Clearly a transition from orality to literacy in the rhetorical culture of the early Church corresponds to a social-historical transition from female/non-literate leadership to subordination of women and the uneducated. But is the correlation causal as Dewey seems to suggest?

Let us work the theory through the rabbinic case. Here we have "a small male elite, free men, heads of households" who create a highly stratified society in which orality is the prized form of cultural mastery. But here, instead, oral performance of tradition is the ticket of admission into the inner circle of *haverim* (I hesitate to translate the term as "buddies," but it is not outlandish). In contrast to what many archaeologists claim to have been the case in other generally contemporary Jewish societies (Brooten; Kraemer: 80–127), the culture of rabbinic discipleship was one in which women and the ignorant (*ammei ha–arets*) could have enjoyed only the most marginal participation. Orality, in the rabbinic setting, clearly has nothing of the Edenic qualities that Dewey seems to imply. The reason, obviously, is that the culture that became Rabbinism had deep filiations with the earlier culture of Jewish scribalism, itself a male preserve as far as we know. Thus, what was mastered orally in rabbinic culture were a male elite's texts, "oral" though they were.

My point is that a more nuanced appreciation of the differences among oral cultures is required before theorizing globally about the differences between "orality" perceived as a monolithic cultural fact and "literacy" perceived as yet another cultural monolith. While Dewey's particular analysis of the early Church stands, in my view, I would caution against whole–sale acceptance of its theoretical underpinnings. What appears to have happened in the early Church is that it *became* scribal (in the fashion of the Roman schools), while the Rabbis inherited what was left of the equally–Hellenized (but Rome–despising) scribal culture of Jewish Palestine.

In sum, fresh conceptions of the hermeneutics of orality have enabled Boomershine and Dewey to open an interesting range of questions about early Christian culture. Moreover, their discussions have important implications for students of early Rabbinism as well. Their stimulating contributions also remind us that the cultural pie of "orality" must be cut with a honed theoretical knife. So, while the Messiah tarries, let the scribes continue their conversation!

WORKS CONSULTED

Alexander, Philip S.
    1991   "Orality in Pharisaic-Rabbinic Judaism at the Turn of the Eras." Pg. 159–84. *Jesus in the Oral Gospel Tradition.* Ed. Henry Wansbrough. Sheffield: JSOT.

Brooten, Bernadette J.
    1982   *Women Leaders in the Ancient Synagogue.* BJS 36. Chico, CA: Scholars.

Carruthers, Mary
    1990   *The Book of Memory: A Study of Memory in Medieval Culture.* Cambridge: Cambridge University Press.

Elman, Yaakov
1994   *Authority and Tradition: Toseftan Baraitot in Talmudic Babylonia.* Hoboken, NJ: KTAV.

Fraade, Steven D.
1991   *From Tradition to Commentary: Torah and Its Interpretation in the Midrash Sifre to Deuteronomy.* Albany: State University of New York Press.

Gerhardsson, Birger
1961   *Memory and Manuscript: Oral Tradition and Written Transmission in Rabbinic Judaism and Early Christianity.* Trans. Eric J. Sharpe. Lund and Copenhagen: C. W. K. Gleerup and Ejnar Munksgaard.

Green, William Scott
1987   "Romancing the Tome: Rabbinic Hermeneutics and the Theory of Literature." Pg. 148-68 in *Text and Textuality (Semeia 40)*: Ed. Charles E. Winquist. Decatur, GA: Scholars.

Jaffee, Martin S.
1992   "How Much 'Orality' in Oral Torah? New Perspectives on the Composition and Transmission of Early Rabbinic Tradition." *Shofar* 10:53-72.
1994   "Writing and Rabbinic Oral Tradition: On Mishnaic Narrative, Lists and Mnemonics." *Journal of Jewish Thought and Philosophy* 4: 123-46.

Kraemer, Ross Shepard
1992   *Her Share of the Blessings: Women's Religions Among Pagans, Jews, and Christians in the Greco-Roman World.* New York and Oxford: Oxford University Press.

Neusner, Jacob
1980   "Oral Tradition and Oral Torah: Defining the Problematic." Pg. 251-71 in *Studies in Jewish Folklore.* Ed. Frank Talmadge. Cambridge, MA: Association for Jewish Studies.
1987   *Oral Tradition in Judaism: The Case of the Mishnah.* New York and London: Garland.

Shinan, Avigdor
1981   "Aggadic Literature Between Oral Recitation and Written Tradition (Hebrew)." *Jerusalem Studies in Jewish Folklore* 1:44-60.

Stern, David
1991   *Parables in Midrash: Narrative and Exegesis in Rabbinic Literature.* Cambridge and London: Harvard University Press.

Strack, H.L. and Stemberger, G.
1991   *Introduction to the Talmud and Midrash.* Trans. M. Bockmuehl. Edinburgh: T&T Clark.

Swartz, Michael
1994   "Book and Tradition in Hekhalot and Magical Literatures." *Journal of Jewish Thought and Philosophy* 3: 189-229.

ORAL, RHETORICAL, AND LITERARY CULTURES: A RESPONSE

Vernon K. Robbins
Emory University

Boomershine's excellent survey introduces the possibility that the discussion of orality and literacy in New Testament texts may finally find its appropriate home in detailed analysis and comparison of analogies and relationships between Israelite-Jewish and Greco-Roman cultures in the context of Mediterranean culture. The special creativity in his investigation lies beyond a discussion of the contexts where Greco-Roman culture and Israelite-Jewish culture were working symbiotically with one another (namely, the Hellenistic era). The creativity comes to full force when he analyzes contexts that reveal significant analogies with one another.

First, after observing the emergence of "writing as a dominant factor in the formation of culture" in Athens (ca. 500 BCE) and the subsequent "watershed between orality and literacy" from the fourth to the third centuries BCE, Boomershine notices the integration of reading and writing in the covenant renewal in Judah in 444 BCE and the subsequent integration of reading and writing "into the fabric of Israel's religious life" from 400 to 300 BCE. This is a profound coincidence that interpreters must investigate further.

Second, Boomershine identifies a significant analogy between the relation of the oral activity of Socrates and Jesus in contexts where writing had become a prominent factor in the formation of culture. This observation is, in my view, directly on target. This insight guided my systematic reading of Plato's *Dialogues* and Xenophon's *Memorabilia* in relation to the Gospel of Mark in *Jesus the Teacher* in the early 1980s (Robbins 1992a, 1994a: 228-42).

Third, Boomershine introduces an intriguing analogy between Plato's disassociation of himself from the poets and the rabbis' disassociation from the literary traditions of the Second Temple period. Dewey, in addition, observes the manner in which Plato wanted to control the "storymakers" (her own discourse changes this to "storytellers").

Boomershine's analysis could be taken yet further by exploring analogies between Xenophon's construction of Book 4 of the *Memorabilia* and the construction of the Gospel of Mark (Robbins 1992a: 60-68, 126-28,

172-73, 206-209; 1994a: 228-42). While Plato's *Dialogues* took oral Socratic tradition in the direction of an exclusive culture with analogies to rabbinic culture, Xenophon's *Memorabilia* took it in the direction of a story account with analogies to the New Testament Gospels. Most of all, however, it is exciting to see a colleague in New Testament studies ready to address these issues. It is natural that these analogies will finally surface when interpreters work seriously with the writings of Walter Ong, since the primary discipline underlying his work is Greco-Roman rhetoric.

Boomershine's analysis could be further enhanced through engagement with Tony Lentz's study of orality and literacy in Hellenic Greece (Lentz). Socrates challenged written traditions with orality and Plato attacked "*both* the oral tradition and writing" (Lentz: 7). The Gospel of Mark is interesting in the context of the tension between Socrates and Plato, since it presents a written account (like the written account of Socrates in Plato's *Dialogues*) that features Jesus as a person who uses "authoritative speech" to challenge the written traditions of the scribes and Pharisees. Kelber (1983), and many following him, have argued that the Gospel of Mark attacks early Christian oral tradition. Few have observed the attack on both oral and written tradition by a Markan Jesus who speaks as though he himself has read the Scriptures the scribes have written (e.g., Mark 2:25; 7:6-7, 10-11; 9:12; 10:2-9; 11:17; 12:10-11, 26, [28-33]; 14:21, 27, 49).

There is even more that can be learned from Lentz's study. When Isocrates aligned himself fully with writing, Alcidamas (ca. 390 BCE), an advocate of orality, used writing as a medium "to attack Isocrates for associating with the written word" (Lentz: 9, 136-44). Matthew's "revision" of Mark's account in the form of a Jesus who "orally" presents extended chapters of teaching is especially interesting in this regard. The Matthean narrator presents an "oral Jesus" through writing that includes extensive recitation of "Scripture" (written text) in its narration. In other words, the Gospel of Matthew is written text that attacks the absence of orality in the Markan portrayal of Jesus at the same time that it advances the medium of "written text" in early Christianity (through an attack on scribes and Pharisees).

Still further advances can be made if interpreters adopt a more refined taxonomy of cultures based on the kind of orality and literacy in them. These essays are weakened by their adoption of a polarization between orality and literacy based on a juxtaposition of two kinds of "pure types": oral culture versus print culture. This produces some unfortunate terminology in Dewey's essay.

The term "nonliterate" occurs fifteen times and "not literate" fourteen times in the essay by Dewey. This terminology results from a polarization of terms in the current discussion, which not only leads to inaccuracy but also obstructs an open discussion of its value-laden presuppositions (see Moore). If a traditional value system presupposes that "nonliterates" are ignorant, Dewey's terminology introduces a "contracultural" inversion of this traditional system (Robbins 1993b: 451-54). In Dewey's essay "nonliterate" refers to people who have never learned to read or write, but it does not simply mean this. Nonliterate leaders are better than literate leaders. They give "spirit-led oral leadership open to all regardless of status or education." Literate leaders, by contrast, have a natural inclination toward evil. They exercise "heirarchical authority" that subordinates "all women," as well as others. This is a form of romanticism that inverts the common tradition that nonliterate people are unintelligent. This inversion re-enacts, with a slightly different emphasis, the romanticism Dibelius perpetuated from the nineteenth century about the oral genius of lowly folk (Mack and Robbins: 10). Dewey's statement presupposes that oral leaders are kinder and better people than literate people. In actual practice, "oral leaders" can be exceptionally hierarchical and some "literate" leaders are exceptionally egalitarian.

The first thing I plead for, therefore, is more precise terminology. We need a refined taxonomy that distinguishes between kinds of speaking, reading, and writing in different contexts. I recommend the following terminology when speaking about culture:

(1) oral culture
(2) scribal culture
(3) rhetorical culture
(4) reading culture
(5) literary culture
(6) print culture
(7) hypertext culture.

This is an expansion of the taxonomy I introduced in a recent volume in honor of George A. Kennedy (Robbins 1991b: 145). Bernard Brandon Scott and Margaret E. Dean's discussion of "recitation" in Mediterranean culture (Scott and Dean: 672-78) as well as a paper written recently by Robert M. Fowler, call for an expansion of my earlier list. I will discuss these cultures in reverse order from their appearance in the list.

Hypertext culture is the newest kind of orality-literacy culture in our midst, according to recent analysts (Fowler). Hypertext culture features "non-sequential writing—text that branches and allows choices to the reader, best read at an interactive screen. As popularly conceived, this is a series of text chunks connected by links which offer the reader different pathways" (Nelson: 0/2; Fowler: 2). Hypertext "demands an active reader," "is fluid, multiple, changing," "has no beginning or ending, no center or margin, no inside or outside," is "multicentered," is "networked text," "collaborative," "antihierarchical and democratic" (Fowler: 2-6).

Neither Jesus nor Paul lived in a hypertext culture. Fowler points out, however, that those of us who use computers regularly may be experiencing what he calls a "second orality." This kind of orality may sensitize interpreters to things they have not been able to see, hear, think, touch, and feel in texts when they were dominated by print culture.

Print culture distributes multiple copies of written text in verbatim form (errors and all). A significant number of people possess exact copies of the same written text, even if they do not read them regularly. The ease with which the wording of passages can be compared with one another creates an environment for "authoritative versions" of written text outside of localized settings in the culture.

Neither Jesus nor Paul lived in a print culture. Multiple copies of exactly the same text did not exist during the first century. As a result, the perception of "text" was different during the first century than it became after the invention of the printing press. This is one of the basic presuppositions of both Boomershine and Dewey, and they both correctly presuppose that there are some interpreters who have not moved away from the images and presuppositions of print culture as they interpret New Testament texts.

Literary culture uses written text as a means of inclusion within its benefits. Ronald Hock's careful analysis of Ulpian's "literary" dinner parties as recounted in Athenaeus's *Deipnosophistae* gives us an excellent place to begin an understanding of literary culture (Hock). Ulpian invited people to dinner and would not let anyone eat until someone could identify a passage in written literature containing the word of the food before them, like "appetizer" (29). Cynulcus, a Cynic participant in this "literary" culture, criticized Ulpian for being a "word-hunter" (ὀνοματοθήρας). The report of the "disputations" (ζητήσεις) in the setting always contain at least one quotation from literature, and Cynulcus, who criticizes virtually everyone else at one time or another, himself regularly quotes one or two lines verbatim from literature (30-35). A literary culture presupposes that people read texts regularly and can recite extensive passages in them from memory. A literary culture can exist without the support of printing presses that produce multiple copies of exactly the same text.

Boomershine presents an excellent summary of Neusner's conclusions about rabbinic Mishnah-Talmud culture. This is a literary culture and, interestingly enough, the date of the cultivation of rabbinic culture coincides with the date of elite literate culture in Rome as described by

Athenaeus's *Deipnosophistae* (the last years of the second century CE). The manuscript traditions of early Christian literature also emerged during this time (late second-fourth centuries), as both Boomershine and Dewey note. Participation in literary culture can create the possibility for certain individuals to begin, at least occasionally, to read silently. One reason for this is that the person often is "looking for" certain words in a text that the reader already knows well. The reader, then, may engage in a process akin to "skimming" a text.

Did Jesus or Paul participate in a literary culture? Boomershine thinks Jesus probably was able to read Scripture. Even if he was able, he would not necessarily be a participant in literary culture. In order to do this, Jesus would have needed to be in a context where he and his associates recited extensive line segments verbatim among one another, like the people at Ulpian's dinners and like the rabbis after the second century CE. Boomershine implies that a literary culture may have developed in second – fourth century Christianity, but his emphasis on the distinctiveness of rabbinic culture leaves the nature of Christian culture at this time unclear. Dewey, influenced by Botha (1992b:22-23), questions Paul's "literacy," by which she would mean that he could neither read nor write. Dewey, then, is proposing that Paul was not a participant in a literary culture. Nor does she posit such a culture in the Pauline communities. She thinks a few people would have read things like letters "to" members of the community; Scripture was possibly read on occasion to them; and some Scripture was used in debate. This is not enough to suggest a significant literary culture in the communities Paul founded.

Reading culture authorizes spoken statement through verbatim reading of written text. In the first instance, reading means "being read to" by someone. Therefore, there are two essential components to a reading culture in late antiquity: a "reciter" and "hearers of the recitation" (Scott and Dean). Reading cultures in late antiquity are local cultures. It appears that people in the inner circle described in Qumran literature read to one another. P. J. J. Botha has gathered significant data concerning reading contexts in antiquity (Botha 1990; 1991a; 1991b; 1992a; 1992b; 1993), and Dewey profitably uses some of his observations as noted above.

Did Jesus hear Scripture read aloud? Most people think he did, and I think this probably was the sole source of his knowledge of Scripture. I myself doubt that he was a reader of Scripture—which, again, would mean that he regularly read "to" other people. Two intriguing passages, Luke 4, which Boomershine discusses, and the Infancy Gospel of Thomas, which he does not discuss, raise the issue of Jesus as a reader. I think the evidence suggests that he did not regularly read to anyone, and he certainly would not have read simply to himself at this time in antiquity (Robbins 1991a: 323-26).

Did Paul hear Scripture and other things read aloud? The answer surely is yes. Did Paul read to others? The evidence is that he did not.

Rhetorical culture features comprehensive interaction between spoken and written statement. In David Cartlidge's words, which Dewey quotes, "The evidence from late antiquity is that oral operations (presentation and hearing) and literary operations (reading and writing) were (1) inescapably interlocked, and (2) they were communal activities" (Cartlidge: 14). In practice this means that writing in a rhetorical culture imitates both speech and writing, and speech in a rhetorical culture imitates both speech and writing (Robbins 1991b, 1993a; Scott and Dean). As Dewey further notes, Ong describes the first century media world as "a manuscript culture with high residual orality" (Ong: 158). This means that Ong's works do not presuppose that first-century Mediterranean culture was an "oral" culture. Rather, first-century Mediterranean culture was a "rhetorical" culture. Ong's works presuppose this as part of his major scholarly discipline, namely Greco-Roman rhetoric.

Boomershine pursues the epistemological dimensions of Jesus' parables, in the tradition of Plato, without using the broader resources of rhetoric in his discussion. Dewey includes some useful comments about rhetoric in her essay, but she also makes some global statements that need to be tested. I will turn below to some of these.

Did Jesus participate in rhetorical culture? This is a question that raises the issue of Jesus' imitation of written text in his speech. Boomershine analyzes a parable that makes no reference to Scripture (written text), and his further discussion of Jesus' speech does not pursue the issue. Did Paul participate in rhetorical culture? Decidedly yes. The issue is how, and we must perform careful rhetorical analysis of the discourse in his letters to answer this question.

Scribal culture reproduces speech or writing for various purposes. A scribal culture is a local culture in the service of certain kinds of officially sanctioned practices or institutions. In the first instance, a scribal culture produces records of grain supplies, accounts of battles and victories, agreements to pay tribute, renting of camelsheds, agreements to clean an irrigation ditch at appropriate times or to support others in particular activities, and laws sanctioned by one person or another. At this stage, the scribal activity creates a "copying" and "editing" culture: a scribe writes down what is seen or heard, editing only as necessary to make things fit.

In the second instance, a scribal culture becomes a "rhetorical scribal culture" producing "progymnastic compositions" (Robbins 1991b; 1993a). "Recitation" is the initial form of progymnastic scribal activity. Moving beyond copying and editing, writers either hear recited or they themselves read aloud a portion of text, then they write either the same or different words (Bonner: 254). The difference between this and scribal copying is that writers have the freedom to write as they wish. The one requirement is that the composition be "clear" (Hock and O'Neil: 95). After learning recitation composition, the writer learns the techniques of addition, expansion, and abbreviation (Hock and O'Neil: 98-103; Robbins 1993a: 118-21). After these stages of progymnastic writing, a person learns the art of "elaboration," which takes the person toward essays and speeches (Mack and Robbins: 31-67; Robbins 1993a: 121-31).

Only in a third instance do writers engage in activities by which they acquire the skills to write "eloquent rhetorical composition" (Bonner: 277-327). The only writer of New Testament texts who clearly achieved this ability is the author of the Epistle to the Hebrews, though the author of Luke and Acts was well on his way. Most of the issues concerning "scribal" activity in New Testament interpretation, therefore, concern "scribal copying" and "scribal progymnastic composition" rather than "eloquent rhetorical composition."

Did Jesus copy in a scribal manner or compose in a progymnastic rhetorical manner? All of our evidence suggests that he did not. Did Paul copy or compose in a progymnastic rhetorical manner? Our evidence suggests that Paul did not himself engage in "scribal copying." Was he involved in progymnastic composition? Two parties usually are involved in such composition. Regularly one person states something aloud and the "scribe" writes down in "as clear a manner as possible" the substance of the person's statement (Hock and O'Neil: 95). Botha thinks Paul participated in the composition of his letters only from the side of the speaker. This would mean that a significant amount of the style in Paul's letters would come from the writer rather than Paul's speech itself. Undoubtedly a majority of New Testament interpreters still presuppose that Paul himself wrote most of his letters. Only detailed analysis of the progymnastic techniques in Pauline discourse could produce an answer to this question, and this kind of analysis is only at its beginning stages in New Testament scholarship (Mack 1990; Sisson). The issue is whether Paul may have alternated between writing and speaking the kind of progymnastic composition that exists in the letters attributed to him, or whether he participated only from the side of the speaker.

Oral culture proceeds on the basis of spoken word alone. This culture has no "written literature" in view (Robbins 1991b: 145). Oral culture as Lord and Ong appropriately have described it refers to a cultural setting in which written texts are not present or presupposed in relation to speech performance. Ong, as indicated above, never presupposed that first-century Mediterranean culture was an oral culture. Rather, it was "a manuscript culture with high residual orality" (Ong: 158). Oral culture exists apart from, thus without any kind of interaction with, written texts. The only kind of "text" that exists is "oral text."

Did Jesus participate in oral culture? Most interpreters attempt to get an emphasis on orality in a context where Scripture is recited in synagogue settings. Boomershine presents a highly ambiguous picture. On the one hand he thinks Jesus could probably read. When Boomershine makes this statement, he seems to stray from his own principle that this would mean that Jesus "read to" other people. His emphasis, instead, is on the kind of knowledge Jesus would have attained by reading (as we do). On the other hand, Boomershine analyzes a parable that has no relation to written text. Again, the concept of a "rhetorical culture" could help Boomershine clarify his position.

Was Paul a vigorous participant in oral culture? Dewey thinks he was, speaking forcefully in marketplaces as well as in community assemblies. Paul himself says he was not a good speaker (e.g., 1 Cor 2:1; 2 Cor 11:6), and it is quite possible that he was not (Merritt: 113-52). Judged from a perspective of "oral culture," he very possibly did not speak well, in contrast to Jesus. On the other hand, quite clearly Paul had significant "progymnastic" skills in the context of "rhetorical culture." I do not agree with the impression Dewey's comments give about the interaction of Pauline discourse with "written text." One of the achievements of Pauline discourse is to "imitate written text." To explain with greater precision what this means, I will turn to the next point.

The most natural way to test our assertions about the orality and literacy of Jesus and Paul is through systematic use of the rhetorical treatises and resources available, from antiquity to the present, to investigate the oral-scribal texture of early Christian texts (Mack 1990; Watson and Hauser). These two essays refer only casually to the rhetorical aspects of early Christian literature, and they never explicitly analyze the oral-scribal texture of these texts. My investigations suggest the presence of the following rhetorical spectrum of oral-scribal texture in New Testament texts (Robbins 1994b:179-81):

(1) reference
(2) recitation
(3) recontextualization
(4) reconfiguration
(5) echo.

This spectrum is informed especially by the discussions of expansion and elaboration of the chreia, narrative, and fable in the Greco-Roman

Progymnasmata (Hock and O'Neil), along with the actual wording in rewritten traditions during the first and second century CE (Robbins 1991b).

Reference is the occurrence of a word or phrase that refers to a personage or tradition known to people on the basis of an authoritative text. "The days of Noah" in Matt 24:37/Luke 17:26 is an example: "As it was in the days of Noah, so will it be in the days of the Son of man." This phrase is an intertextual reference that evokes the story of Noah. This reference does not replicate any actual "text" of the story. Reference like this can occur in strictly oral culture, namely where nothing but "oral text" exists, and it is also common in rhetorical culture. There is no reference like this in the parable Boomershine analyzes to describe the epistemological revolution in Jesus' speech. Does Boomershine think Jesus spoke this saying about Noah (cf. Funk and Hoover: 251, 365-67)? He does not discuss the presence or absence of "scriptural wording" in Jesus' speech. Paul's discourse contains references to people like Abraham and traditions like "covenant." Dewey says these are "secondary" in all of Paul's letters except Romans and Galatians. This assertion needs to be tested through systematic analysis.

Recitation extends beyond the use of a word or phrase that refers to something in Scripture. Recitation is an extensive phenomenon, for it includes the transmission of both speech and narrative, either from oral or written tradition, in exact or different words from which the person has received them. Recitation (ἀπαγγελία) is the first exercise Theon discusses in his section on the chreia (Hock and O'Neil: 94-95; Robbins 1993a: 120).

(a) Recitation may replicate exact words of a written text. An example is Mark 7:10a: For Moses said, "Honor your father and your mother." This is an especially interesting example, since it replicates a string of eight words that stand in common between Exodus 20:12 and Deut 5:16 (Dean-Otting and Robbins: 113). This is a verbatim wordstring that people easily and regularly commited to memory in antiquity. The attribution to Moses signals the awareness of a written text that was probably read regularly to people in the synagogue. The transmission of such a verbatim string of words in the context of a clause of attribution (making it a "chreia") is a common characteristic of rhetorical culture, and discourse like this is attributed both to Jesus and Paul in New Testament texts.

(b) Recitation may occur with an omission of words that gives the word string the force of an authoritative judgment. An example is 1 Corinthians 1:31. The verse reads: Therefore, as it is written, "Let him who boasts, boast in the Lord." This verse is an abbreviation of:

"But *in this let him who boasts boast*, understanding and knowing that I am *the Lord* who does mercy and justice and righteousness on the earth; for in these things are my will," says the Lord (Jeremiah 9:24).

Gail O'Day's interesting article on this passage lacks any mention of a "rhetorical" use of this wording from Jeremiah 9. This usage supports Dewey's case that a "literary culture" is not governing the use of words in Pauline discourse. There is explicit reference to the presence of these words in a written text, yet the recitation selects and/or rearranges the words to give them the force of an authoritative judgment. Systematic analysis of this in Pauline discourse could be especially beneficial to test Dewey's assertions. This is common usage in rhetorical culture, and New Testament texts attribute this kind of discourse both to Jesus and Paul.

(c) A third way is to speak or write a recitation in words that are different from an "authoritative" version. Theon describes this as reciting "in the same words or in others as well" (Hock and O'Neil: 95). An excellent instance of this exists in Paul's recitation in 1 Cor 9:14 of the command of the Lord "that those who proclaim the gospel (τοῖς τὸ εὐαγγέλιον καταγγέλλουσιν) should get their living (ζῆν) from the gospel (ἐκ τοῦ εὐαγγελίου). This exists in written text in the following form:

For the laborer is worthy of his food/reward (Matt 10:10/Luke 10:7).

This is an instance of Pauline recitation "in different words" from the tradition. The words, in fact, are characteristic Pauline words. The verb καταγγέλλουσιν (to proclaim) is not customary in early Christian discourse outside of Paul's writings, and the noun εὐαγγέλιον (gospel) does not occur in the earliest strata of sayings attributed to Jesus (Kloppenborg: 220; Mack 1993). Pauline discourse uses "its own words" freely in quotations of the Lord Jesus, but it appears that it does not use "its own words" so freely with written biblical text. Systematic analysis of this, also, would be important to test Dewey's assertions. It appears that 1 Corinthians, at least, seriously challenges some of Dewey's conclusions about the relation of Pauline discourse to written biblical text. Pauline discourse includes many exact words from written biblical text, and this is a phenomenon she does not address in her statements about the "primary" or "secondary" nature of Paul's use of Scripture.

(d) A fourth way is to recite an episode using some of the narrative words in biblical text plus a saying from the text. Acts 7:30-32 reads as follows:

> Now when forty years had passed, *an angel appeared to him* in the wilderness of Mount Sinai, *in the flame* of a *burning bush*. When *Moses* saw it, he was amazed at *the sight*; and as he approached to look, there came the voice of the Lord: *"I am the God of Abraham, Isaac, and Jacob." Moses* began to tremble and did not dare to look.

This recitation contains words (underlined) that appear in Exodus 3:2-6. This is an excellent example of recitation in an abbreviated form, which Theon discusses as a characteristic rhetorical activity (Hock and O'Neil: 100-101). The recitation not only abbreviates the narrative wording. In Exodus 3:6 the saying of the Lord reads:

> I myself *am the God* of your father, the God *of Abraham, and* the God of *Isaac, and* the God of *Jacob*.

The recitation in Acts replicates only the underlined words in the saying. This abbreviated recitation suggests the presence of the expanded written version somewhere in the vicinity of this composition. The abbreviated account does not vary "factually" from the written version. There is no special concern to replicate extended word strings in verbatim form, but neither is there any embarassment about replicating words exactly. There is freedom to use one's own words to recite the account in a manner that fits the rhetorical context and that gives the recitation an appropriate function in its context (Robbins 1991b). This kind of recitation is frequent in Luke and Acts. It would be helpful to test the genuine and deutero-Pauline letters for the presence of this phenomenon.

(e) A fifth way is to recite a narrative in substantially one's own words. Mark 2:25-26 is an example:

> And he said to them, "Have you never read what *David* did when he and the ones *with* him were hungry and in need of food? He entered the house of God, when Abiathar was high priest, and ate *the bread of the Presence*, which it is not lawful for any but *the priests* to *eat*, and he gave some to his companions."

Words that occur in 1 Samuel 21:1-6 are underlined. The remaining words are different from the biblical text. A remarkable feature of this recitation is that it does not get the story quite right (Mack and Robbins: 114-17; Dean-Otting and Robbins: 99-105). This is an abbreviated recitation in rhetorical culture that reveals no close relation to the written version. This recitation replicates only words that are easily transmitted in oral transmission apart from any "authoritative" version of the text, and it contains a significant number of variations from the written text that a "literary" culture would consider to be "errors." Despite these "oral" characteristics, interpreters regularly attribute the composition of this to an early Christian scribe rather than Jesus (Funk and Hoover: 49). Boomershine says nothing about a text like this. Are there any recitations of episodes in Pauline discourse that exhibit this kind of "factual" variation?

(f) A sixth way is to summarize a span of text that includes various episodes. The full text of Luke 17:26-27 reads:

> Just as it was in the days of *Noah*, so it will be in the days of the Son of Man. They were eating and drinking, and marrying and being given in marriage, until the day Noah entered the ark, and the flood came and destroyed them all.

This recitation presents a summary of the biblical text in Genesis 6:1-24. There is no reference to "eating and drinking" in the biblical account. This appears to be a result of the characterization of the Son of man's "eating and drinking" (Matt 11:19/Luke 7:33). The reference to "marrying and being given in marriage" summarizes Gen 6:2-4, which emphasizes the marrying between "sons of God" and "daughters of men." In addition, the biblical text features Noah and all of his household entering the ark (Gen 7:1, 7), while the recitation focuses on Noah alone. There is no evidence of direct interaction between the wording in this saying attributed to Jesus and wording in the biblical text of the account. The wording of the saying is characteristic of oral expansion in a rhetorical culture, without concern for wording in the actual written text of the account. Is this phenomenon characteristic of Pauline discourse as well as discourse in the Gospels?

Recontextualization, in contrast to recitation, presents wording from biblical texts without explicit statement or implication that the words "stand written" anywhere else. An excellent example is Mark 15:24:

> And they crucify him
> and they divide his garments
> casting lots for them, who would take what.

The biblical text it recontextualizes contains the following wording:

> They divided my garments among themselves
> and for my outer garment they cast lots (Ps 22:19 [LXX: 21:19]).

The Markan recitation recontextualizes wording from the psalm, revising the tense and syntax to create a three-step statement out of *parallelismus membrorum* (Robbins 1992b:1176-77). The Markan text gives no indication that these words exist anywhere else in a written text. This form of writing, which significantly replicates word-stems in a new syntactical construction, is characteristic of both oral and written composition in a rhetorical culture (Robbins 1991b). Again, what is the nature of "recontextualization" in the authentic and deutero-Pauline letters?

Reconfiguration refers to the restructuring of an antecedent tradition. Reference, recitation, and recontextualization may or may not be present in the context of reconfiguration. An excellent example exists in the reconfiguration of Psalm 22 in the broader context of Mark 15. Significant reinscription of wording from Psalm 22 occurs in Mark 15:24, 29-32, 34. The recontextualization of Ps 22:19 in Mark 15:24 has been discussed above. Mark 15:29-32 recontextualizes language from Ps 22:7-9 in the form of "expansion composition" that produces a three-step scene featuring the mocking of three groups: (a) people passing by (15:29); (b) chief priests with scribes (15:31); and (c) the two thieves crucified alongside Jesus (15:32) (Robbins 1992b:1177-78). Mark 15:33-39 contains recontextualization of the opening verse of Ps 22. In this instance, the Markan text attributes the words in Aramaic to Jesus, forming a chreia statement, and to this the text adds a parenthetical comment that translates the statement into Greek (Robbins 1992b:1178). The net result of this recontextualization is a "reversal of the order" of the scenes in Ps 22. Given the nature of the scenes and the content of Ps 22:1, the reversal of the order produces a reversal of the rhetoric. Mark 15 reconfigures an account of a suffering person who expresses hope that he will be saved into an account of a crucified person who expresses despair just before he dies (Robbins 1992b:1178-81).

It would be unlikely that such a reversed use of Ps 22 would occur in oral composition. In other words, here we have, it seems to me, excellent evidence of scribal rather than oral progymnastic composition as the process by which this version of the text was produced. What is the nature of this phenomenon in Pauline and deutero-Pauline discourse?

Echo occurs when a word or phrase evokes, or potentially evokes, another text. Richard Hays's recent study uses this term, but the analysis addresses many different phenomena without distinguishing rhetorically among them. The nature of echo assures that scholars regularly will debate the presence or absence of the phenomenon in the text under consideration. One of the most interesting instances of echo in recent New Testament scholarship has been Burton L. Mack's discovery of the echo of *paideia* in the planting of the seeds in Mark 4:1-34. He presents the following Greco-Roman texts to support his case:

> The views of our teachers are as it were the seeds. Learning from childhood is analogous to the seeds falling betimes upon the prepared ground (Hippocrates, III).
> As is the seed that is ploughed into the ground, so must one expect the harvest to be, and similarly when good education is ploughed into young persons, its effect lives and burgeons throughout their lives, and neither rain nor drought can destroy it (Antiphon, fr. 60).
> Words should be scattered like seed; no matter how small the seed may be, if it once has found favorable ground, it unfolds its strength and from an insignificant thing spreads to its greatest growth (Seneca, Epistles 38.2).
> If you wish to argue that the mind requires cultivation, you would use a comparison drawn from the soil, which if neglected produces thorns and thickets, but if cultivated will bear fruit (Quintilian, V.xi.24) (Mack and Robbins: 155-56; Mack 1988:159-60).

The echo of *paideia* in Mark 4 undoubtedly represents the kind of "cultural" intertexture Abraham J. Malherbe has so well outlined with the relation of Pauline discourse to both Hellenistic-Jewish and Greco-Roman moral philosophical discourse (Malherbe 1987; 1989).

In the context of this rhetorical spectrum of oral-scribal intertexture in New Testament texts, we have an opportunity to pursue systematically the questions Boomershine and Dewey raise about Jesus and Paul. The issues, however, concern many more people than Jesus and Paul. Both orality and literacy were "group" activities. Who, then, was speaking and who was writing? Whose speech was imitating writing and speech, and whose writing was imitating writing and speech? These are intriguing questions that can shed new light on our understanding of first-century Judaism and Christianity.

WORKS CONSULTED

Andersen, Øivind
    1987   "Mündlichkeit und Schriftlichkeit im frühen Griechentum." Pp. 29-44 in *Antike und Abendland: Beiträge zum Verständnis der Griechen und Römer und ihres Nachlebens*, vol 33. Eds. Albrecht Dihle, Wolfgang Harms, et al. Berlin: Walter de Gruyter.
    1990   "The Making of the Past in the *Iliad*." *Harvard Studies in Classical Philology* 93: 25-45.

Bonner, Stanley F.
    1977   *Education in Ancient Rome: From the Elder Cato to the Younger Pliny*. Berkeley and Los Angeles: University of California Press.

Botha, Pieter J. J.
    1990   "Mute Manuscripts: Analyzing a Neglected Aspect of Ancient Communication." *Theologica Evangelica* 23: 35-47.
    1991a   "Mark's Story as Oral Traditional Literature: Rethinking the Transmission of Some Traditions about Jesus." *Hervormde Teologiese Studies* 47: 304-31.
    1991b   "Orality-Literacy Studies: Exploring the Interaction between Culture and Communication Technology." *Communicatio* 17: 2-15.
    1992a   "Greco-Roman Literacy as Setting for New Testament Writings." *Neot* 26: 195-215.
    1992b   "Letter Writing and Oral Communication in Antiquity: Suggested Implications for the Interpretation of Paul's Letter to the Galatians." *Scriptura* 42: 17-34.
    1993   "The Verbal Art of Pauline Letters: Rhetoric, Performance and Presence." Pp. 409-28 in *Rhetoric and the New Testament: Essays from the 1992*

Heidelberg Conference. Eds. Stanley E. Porter and Thomas H. Olbricht. Sheffield: Sheffield Academic.

Cartlidge, David R.
1990 "Combien d'unités avez-vous de trois à quatre?: What Do We Mean by Intertextuality in Early Church Studies?" Pp. 400-11 in *SBLASP*. Ed. David J. Lull. Atlanta: Scholars.

Dean-Otting, Miriam and Vernon K. Robbins
1993 "Biblical Sources for Pronouncement Stories in the Gospels." *Semeia* 64: 95-115.

Funk, Robert W., Roy W. Hoover et al.
1993 *The Five Gospels: The Search for the Authentic Words of Jesus.* New York: Macmillan.

Fowler, Robert M.
1994 "How the Secondary Orality of the Electronic Age Can Awaken Us to the Primary Orality of Antiquity, or What Hypertext Can Teach Us About the Bible." Presented at the Annual Meeting of the Eastern Great Lakes Biblical Society, April 14-15. *Interpersonal Computing and Technology: An Electronic Journal for the 21st Century* 2/3: 12-46.

Hays, Richard B.
1989 *Echoes of Scripture in the Letters of Paul.* New Haven & London: Yale University Press.

Hock, Ronald F.
1990 "A Dog in the Manger: The Cynic Cynulcus among Athenaeus' Deipnosophists." Pp. 27-52 in *Greeks, Romans, and Christians: Essays in Honor of Abraham J. Malherbe*. Eds. D. Balch, E. Ferguson, and W. Meeks. Minneapolis: Fortress.

Hock, Ronald F. and Edward N. O'Neil
1986 *The Chreia in Ancient Rhetoric. Volume I. The Progymnasmata.* Atlanta: Scholars.

Kelber, Werner H.
1983 *The Oral and the Written Gospel: The Hermeneutics of Speaking and Writing in the Synoptic Tradition, Mark, Paul, and Q.* Philadelphia: Fortress.

Kloppenborg, John S.
1988 *Q Parallels: Synopsis, Critical Notes, and Concordance.* Sonoma, CA: Polebridge.

Lentz, Tony M.
1989 *Orality and Literacy in Hellenic Greece.* Carbondale and Edwardsville: Southern Illinois University Press.

Mack, Burton L.
1988 *A Myth of Innocence: Mark and Christian Origins.* Philadelphia: Fortress.
1990 *Rhetoric and the New Testament.* Minneapolis: Fortress.
1993 *The Lost Gospel: The Book of Q and Christian Origins.* San Francisco: Harper San Francisco.

Mack, Burton L. and Vernon K. Robbins
    1989   *Patterns of Persuasion in the Gospels*. Sonoma, CA: Polebridge.

Malherbe, Abraham
    1987   *Paul and the Thessalonians: The Philosophic Tradition of Pastoral Care*. Philadelphia: Fortress.
    1989   *Paul and the Popular Philosophers*. Philadelphia: Fortress.

Merritt, H. Wayne
    1993   *In Word and Deed: Moral Integrity in Paul*. New York: Peter Lang.

Moore, Stephen D.
    1992   "Deconstructive Criticism: The Gospel of Mark." Pp. 84-102 in *Mark and Method: New Approaches in Biblical Studies*. Eds. Janice Capel Anderson and Stephen D. Moore. Minneapolis: Fortress.

Nelson, Theodor Holm
    1993   *Literary Machines 93.1*. Sausalito, CA: Mindful.

O'Day, Gail R.
    1990   "Jeremiah 9:22-23 and 1 Corinthians 1:26-31: A Study in Intertextuality." *JBL* 109: 259-67.

Ong, Walter J.
    1982   *Orality and Literacy: The Technologizing of the Word*. London: Methuen.

Robbins, Vernon K.
    1991a   "The Social Location of the Implied Author of Luke-Acts." Pp. 305-332 in Neyrey (ed.), *The Social World of Luke-Acts*. Peabody, MA: Hendrickson.
    1991b   "Writing as a Rhetorical Act in Plutarch and the Gospels." Pp. 157-186 in *Persuasive Artistry: Studies in New Testament Rhetoric in Honor of George A. Kennedy*. Ed. Duane F. Watson. Sheffield: JSOT.
    1992a   *Jesus the Teacher: A Socio-Rhetorical Interpretation of Mark*. Rpt. Minneapolis: Fortress. First edition, 1984.
    1992b   "The Reversed Contextualization of Psalm 22 in the Markan Crucifixion: A Socio-Rhetorical Analysis." Pp. 1161-1183 in *The Four Gospels 1992. Festschrift Frans Neirynck*, vol 2. Ed. F. Van Segbroeck, C.M. Tuckett, G. Van Belle, J. Verheyden. BETL 100. Leuven: Leuven University Press.
    1993a   "Progymnastic Rhetorical Composition and Pre-Gospel Traditions: A New Approach." Pp. 111-147 in *The Synoptic Gospels: Source Criticism and the New Literary Criticism*. Ed. Camille Focant. BETL 110. Leuven: Leuven University Press.
    1993b   "Rhetoric and Culture: Exploring Types of Cultural Rhetoric in a Text." Pp. 443-463 in *Rhetoric and the New Testament: Essays from the 1992 Heidelberg Conference*. Eds. Stanley E. Porter and Thomas H. Olbricht. Sheffield: Sheffield Academic.
    1994a   *New Boundaries in Old Territory: Form and Social Rhetoric in Mark*. Ed. David B. Gowler. Emory Studies in Early Christianity 3. New York: Peter Lang.
    1994b   "Socio-Rhetorical Criticism: Mary, Elizabeth, and the Magnificat as a Test Case." Pp. 164-209 in *The New Literary Criticism and the New*

Testament. Eds. Elizabeth Struthers Malbon and Edgar V. McKnight. Sheffield: Sheffield Academic.

Scott, Bernard Brandon and Margaret E. Dean
1993 "A Sound Map of the Sermon on the Mount." Pp. 672-725 in *SBLSP* 32. Ed. Eugene H. Lovering, Jr. Atlanta: Scholars.

Sisson, Russell B.
1993 *The Apostle as Athlete: A Socio-Rhetorical Interpretation of 1 Corinthians 9.* Unpublished PhD. dissertation. Atlanta: Emory University.

Watson, Duane F. and Alan J. Hauser
1994 *Rhetorical Criticism of the Bible. A Comprehensive Bibliography with Notes on History and Method.* Biblical Interpretation Series 4. Leiden: Brill.

II

PAUL AND PERFORMANCE:
SPECIFIC TEXTS

PAULINE VOICE AND PRESENCE AS STRATEGIC COMMUNICATION

Richard F. Ward
Yale Divinity School

ABSTRACT

The reciter of Paul's four-chapter letter (2 Cor 10-13) played a significant role in the conflict between Paul and the Corinthian "superapostles." Methods drawn from the discipline of performance studies illumine a critical encounter between two rival apostolates in the early Christian missionary movement. When one apostolate, distinguished by skill in oral performance, accuses Paul of being weak in speech and bodily presence, he constructs an effective counter-performance: Paul's letter, as recited by his emissary, becomes Paul's way of being present in the Corinthian community. This presence, as embodied by the reciter of the letter, is powerful enough to undercut the charges brought by Paul's opponents and to support Paul's claim to apostolic authority in the Corinthian church.

As an historian of performance, I am interested in how bodily presence and speech became issues in Paul's conflict with the Corinthian superapostles in the 50's CE. From the information presented in 2 Cor 10:10 and 11:6, it appears that Paul was deemed ineffective in some form of public speech and that his inability to perform in this way jeopardized his claim to apostolic authority at Corinth. Of course, we will never finally know what mode of oral presentation is referred to here. But there are some things we *can* consider. First, we have a letter and we know from our knowledge of performance history that such letters were written to be read aloud.

> A man read even a private letter aloud in a low voice. This practice obviously had great influence on epistolary convention and style. It also helped to make the letter addressed to an individual or group an easy and natural vehicle for philosophical or religious discussion or exposition (McGuire, 150).

Second, the discipline of performance studies lends us an experiential understanding of what happens within the matrix of text, reciter, and audience when a written text, such as a letter, is orally performed. Part of my method of studying this letter has been to perform it in a variety of contexts. Oral performance is a means of transforming silent texts into sounds and movement through the mediums of speech and gesture. It is a way in which the author-in-the-work becomes an audible presence by means of the speech and movement of the presenter. This is why the performance of Paul's letters contributes some important insights into the sociopolitical dynamics that govern his relationships with those he addresses. For example, I believe that the recitation of Paul's four-chapter letter (2 Cor 10-13) was a counter-performance through which Paul shrewdly and creatively re-established a powerful parousia in the Corinthian church. This event helped to form a basis for reconciliation between Paul and the Corinthians by refurbishing Paul's credibility as a Christian apostle.

The group of itinerate missionaries who came to Corinth in the 50's CE attacked Paul's credentials on many fronts; perhaps the most devastating charge was a personal attack on his ability to communicate the Gospel. Paul actually quotes his opponents in 2 Cor 10:10: They say, 'His letters are weighty and strong, but his bodily presence is weak, and his speech is of no account' (RSV). In the opinion of these rivals, Paul's *parousia*, that is, his very way of being in that church communicated weakness; his *logos*, that is, his speech, was empty or of no account. Apparently these categories of oral performance were being established as criteria for evaluating Paul's effectiveness as a Christian leader.

PAUL'S OPPONENTS IN THE HISTORY OF RECITATION

The identity of these opponents remains the subject of considerable debate. I will not review all of the attempts to link this group of missionaries with other figures in the early Christian missionary movement. Dieter Georgi's hypothesis, as presented in *The Opponents of Paul in Second Corinthians*, is best for highlighting the importance of oral performance in the struggle for apostolic authority at Corinth. Georgi points out that since the missionary activity of the diaspora did not have a central organization, the service of worship in the synagogue was the magnet that drew potential converts. The central feature of this public event was the oral performance and exegesis of scripture. Performance of sacred stories and subsequent oral interpretations made the faith of Judaism accessible to outsiders and helped to assimilate pagans into the communities of worship. A loose network of "oral exegetes" was established to travel about and offer oral performances and interpretations of texts in the communities (91). Georgi identifies the superapostles as part of this network.

One remarkable feature in the careers of these wandering preachers is that they were expected also to perform outside the synagogue. Synagogue officials saw the value in having a talented oral performer soliciting financial support just outside the synagogue. Such performances attracted the attention of potential converts. For the preacher, the attention brought financial reward, prestige, and reputation (Georgi: 101-2). The wandering preacher would not only attract attention to his or her gifts as a performer, but also to the diety that she or he represented.

The centerpiece of these performers' repertoire was the oral intepretation of sacred scripture. These exegetes were:

> capable of setting free the spirit bottled up in the composition of holy scripture . . . Insofar as they themselves did not create the text which is to be interpreted, the source of the spirit, they are subordinated to it. But insofar as the spirit speaks through their exegesis, they were quite equal to the prophets of old (Georgi: 111).

Public worship revolved therefore around this release of the spirit through the exegetes' performances. The synagogue ceremony, then, was the occasion for highly theatrical activity. Numerous people were included in the ceremony, even if they only accompanied the action with applause. The synagogue became a spiritual theater.

The taste for theatrical activity encouraged architects to design appropriate structures. Epiphanus compares the architecture of one particular synagogue to a theater:

> There is a proseuche in Sichem, which is now called Neopolis, outside the city on the plain, at about a distance of two milestones, built by the Samaritans, who imitate the Jews in all things, like a theatre in the open air and a spot which lies free under the sky (*Haereses* 80.1; quoted in Georgi: 113).

Even a closed synagogue's structure encouraged theatricality. "There was . . . an open area extending from the front into the center, a kind of stage where the participants in the liturgy could act" (Georgi: 113). It is clear from these sources that worshipers in these synagogues encouraged and even expected highly developed, oral presentations of Yahweh's Word. Oral performance provided immediate access to the spirit of God; true worship depended on the release of Yahweh's spirit, which was achieved by the oral interpretation of sacred texts. Performers who possessed particular skill in this art were prophets who represented God.

PAUL'S OPPONENTS IN THE CONTEXT OF PERFORMANCE HISTORY

Georgi's profile of the superapostles helps to place them within the performance world of the first-century Christian church. Christian worship in the Pauline era was characterized by various modes of oral performance. One of the most common was the telling of gospel traditions in early Christian worship. Eusebius records that the oral performances of gospels were central events in early Christian worship:

> A great light of religion shone on the minds of the hearers of Peter, so that they were not satisfied with a single hearing or with the unwritten teaching of the divine proclamation, but with every kind of exhortation besought Mark, whose Gospel is extant, seeing that he was Peter's follower, to leave them a written statement of the teaching given them verbally, nor did they cease until they had persuaded him, and so became the cause of the Scripture called the Gospel According to Mark (49).

Though this account of Markan authorship is contested, the description is an authoritative report of how the gospel would have been orally rendered. Amos Wilder adds a piece to our understanding of what these performances might have been like:

> When we picture to ourselves the early Christian narrators we should make full allowance for animated and expressive narration . . . oral speech also was less inhibited than today . . . when we think of the early church meetings and testimonies and narrations we are probably well guided if we think of the way in which Vachael Lindsay read or of the appropriate readings of James Weldon Johnson's *God's Trombones* (56).

Recitation of oral traditions in early Christian worship was emotionally expressive. It reflected the involvement of the performers with the stories themselves and prompted a wide range of emotional responses from the audiences. If the teller was successful in involving the audience with the story, he or she might expect them to become involved in the performance of the story, singing along, humming, or even accompanying the tellings with musical instruments (Boomershine: 11). During Christian worship, one performer might be charged with the telling, even though the entire community would come to know the stories well enough to tell them. The effect of these tellings was the constitution of a community. Christian worship became occasions where disparate cultural groups bonded together around the recitation of oral traditions. Jews, Greeks, and other Gentiles learned to identify with the traditions, interpreting them in light of the issues they faced (Boomershine: 35-36).

Christian storytellers resembled the oral singers studied by Albert Lord in *The Singer of Tales*. To see how the early Homeric rhapsodes might have developed their art, Milman Parry and Lord studied epic singers in Yugoslavia to understand how epics were composed and transmitted in pre-literate cultures:

> Oral epic song is narrative poetry, composed in a manner evolved over many generations by singers of tales who did not know how to write. It consists of the building of metrical lines and half-lines by means of formulas and

formulaic expressions and of the building of songs by the use of themes (Lord: 4).

A formula is a group of words that is regularly employed under the same metrical idea (30). The earliest rhapsodes (of which Homer was a prototype) were agents of composition, poets for whom singing, performing, and composing were parts of the same creative act. The oral singer accumulates through the years a vocabulary of these formulas and, in the act of utterance, he or she is actually creating the epic. The singer's performance is conditioned by the context of the utterance. The oral singer varies the length and emphases according to the needs of the occasion. Walter Ong states that "All epics are structured around certain themes; the summoning of the council, the arming of the hero, the description of the hero's mount" (24). Ong goes on to explain that each epic singer has his own massive store of these themes, which he weaves together with ease. The oft-repeated formulas, 'rosy-fingered dawn' or 'wine-dark sea,' are metrically manageable (25). To the modern ear, these performances might sound like singing. However, singing carried a different connotation in that culture than it does today. Donald Hargis, an historian of performance, suggests that the best analogue in our culture to these performances is the talk-song from musical comedy (389).

Gospels, like oral epics, were composed anew at each performance; tellers improvised along story lines and using oral formulas just as the earliest Greek rhapsodes had done with Homeric epics. The Christian storyteller would be expected to acquire a repertoire of story lines and formulas to use in recomposing gospels at each telling. Christian performers of sacred stories must have drawn upon the standards of excellence in performance behavior that were dominant in Greco-Roman culture.

The best source we have for determining standards for oral performance of literature in this period is Quintilian's *Institutio Oratoria*.[1] Quintilian taught that when the good speaker took the stage, his neck was straight, not bent backward, so that his throat would be relaxed. His shoulders would be relaxed, not contracted or raised. The audience would get a clue to the speaker's attitude toward delivery by looking at the speaker's eyes. Quintilian stressed that the "eyes would reveal the temper of the mind, even without movement" (285). The speaker's weight would be evenly distributed over his feet. Quintilian warned against placing the right foot forward or against "straddling the feet . . . when standing still"

---

[1] I am indebted to Cobin (1958) for a discussion of the relevance of Quintilian's *Institutes* to the historical studies in the performance of literature. The use of the masculine pronoun reflects Quintilian's cultural perspective that the discipline of public oratory was practiced by men.

(311). When the speaker moved out of the standing position, he would move diagonally, keeping his eyes fixed on the audience, and would avoid swaying to the right or the left. Since his garb would certainly be noticed, the speaker's attire must be "distinguished and manly." He would pay particular attention to the cut of his toga, the style of his shoes, and the arrangement of his hair. As he stood, the speaker would raise the thumbs of his hands and slightly curve his fingers, unless he was holding a manuscript. The reciter would bring a good deal of natural talent to the process of preparing for performance. His "natural gifts" would include a good voice, excellent lungs, and good health. Audiences would note the reciter's natural charm and would be aware of his good character. Such traits were essential for the good performer.

In Quintilian's teaching, the voice and body are shaped by the emotional values of the piece in performance. Sound and movement are keys to what the speaker is experiencing himself. An audience will be able to determine degrees of sincerity and insincerity by listening to the tone of the voice and by watching the speaker's movement. "For the voice is the index of the mind and is capable of expressing all varieties of feeling" (277). Gesture is adapted to suit the voice, though movements are also full of meaning (279). Quintilian insists on integration between voice and movement. "If gesture is out of harmony with the speech . . . words fail to carry conviction" (281). Certain emotional attitudes stimulate corresponding patterns of movement in performance. For example, an arm slightly extended, with shoulders thrown back, and fingers opening as the hand moves forward will highlight "continuous flowing passages" (289). Qualities of restraint and timidity are often conveyed by slightly hollowing the hand as if making a vow, moving it to and fro lightly, and swaying the shoulders in unison. For wonder, the head turns upward and fingers are brought into the palm, beginning with the little finger first (297).

In preparing to perform, then, the reciter must bring all his natural gifts to bear. He must be thoroughly acquainted with his piece and work to internalize its performative values. Each letter had a particular sound that suited it; the natural voice should not be over-laid with a fuller sound. Vocal production should be supported from the lungs, not the mouth, and the final syllables of words should not be clipped. He warns that sometimes the personality of the reciter overshadowed the value of the text. Finally, Quintilian emphasized that a reciter sparks interest in a text because he "stimulates us by the animation of his delivery, and kindles the imagination, not by presenting us with an elaborate picture, but by bringing us into actual touch with the things themselves" (11, 13).

Though the Christian movement preferred orality as its repository for sacred stories, its leaders freely employed the art of writing. Texts (such as written gospels or letters) recited or orally composed in Christian worship harkened back to the immediacy of oral discourse. Letters served orality and were thus returned to oral space by way of the public reader.

While Quintilian's *Institutes* were designed to train the orator of the first century CE, they do present principles that set the standard for a variety of modes of oral performance, including the public performance of an apostolic letter or an oral gospel. Quintilian saw the performer as an instrument for embodying the images presented by both oral and written materials. Through the skillful use of voice and gesture, the representation of felt emotional values, and the thorough knowledge of the style and content of a given text, the oral performer in Greco-Roman culture embodied potent voices present in both oral and written material.

Probably the Corinthians in particular had a healthy appetite for excellence in oral performance since they lived near the site of the Isthmian games, one of the great festivals where oral poets, dramatists, musicians, and athletes had come every two years for centuries to compete for top awards and prestige. At the time of Paul's visit, the Isthmian games were under Corinthian sponsorship and were being held in a newly restored stadium and theater facility. It is possible that one member of Paul's Corinthian congregation was the civic official named Erastus who made a substantial contribution to the renovation of the theater.[2] The Corinthian Christians may well have appreciated trained oral performance, such as the superapostles seem to have provided.

The text of 2 Cor 10-13 strongly suggests that the apostle Paul was at this point in his career in danger of losing his following at Corinth to these performers of the word. Apparently, they had made his ineffective speech and presence cause for the Corinthians' concern. If Paul could not himself render the gospel, could he be deemed an authentic bearer of the good news? Paul's problem was how to establish a presence in the Corinthian community that recaptured their attention and loyalty. This is where the *reciter* of Paul's four-chapter letter plays a significant role in the politics of performance in the Corinthian church.

---

[2] Broneer (20) notes that in Rom 16:23, Paul salutes a man named Erastus. There is an inscription on the pavement of the road that leads up to the theater honoring the contribution of a Corinthian freedman named Erastus sometime in the middle of the first century CE. There is a strong possibility that the man Paul addresses in Rom 16:23 is the same man who laid the pavement leading to the theater. For a dissenting view see Cadbury.

The Letter and Presence

Robert Funk has observed that in the early Christian church, the apostle's means of exercising power and influence was dependent upon his establishing apostolic parousia in that community. Parousia or presence in a church during a time of crisis gave that apostle social visibility and political authority. Since early Christian missionaries were itinerates, it was not always possible for them to be physically present when difficult situations arose, so the early missionaries employed other means of establishing their presence.

Sending an emissary to read a letter aloud was one of the most effective ways of establishing parousia in the early churches. When the apostle could not visit the church himself, he would commission an emissary to represent him to the members of the congregation. This chosen envoy often carried a letter from the apostle that recommended the emissary as an authoritative substitute for the apostle. Paul, like other ancient epistolers, was dependent upon trusted carriers to deliver his letters to recipients. Martin McGuire writes: "The personal representative or messenger, the visitor or traveller, were almost the sole means of communication between nations and individuals" (185). Before sending the letter, the author would "brief the carrier on the contents of the letters entrusted to them and also make supplementary reports on matters that were not set down in writing" (185). Receiving a letter meant hearing both a message conveyed on behalf of the sender and a written document. Letters, therefore, bore a kinship with oral messages; like oral messages, the sender's name was placed in the beginning. The written document authenticated the messages. The carrier could also provide information about the author of the letter. The letter, then, as written and conveyed, was a major way Paul overcame his separation from his churches. "We also gain a sense of the importance of his emissaries or letter carriers: they receive authority to convey the letters to expand upon them, and to continue Paul's work" (Doty, 37).

Paul likely intended that his emissary to Corinth would not only recite but interpret the contents of 2 Cor 10-13 to the Corinthians. Doty suggests that because of political intrigue and the vulnerability of the postal system, the letter writer was careful to entrust the *real* message of the letter to the carrier, not merely to the text of the letter itself (45-46).

> Paul, who made such a point of indicating his trust in those carriers (co-workers), did not think of his written letters as exhausting what he wished to communicate. He thought of his associates, especially those commissioned to carry his letters, as able to extend his own teachings (45-46).

Doty wonders further:

if the Pauline letters may not be seen as the essential part of the messages Paul had to convey, pressed into brief compass as a basis for elaboration by the carriers. The subsequent reading of the letters in the primitive Christian communities were occasions for full exposition and expansion of the sketch of the material in the letters (46-47).

In other words, the oral rendering and interpretation of the letters completes the apostle's *logos* for the church.

The church receiving the letter would expect the emissary to read it aloud to the congregation. Doty and other epistolary theorists agree that the letters were written by an author who was conscious of his responsibility as an apostle in the congregation and thus fully intended such letters to be read aloud to the gathered community.[3] At Corinth, the oral performance of the letter has particular significance to the Pauline apostolate; since Paul's bodily presence had been deemed weak, Paul establishes a new presence, that of Paul-in-the-letter, which, when embodied by the reciter, gave Paul restored visibility in the community.

PERFORMANCE AND THE POWER OF EMBODIED PRESENCE

Alla Bozarth-Campbell's incarnational metaphor for performance helps explain how composers of texts become present when those texts are performed. Like all texts prepared for public reading, the letter achieves its entelechy in oral performance. When it is rendered orally, the form of the letter is transformed into a presence that is embodied by the reciter. Bozarth-Campbell explains what happens when texts are transferred from surface structures to oral space:

> Through dialogue the phenomenon of interpretation may come to reveal what was hidden in itself, to show its own processes of rendering what was invisible and inaudible in literature both visible and audible in a dynamic presence (3).

For Bozarth-Campbell, the oral performance of any text is a process that creates a "new being by bringing two separate beings together in an incarnation" and "this process leads to an event which constitutes a transformation of all who participate in it" (13). In other words, the body of the performer meets with the body of the text through the mediums of speech and movement in order to create the new body of the text-in-performance. This process has several phases: the creation of the literary work (which Bozarth-Campbell calls the poem), the matching between the poem and the reader (whom she calls the interpreter), and the

---

[3] For a full discussion on this point see Doty (25-27).

communion between the audience and the new being, the incarnate body that is created by the interaction of poem and performer.

Bozarth-Campbell's framework provides a basis for discussing how the rendering of Paul's letter by a trusted emissary established a new, more powerful Pauline presence in the Corinthian church. She states that the primary task of the interpreter (hereafter referred to as the performer) of the work is to create a presence, and to create it so fully that it can contain and involve the audience (18; see also Bacon: 165). Performers must know the piece, not just its parts in isolation, but the feel of the whole. For example, when Paul's emissary stood before the Corinthians to speak the letter, he would have internalized the contents of the letter and would be prepared to interpret the whole of Paul's logos to the Corinthians. This reciter was probably Titus, given his relationship with the church of Corinth (2 Cor 8:16), or perhaps the brother who is mentioned as famous among all the churches for proclaiming the good news (8:18). In any case, Paul must have carefully considered the ability of his reciter to render his text in accordance with the standards of excellence of the time. Titus or some other emissary, through the skillful rendering of Paul's letter, intended to guide the audience through an *experience* of the situation from Paul's perspective.

To render Paul's text effectively, the reciter would have to have, in Quintilian's words, "natural gifts," including a good voice, a measure of charm, and good character. The reciter would have to convey effectively the emotional values of the letter and allow those values to shape vocal production and physical movement. Only then would Paul's authorial presence be embodied in performance. As the letter's performer allowed the body and voice to represent the passions invested in the piece, a process of transformation could begin:

> It is in this moment of existence that relationship between interpreter and text takes on the properties of vivid presence in the power of performance, when all things come together to effect a quality greater than the sum of them as separate (Bozarth-Campbell: 40).

If the first act in creating Paul-in-the-letter was composing it, the second act was the performer's enfleshing of the presence. Paul's word was transformed from silent surface structures into the mode of being known as flesh by the emissary's performance of Paul's word. In making the word become flesh, the interpreter makes herself or himself into the word, takes the word as poem into her or his body, continues the creation process begun by the poet (Bozarth-Campbell: 52). The purpose of performing a text is to allow the poem to achieve fullness through the performer's body. Given the conventions of performing letters in antiquity, we can imagine the reciter giving Paul's letter fullness, not simply by rendering the written word but by adding oral commentary in the spirit and attitude of Paul himself. The emissary's performance of Paul's letter allowed it to become "a more truly present word, authenticated by a living voice" (Bozarth-Campbell: 75).

The challenge for Paul was exactly this: by means of an effective counter-performance, could Paul demonstrate his ability to be present in the same lively and authoritative way as his opponents? If the superapostles could bring the audience into sacred acoustical space by means of their recitation of texts, Paul could show a different, more powerful image of himself through the performance of his letter.

Bozarth-Campbell suggests that performers of texts become icons for the new body or presence created in performance. "The interpreter's presence—as the embodiment of the poem—constitute a kind of image-meaning, or a sacramental meaningfulness" (103). If Georgi's profile is correct, then Paul's opponents had become icons for the presence of such divine figures as Moses and Jesus. The performer of Paul's letter became an icon for the apostolic presence of Paul, a presence deemed powerful by both the Corinthians and Paul's opponents. The letter-in-performance demonstrated to the Corinthians that Paul's voice and presence could be very strong indeed and certainly quite different from the poor self-presentations Paul had given during his visits. Thus Paul's emissary, as the icon of Paul-in-the-letter, would be able to put the audience in the presence of the holy in a way Paul's opponents did in their performances and thereby place the Pauline apostolate on equal ground with its rivals. The embodiment of Paul-in-the-letter was an act that collapsed the distance between Paul, performer, and audience; this incarnation of the letter's persona transformed the Corinthian audience and established the basis for a renewed relationship between the church and Paul.

> Performance as icon . . . alters the very perception of being. One cannot look deeply into the eyes of an icon and ever see the world in exactly the same way again. The icon changes one by bestowing the vision of another world . . . to enter the world of the icon is to take on that world by spontaneous and largely unconscious response to it (Bozarth-Campbell: 118).

The Corinthian audience changes by seeing the Apostle Paul in a new way. The performer shows the persona of the letter, a fool who is speaking with enormous power (2 Cor 11:1, 16, 17; 12:11). This embodied voice lampoons the social order that the Corinthians have set up under the leadership of the rival apostolate. By looking at the situation through Paul's eyes, the Corinthians' perception of Paul's legitimacy as a Christian apostle may have changed.

CONCLUSIONS

Alla Bozarth-Campbell's incarnational metaphor for the performance of literature grants us insight into a strategy by which the Pauline apostolate could re-establish an authoritative parousia in the Corinthian church. Paul created the word for the church; the oral interpreter of Paul's letter (a sympathetic emissary) gave that word its body in performance before the community. The creation of this new body can be viewed as a counter-performance to the effective recitations offered by Paul's rivals, which implicitly demeaned Paul's presentations. The effect of the performance was to re-establish Paul as a potent and powerful voice within the Corinthian community.

WORKS CONSULTED

Bacon, Wallace
    1972   *The Art of Interpretation*. New York: Holt.

Boomershine, Thomas E.
    1985   *Biblical Storytelling*. Unpublished manuscript.

Bozarth-Campbell, Alla
    1979   *The Word's Body: An Incarnational Aesthetic of Interpretation*. Tuscaloosa: Alabama University Press.

Broneer, Oscar
    1962   "The Apostle Paul and the Isthmian Games." *BA* 25:1-31.

Cadbury, Henry
    1931   "Erastus of Corinth." *JBL* 50:42-58.

Cobin, Martin T.
    1958   "An Oral Interpreter's Index to Quintilian." *Quarterly Journal of Speech* 44:61-66.

Doty, William G.
    1973   *Letters in Primitive Christianity*. Philadelphia: Fortress.

Eusebius
    1989   *The History of the Church from Christ to Constantine*. Trans. G. A. Williamson. London: Penguin.

Funk, Robert
    1967   "The Apostolic Parousia: Form and Significance." Pp. 249-69 in *Christian History and Interpretation: Studies Presented to John Knox*. Ed. W. R. Farmer, C. F. D. Moule, and R. R. Neibuhr. Cambridge, England: Cambridge University Press.

Georgi, Dieter
    1986   *The Opponents of Paul in 2 Corinthians*. Philadelphia: Fortress.

Hargis, Donald
    1970   "The Rhapsode." *Quarterly Journal of Speech* 56:388-94.

Lord, Albert
    1960   *The Singer of Tales*. Cambridge: Harvard University Press.

McGuire, Martin R. P.
    1960   "Letters and Letter Carriers in Ancient Antiquity." *Classical World* 53:148-99.

Ong, Walter J.
    1967   *The Presence of the Word: Some Prolegomena for Cultural and Religious History*. Minneapolis: University of Minnesota Press.

Quintilian
    1963   *Institutes for the Orator*. Trans. H. E. Butler. Vol. IV. Cambridge: Harvard University Press.

Wilder, Amos N.
    1971   *Early Christian Rhetoric: The Language of the Gospels*. Cambridge: Harvard University Press.

A RE-HEARING OF ROMANS 10:1-15

Arthur J. Dewey
Xavier University

ABSTRACT

The pioneering work of Werner Kelber (1983) provided the critical starting point for this paper, which refines the oral/written distinction describing Paul's epistolary strategy. A nuanced "oral" reading of Romans 10 suggests that Paul, by employing the written medium (Deut 30:12-14) within an oral performance, was intent on playing to the utopian dreams and desires of the first century. In contrast, Philo's use of Deut 30:11-14 in *De Virtutibus* 180-85, *Quod Omnis Probus Liber Sit* 62-73, and *De Specialibus Legibus* 14:160-169 allows us to see that there was another way of combining the written and oral media. In their own ways, both writers were attempting to declare that genuine access to ultimate power was within the grasp of their listeners. Yet, for Paul the use of Deut 30 serves as a subversive oral message to the non-elite, while for Philo the message is meant to encourage the literate to participate in a gradual transformation.

INTRODUCTION

The intent of this paper, as intimated by the title, carries forward on an expanding wavelength. My "re-hearing" begins with a critical appraisal of Werner Kelber's pioneering analysis of orality in Paul (1983). In bringing the ground-breaking work of Walter Ong, S.J. (1970) to bear on the Pauline material, Kelber was able to detect the oral dimension of Paul's letters. In addition, Kelber made initial suggestions as to the social conditions and implications of Paul's mode of communication. However, the oral/written distinction, which Kelber originally used to understand Paul's acoustic field in absolute opposition to the regimentation of the "letter," needs a nuanced critique.[1] Paul's epistolary strategy assumed that the two types of communication media were powerful means. Both speech and manuscript were embedded in the understanding of the transmission of power in the ancient world. As we shall see, it was not a simple opposition (even with Paul's letters) between orality and

---

[1] As his present articles in this volume demonstrate, Kelber has moved from the more absolute position that bears the brunt of my criticism in this paper. His present position would seem to coincide with my nuanced reading of Paul and Philo.

writtenness. Rather, the use of either medium signaled the reach for power, the attempt to gain access to the sources of power and patronage in the ancient world. What is of capital interest is to determine why and how Paul uses the written medium within an oral stance. To see this I shall return to Romans 10 for a rereading. Here I contend that Paul did not simply use the manuscript tradition but actually purported to allow it to speak, as it were, for the first time, in and through the very presence of the trusting community. In contrast to Kelber, who saw Paul as an "oral traditionalist" (Kelber: 177), setting an oral performance against the externalities of a chirographic culture, I shall argue that Paul was playing creatively to the utopian desires of his audience and of the first century in general.

It is in light of this larger discussion that Philo is introduced. A comparison of how Paul and Philo employed Deut 30:11-14 will show that their selections of this passage were politically decisive. We shall see that both Philo and Paul, though working in different directions, challenged their respective listeners to an active and immediate response in a world where power, resources, and control were assumed to be in the hands of an elite few. Both Paul and Philo utilize, although in ways distinct from one another, the powers of the written and oral means of communication. Each in his own way was declaring that access to genuine power, to the desired patron, was right before the engaged listener.

Werner Kelber And The Battle Of Technologies

With the exception of my own dissertation (1982), only Werner Kelber has attempted to apply the recent discussion of orality to the writings of Paul. Kelber drew upon the work of Walter Ong who had noted that an oral performance produces an interior response quite distinct from a chirographic experience. The world of sound is experienced as *going on*. It delivers an interior or interiorizing experience that is percussive, not superficial. The actual underlying or interior relationships determine the effect the sound has. Sound reveals the interior without the necessity of physical invasion. Sound situates people in the middle of actuality, in a world with echoes, both past and to come, in a world of voices. In light of this, one can begin to see that even space takes on a different sense. Acoustic space is apprehended in terms of sounds and echoes, which are not spread out in front of the listeners but are diffused around them. The hearer is situated in the center of the acoustic field not in front of it. Acoustic space is in a way a vast interior in the center of which listeners find themselves together with their interlocutors. This means that space is not the neutral environment of Newton but a kind of vast interiority, a cosmic echo chamber. Time also has a different ring to it, for one can exist in this acoustic realm without time limit as long as the conversation is going on (Ong: 111-75).

In light of this understanding of "acoustic space," Kelber argued that Paul's gospel is an oral phenomenon, which aims at "interiorizing the essentially invisible," not at objectifying the communication of a transcendent God (Kelber, 142). Paul would communicate directly to the human heart, not through externals. For Paul life is allied with sound/hearing. The gospel "is ... operationally defined in oral terms, not by association with writing and reading" (144). Kelber correctly noted that the gospel is to be linked primarily with its effect upon its hearers. Indeed, Kelber made a most important connection between spirit (pneuma) and sound:

> In the background lurks the phenomenological connection between sound and spirit or breath, although Paul has not consciously reflected on it. . . . spoken words owe their very existence to spirit, the breath of life. . . . speech is fluid, hence living, and not subject to the written regimentation of textualization (145).

It is in keeping with Kelber's assessment of the NT writings he treated in *The Oral and the Written Gospel* that he would juxtapose the vitality of the oral with the "regimentation" of the written. As I shall attempt to demonstrate, I regard this absolute distinction between the oral and written with misgiving. While the oral/written distinction is important for Paul, it is not to be understood in terms of such stark opposition. On the contrary, the distinction has merit for Paul because it expresses concisely how the two media of communication functioned as different avenues of conveying power and breaking through the boundaries of space and time. For Paul it was a question of how power was to be conveyed and what sort of access people might have to it. Neither for Paul nor for his contemporaries was the written mode impotent; it was exactly the opposite in the understanding of the ancient world:

> . . . precisely as written, Scripture indicates the presence of a living tradition. Scripture comes to be seen as a conveyance of the power of tradition, functioning as a storehouse for tradition, as well as the very means of breaking through the boundaries of space and time to come upon eternity (Dewey 1982: 95).

The oral interpretation of Scripture became a way of gaining access to divine patronage. As we shall see below, a comparison with Philo's understanding of the internalization of law as embodying the political/philosophical ideals of the day will help us see how the activity of interpretation can provide a means of access for those willing to participate (Dewey 1982:88-107).

Kelber also stressed the social effect of an oral performance. Here he initiated the critical discussion regarding the social assumptions and vision supporting such oral behavior. We shall continue to explore this below. As Kelber noted, spoken words create an audience. But this created acoustic space is hardly simple. A "tense world of personal loyalties and betrayals" (147) is part and parcel of the audience's cultural situation. Thus, the appearance of opposing parties (as happens quite often in Paul's letters) would have a divisive effect, since there is a competition for acoustic space. This would raise the question of competitive dissonance. In sum, the intent of Paul's message is to create an ethos of participation, an orbit, a sphere of influence, or, in Walter Ong's terms, "an acoustic field" (Ong: 163).

In contrast to this acoustic realm, Kelber set up the "written law." He contrasted, for example, Abraham's inward hearing of faith (orality) with the "externalization" (writtenness) of the Word of God (Gal 3:1-14).[2] I would simply point out that this contrast might well be based upon chirographic distinctions (where surface and sub-surface occur) noted above and not upon oral experience. While Kelber made an important connection between writtenness and Law and noted that this connection does not refer to some legalistic character of the Law but to the sense of its written totality and complexity, he failed, in my opinion, to bring in the fundamental issue of the power conveyed through this written tradition. The reason for this is that Kelber explained the oral/written dialectic in Paul according to Ong's modern category distinctions (154-155). But that does not work. The written text in the ancient world was not silent; rather, it was read aloud, indeed performed, and in so doing actually increased the potential of conveying a tradition through the audience's participation. Again, the question is not simply one of orality versus writtenness but of how power was to be conveyed and augmented.[3] What would it mean if one medium for communicating the tradition had dominance? Whether the manuscript medium determined the oral experience or vice versa, the underlying question would be: would either medium deliver the desired access and power to its audience?

Finally, Kelber speculated as to whether Paul has admitted the disjunctive force of writing into the fiber of his own theology, insuring what eventuates as the "rupture of the oral synthesis" (168-169). Again, this speculation misses the mark. It is somewhat misleading since it does

---

[2] What I have demonstrated in my dissertation (Dewey 1982:52-69, 127-134, 196-200), Kelber notes, namely, the association of hearing/faith/proclamation of righteousness/blessing/promise of Spirit (152).

[3] In light of the question of power conveyed through an oral or written medium, it is interesting to note that Kelber overlooks the oral properties of curse and the function of the Law as curse in Gal 3.

not take into account the dialectical relationship that occurs whenever there is a mix of technologies. Georgi has documented quite well the positive use of the written tradition in Hellenistic Judaism as a conveyance of power (1986). In my own work I have argued for a dialectical employment of both oral and written media (1982:88-153) to convey the power of the spirit (pneuma). Once a new medium has made its cultural appearance, the old medium does not die out, nor does it exist independently of the new; on the contrary there now exists the possibility to use the old in light of the new and vice versa. Just as in the electronic age one can use the skills of the typographic culture to direct and shape the electronic communication, so also the oral can determine the shape of the chirographic, thereby allowing the oral medium to perform in ways not possible within a totally oral environment. Moreover, the use of a more "conservative" medium may well signal not the presence of an oral traditionalist in the sense of a political reactionary. Instead one may wonder whether the use of an "oral stance" could signal an alternative or even utopian vision.[4]

REREADING ROMANS 10

Kelber has called this passage, Rom 10:14-17, the *locus classicus* of the oral hermeneutics of sound, where "the oral gospel partakes in the itinerant mode of apostolic action" (149). In my translation[5] of Romans, I have underscored the oral and written clues in the material. Of course, we cannot overlook the point that the entire piece was orally delivered and interpreted.

(14) Now, then, how can they *appeal* to someone
 whom they haven't *trusted*?
How can they trust one they haven't *heard about*?
How can they *hear* without someone *announcing* [it]?

(15) How can they *announce* unless they are sent?
 Just as it's *written*:
"How welcome are the feet of those who *deliver* good *news*."

(16) But not all listen to the *news*.
 Isaiah says:
 "Lord, who believed what they *heard* from us?

---

[4] For more on Paul's utopian vision see Dewey 1987, 1994.

[5] All translations of Romans are mine. Unless noted, the translations from Philo are from the Loeb edition. Translations from the Hebrew Scriptures are taken from the RSV.

(17) Trust, thus, comes from actually *hearing*,
hearing through the word of Christ.

There is, however, much more to be mined in Romans 10 beyond citing vv. 14-17 as an oral *locus classicus*. Indeed, it is imperative that we listen once more to this chapter in order to begin to pick up further nuances of this material. As noted above, Kelber pointed to the social situation of an oral performance. Not only do we have the creation of an acoustic space, but we may discern ways in which Paul is trying to negotiate social relationships, where the question of power comes into play. Certainly in the verses just cited, we can see the outline of a communication system (vv. 14-15), founded upon the relationship of trust (vv. 14, 16). At the same time, it is quite significant that Paul even brings the written world into this oral chain of communication. It is, thus, not simply a sharp dichotomy of orality vs. literacy; rather, a fascinating dialectic is underway. Indeed, the sounds we pick up may well be echoes of surrounding cultural forces, reverberations of present (or hoped for) social relations.

Chapter 10 resumes Paul's dialogue with his Roman correspondents:

(1) *Comrades*,
my heart's desire and *prayer* to God is for their well-being.

(2) I *swear* they have desire for God but not understanding.

(3) For, in being unaware of the proper relation with God,
and in attempting to maintain their own,
they haven't come to terms with the proper relationship with God.

(4) Christ is the point of [the] tradition,
for a solid relation with everyone who trusts.

Verse 1 begins directly with a public communication. Such a public prayer allows the audience (and us) to see the inside of a first-century personality (Malina: 64-67), whose innermost wishes and prayers were usually manifest only in God's sight (ἡ μὲν εὐδοκία τῆς ἐμῆς καρδίας καὶ ἡ δέησις πρὸς τὸν θεὸν [v. 1]). Now this mentioning of the heart is crucial since it is part and parcel of the oral mode, as Kelber notes:

> The heart is the central organ of reception that facilitates communication with Spirit and gospel. Spoken words enter the human heart and enjoy privileged participation in human actuality . . . what enters the human heart affects a person's whole being. In broader hermeneutical perspectives, spoken words are experienced personally and more directly than written words. Sound has a pervasive quality; it permeates one's whole physical existence (146).

In addition, this prayer sends echoes throughout the surrounding material. The main burden of Rom 9-11 is maintained, as Paul publically expresses his fondest wish for his kinfolk's well-being (ὑπὲρ αὐτῶν εἰς σωτηρίαν [v. 1]). In fact, this declaration of his intention has a public or forensic character. "I swear" (μαρτυρῶ [v. 2]) orally confirms this public pose by Paul. He then attempts to explain why the discrepancy among his kin exists. Paul asserts that his people have the desire (ζῆλον θεοῦ ἔχουσιν) but not the understanding (ἀλλ' οὐ κατ' ἐπίγνωσιν). In effect, they have established their own situation instead of perceiving the correct order under God (v. 3). Paul's use of "proper relationship" (δικαιοσύνη) would indicate that Paul's kin were unaware of what Paul saw as the proper social relationship, namely the patron/client relation, where this particular patron is infinitely superior. Verse 4 makes it clear what Paul understands the correct understanding of this relationship to be. From Paul's perspective genuine solidarity between God and humanity comes through recognizing Christ as "the point of the tradition" (τέλος γὰρ νόμου χριστὸς εἰς δικαιοσύνην). What should not be lost on us is that this issue was not a simple theoretical one; rather, it was a matter of speaking about access to the true patron/client relationship, which could guarantee fundamental stability in a world where there were few safety nets. Moreover, "everyone who trusts" (παντὶ τῷ πιστεύοντι) would indicate universal access to this primordial relationship.

It is only after Paul declares that Christ is "the point of the tradition" that he explicitly draws upon the written tradition, quoting a text:

(5) Now *Moses writes* about the relationship from tradition:
"The person who does these things will live by them."

Paul does so in order to make a distinction between "the relationship from tradition" (ἡ δικαιοσύνη ἡ ἐκ [τοῦ] νόμου) and "the relationship of trust" (ἡ δὲ ἐκ πίστεως δικαιοσύνη). Most crucial for our investigation is that Paul personifies *Dikaiosune*, the "proper relationship."

(6) But the *relationship of trust says*:
"Don't *say* in your heart,
who will climb up to the sky?"
which is to say, to bring Christ down.

(7) "Or who will plunge into the abyss?"
which is, to bring Christ back from the dead.

(8) But what does *she say*?
"Near you is the *word—in your mouth—*in your heart,"
that is, the *word* of trust that we *announce*.

Certainly there is a sharp contrast between v.5 and the correction delivered by personified Dikaiosune: "But the relationship of trust says"; ἡ δὲ ἐκ πίστεως δικαιοσύνη οὕτως λέγει (v. 6).[6] Here Paul gives a new voice (*Dikaiosune*) to the tradition, which transforms the understanding of the written tradition. At the same time, he evokes what the audience would recognize as theirs already. They already experience this relationship of trust. In effect, then, Paul names their present condition of trust. Indeed, one might even read v. 5 in a utopian vein, whose promise comes to realization in the following oral experience (vv. 6-11). Furthermore, it should be underscored that the citation of the written tradition was an evocation of power. And only a stronger force, personified *Dikaiosune*, would have been able to speak more authoritatively. Indeed, *Dikaiosune*, "genuine solidarity," speaks directly to and through the communal experience of the Roman community.

It is interesting that the words upon the lips of *Dikaiosune* come from Deut 30:12-14. In its original context Deut 30:12-14 speaks of a remarkable transcending of limitations so that the covenant of God can be kept. As we shall see below, this note of transcending limits in Deut 30 figures prominently in the Hellenistic Jewish mission. In effect, the outreach already present in the Deuteronomic material was revived by first-century interpreters. Rom 10:6-8, apparently playing upon this missionary usage, make two essential points. First, there is an immediate interpretation or application of the Deuteronomic verses. Second, this application is tied in with the experience of the early Jesus mission.

(6) But the relationship of trust says: (Pauline personification)
"Don't say in your heart,   (Deut 9:4)
who will climb up to the sky?"   (Deut:30:12)
which is to say, to bring Christ down.   (Mission language applied)

(7) "Or who will plunge into the abyss?"   (Deut 30:13)
which is, to bring Christ back from the dead.   (Mission language applied)

(8) But what does she say?   (Pauline personification)
"Near you is the word—in your mouth
—in your heart,"   (Deut 30:14)
that is, the word of trust which we announce.   (Mission language applied)

This material interweaves tradition and application; Deut 30 is connected directly with the message that Paul delivers and presumes the community shares. This rhetorical application is meant to echo the oral and

---

[6] In Gal 3:8 Paul personifies "Scripture" (ἡ γραφή) as foreseeing the fruition of the promise to Abraham (Dewey 1982:54).

interiorized experience of the believers (v. 9), to which even the written tradition bears witness (v. 11):

(9) Because if you *confess with your mouth*
  "JESUS IS LORD!"   (liturgical language)
  and trust in your heart
    that "God raised him from the dead,"   (liturgical language)
      you will be all right ...

(10) For the *written* tradition *says*:
  "No one who trusts in him will be shamed."

Reading vv. 6-8 more closely, we can see that personified *Dikaiosune* speaks directly to the individual to deliver enlightenment: "Don't say in your heart" μὴ εἴπῃς ἐν τῇ καρδίᾳ σου (v. 6). The worries from Deut 30:12-14 continue to resound and to need clarification in the present vocabulary of the community. Thus, "who will climb up to the sky?" (τίς ἀναβήσεται εἰς τὸν οὐρανόν [v. 6]) is immediately interpreted by "which is to say, to bring Christ down" (τοῦτ ἔστιν χριστὸν καταγαγεῖν [v. 6]). And "who will plunge into the abyss?" (τίς καταβήσεται εἰς τὴν ἄβυσσον [v. 7]) receives a further note, "which is, to bring Christ back from the dead" (τοῦτ ἔστιν χριστὸν ἐκ νεκρῶν ἀναγαγεῖν [v. 7]). Paul then resumes the voice of *Dikaiosune* in asking "what does she say [mean] (ἀλλὰ τί λέγει; [v. 8]) by "Near you is the word—in your mouth—in your heart" (ἐγγύς σου τὸ ῥῆμά ἐστιν ἐν τῷ στόματί σου καὶ ἐν τῇ καρδίᾳ σου [v. 8]). To which a response is given that echoes the very message of Paul: "that is, the word of trust which we announce" (τοῦτ ἔστιν τὸ ῥῆμα τῆς πίστεως ὃ κηρύσσομεν [v. 8]).

Verse 9 continues to work upon what Paul rhetorically anticipates to be the experiential basis of his audience.

(9) Because if you *confess with your mouth* "JESUS IS LORD!"
  and trust in your heart that "God raised him from the dead,"
    you will be all right.

Both "Jesus is Lord" (κύριον Ἰησοῦν) and "God raised him from the dead" (ὅτι ὁ θεὸς αὐτὸν ἤγειρεν ἐκ νεκρῶν) may well come from common liturgical language (note ὁμολογήσῃς; cf. John 9:22). If so, then Paul not only would be appealing to their own experience but would be demonstrating inductively that *Dikaiosune* herself is speaking from the midst of their own situation, that is, from their experience of a trusting relationship with God. Thus, we are not simply dealing with a recitation of creedal formulae. Rather, the alternating utterances on the lips of Paul and of the community would manifest the soundness of genuine inner relationship (*Dikaiosune*). In an oral situation people are placed in the buzz of things.

By writing these lines for delivery, Paul hopes that his audience would find themselves in the midst of this acoustic field. He anticipates that they would discover that they are part of what is going on and what is going on is this genuine relationship named *Dikaiosune*. The true sound (Christ, cf. vv. 4, 6, 7, 9) reveals the interior of tradition (νόμος). In fact, from Paul's perspective, once this point is *felt*, then the community can recognize that everything and everyone can resound with this sense. Even the written tradition can be overheard proclaiming this:

(10) Trusting in one's heart results in genuine relationship
and *confessing with one's mouth* brings well-being.

(11) For the *written* tradition *says*:
"Everyone who trusts in him will not be shamed."

This citation (v. 11) of Isa 28:16 has implications in regard to universal access. Paul fills out Scripture by adding "everyone" (πᾶς) to universalize its meaning (πᾶς ὁ πιστεύων). In vv. 12-13 we continue this universal impetus by the complete reevaluation of social distinctions. Indeed, there can be no social distinction ("Nor is there any social distinction;" οὐ γάρ ἐστιν διαστολὴ [v.12]) since this relationship manifests the true universal patron:

(12) Nor is there any social distinction between Jew and Greek—
the same Lord is Lord of all,
enriching all who *appeal* to him.

(13) For "everyone who *appeals* in the Lord's *name* will benefit."

Everyone (πᾶς) can call upon, that is, petition the Universal Patron, who gives generously and freely upon the establishment of this relationship. The utopian dream, inaugurated by Alexander the Great, the hope that people can enter into a commonwealth of communication and humanity (cf. Gal 3:28), appears to be an effective possibility (Georgi: 1976:29-30). According to Paul a surplus enters the cosmic economy. It is extended to all, not just to an elite or a privileged group.

In addition, v. 13 is not simply a citation of Joel 3:5 (LXX). Once again Paul uses a written tradition voicing a basic possibility for those who would take this to heart. From Paul's rhetorical vantage point, the utopian vision of Joel 3:5 brings home a point that would reverberate in the experience of the Roman communities. In fact, the phrase "appeals in the Lord's name" (ἐπικαλέσηται τὸ ὄνομα) would carry with it overtones of the common experience of an appeal to a superior by someone who has been empowered or initiated to do so (Eisenstadt and Roniger: 58). Of course, in any patron/client relation it was vital to use the proper address for effective access. And in v. 9 we have the proper name ("Jesus" or "Christ" in vv. 4, 6, 7).

Moreover, the continued advance of this universal message is brought about through the agency of missionaries like Paul (vv. 14-15):

> (14) Now, then, how can they *appeal* to someone whom they haven't trusted?
>> How can they trust one they haven't *heard about*?
>> How can they *hear* without someone *announcing* [it]?
>
> (15) How can they *announce* unless they are sent?
>> Just so, it is *written*:
>>> "How welcome are the feet of those who *deliver* good *news*."

Verse 14 once more demonstrates the interdependent reality of Paul's oral mission, that is, the "relationship of trust" that can only come about through human communication, reaching right into the Roman community. Verse 15 again employs the written tradition to reiterate and throw light upon the mission effort. The very words of Scripture speak to the efforts of people like Paul. Indeed, the person who delivered Paul's letter is indirectly referred to, if one understands the implications of such words coming true in the audience's presence. The beat goes on. And on. For the succeeding verses in Romans 10 continue Paul's oral performance, enlisting the written tradition. Isaiah speaks up to cast light on the present situation (v. 16b). Verse 17 plays totally within the terms of oral experience. Verse 18b brings Ps 19:4 into this argument, while vv. 19, 20-21 allow Moses and Isaiah further utterance. Quite significantly v. 21 would allow the deliverer of the letter an opportunity for a dramatic gesture of open arms.

> (16) But not all listen to the *news*.
>> *Isaiah says*:
>>> "Lord, who believed what they *heard* from us?"
>
> (17) Trust, thus, comes from actually *hearing*,
>> hearing through the *word* of Christ.
>
> (18) But, I say, did they not *hear*?
>> Of course!
>>> "Their *voice* went out to all the earth
>>> to the ends of the world their *words*."
>
> (19) But, I say, didn't Israel understand?
>> First *Moses says*:
>>> "I will make you envious of a non-people.
>>> I will make you angry over a foolish people."

(20) Then *Isaiah* dares to *say*:
> "I was found by those not looking for me.
> I revealed myself to those who did not ask for me."

(21) But regarding Israel *he says*:
> "All day long I held out my hands
> to a disbelieving and contrary people."

It is rather evident from what I have noted in Romans 10 that Paul is quite vigorous in his employment of oral experience. To recapitulate: Paul's public oath and prayer, his personification of *Dikaiosune*, his application of Deut 30:12-14 (which highlights oral experience), his enfolding of written Scripture within the oral field of argument, his anticipation of the oral experience of his audience (including the notion of appeal to a superior), and his appreciation of the oral lines of communication of the Jesus mission, all of these suggest a decidedly oral bias. Romans 10 needs to be performed orally to be truly understood, for Paul apparently wants an interplay between the performer of the letter and the audience. Paul's choices from written tradition, his rhetorical anticipation of the experience of the community as well as their communal expressions, and his awareness of the chain of human communication at the heart of the Jesus mission would argue for such an appreciation between the letter's performer and the Roman community. The very language is set up to echo the experience of the community. Thus, Romans 10 can be viewed as a contrapuntal or antiphonal piece (although we have only fragments of the other side's voice), which intends to play the words of the congregation and of Scripture on a variety of lips. An echoing effect is created that confirms and legitimizes the writer's and audience's experience. Perhaps, it may be better said that, if Paul's rhetoric works, the true experience of relationship would be discerned and felt in the oral interaction itself. I have also pointed out how Paul has included the written tradition within the orbit of the oral phenomenon, subordinating it to his argument. Moreover, in closely reading Romans 10 we have begun to see that Paul was not preoccupied with linguistic distinctions but with the more substantial problems of power and universal access to the divine patron. It would be helpful now to see how another Jewish thinker handles both the Deuteronomic tradition and the questions of power and access. We shall now turn to Philo, who presents another utopian perspective.

IV. PHILONIC STRAINS

In a short exhortation to repentance (*De Virt.* 175-182) Philo entreats "everyone everywhere" to live a life of piety and justice (εὐσεβεία καὶ δικαιοσύνῃ). While the call to true citizenship in the best of commonwealths is for Jew and gentile alike, the brunt of this piece is intended for prospective proselytes (ὁ ἐπηλύται). The summons to repentance (εἰς μετάνοιαν) is not separated from other concerns in life; the formation of the proper Creator/creature relationship through repentance is directly connected with the question of good government (180). True worship of the "One who is" brings the proselyte to true citizenship/virtue. Political life is embedded in the fundamental relationship with the divine. And in moving into this relationship, the proselyte moves from "ignorance to knowledge, from senselessness to sense . . . from injustice to justice, from timidity to boldness" (ἐξ ἀμαθίας εἰς ἐπιστήμην, ἐξ ἀφροσύνης εἰς φρόνησιν. . . ἐξ ἀδικίας εἰς δικαιοσύνην, ἐξ ἀτολομίας εἰς θαρραλεότητα *De Virt.* 180).

Counselling a reformation of one's life, Philo introduces his interpretation of Deut 30:11-14:

> He tells us that the thing (τὸ πρᾶγμα) is not over great, not very distant, neither in ether far above nor at the ends of the earth, nor beyond the great sea, that we should be unable to receive it, but very near, residing in three parts of our being, mouth, heart, and hands, thus symbolizing words and thoughts and actions, for the mouth is a symbol of speech, the heart of thoughts and intentions, the hand of action, and in these three lies happiness (*De Virt.* 183).

Deut 30:11-14 reads:

> For this commandment which I command you this day is not too hard for you, neither is it far off. It is not in heaven, that you should say, "Who will go up for us to heaven, and bring it to us, that we may hear it and do it?" Neither is it beyond the sea, that you should say, "Who will go over the sea for us, and bring it to us, that we may hear it and do it?" But the word is very near you; it is in your mouth and in your heart, so that you can do it (RSV).

It is apparent that Philo paraphrases Deut 30:11-14. Noteworthy modifications are: the inclusive sense of the first person plural (καθ' ἡμᾶς), the explanation accompanying the paraphrase "that we should be unable to receive it," and the interpretation of mouth, hands (added), and heart as symbolizing the totality of a person. Each interpretive move is made to make Deut 30:11-14 accessible to Philo's audience. Indeed, enactment of this exhortation is seen as complying with the "divine oracle" (ἐχρήσθη τὸ λόγιον ἐκεῖνο) of Deut 26:17, 18. Philo writes:

> Whence in full harmony with what was spoken [i.e., Deut 30:11-14] that oracle was given: "Today you have chosen God to be your God and the Lord

has chosen you today to be his people." (ὅθεν εὖ καὶ συμφώνως τοῖς εἰρημένοις ἐχρήσθη τὸ λόγιον ἐκεῖνο· τὸν θεὸν εἵλου σήμερον εἶναί σοι θεόν, καὶ κύριος εἵλατό σε σήμερον γενέσθαι λαὸν αὐτῷ De Virt. 184 [My translation]).

Here written tradition speaks in oracular fashion to confirm what is offered the prospective repentant.[7] Philo intentionally evokes the oral features of this written tradition. At the same time, Philo has introduced explanations that go beyond mere memorization of Scripture to call for thoughtful application. Philo, further, couches the anticipatory action of the divine towards the true worshipper within the imagery of the patron/client relationship:

> Glorious is this reciprocation (ἀντίδοσις) of choice, when a human hastens to serve the Existing One, and God does not delay to take the supplicant on and anticipates the will of the one who honestly and sincerely enters into his service (De Virt. 185).

From this relationship the true worth of the worshiper becomes clear. A person's real value is equal to that of a complete nation (De Virt. 185). The terms used ("in real value"/δυνάμει, "equal worth"/ἰσότιμος) to describe the true worshipper's value play upon the terms' first-century economic undertones (De Virt. 185; LSJ 452 [II.1-2]; 840). In other words, Philo is using words that would suggest enhanced social status.

In addition, in Quod Prob. 62-73 we find a most interesting connection with Deut 30:11-14 in a Philonic contrast between the spheres of virtue and vice. Before the introduction of the Deuteronomic allusion, we hear a description of life lived according to the extractive economy of the Empire:

> As it is, for the sake of money we ransack every corner and open up rough and rocky veins of earth, and much of the low land and no small part of the high land is mined in the quest of gold and silver, copper and iron, and other like substances (65).

Note how this continues with allusion to Deut 30:11-14. I have emphasized the obvious connections:

> The empty-headed way of thinking, deifying vanity, dives *to the depths of the sea*, searching whether some fair treasure to delight the senses lies hidden there.... But for wisdom or temperance or courage or justice, no journey is taken by land, even though it gives easy travelling, *no seas are navigated*, though the skippers sail them every summer season. Yet what need is there of long journeying on the land or voyaging on the seas to seek and search for virtue, whose roots have been set by their Maker *ever so near us*, as the wise

---

[7] In De conf. ling. 197, Philo cites Deut 30:4 to point out that the present proclamation (κήρυγμα) is made clear by the oracles (οἱ χρησμοί) in which it is declared (*again oral*) that the true commonwealth begins: "if your διασπορά is from one point in heaven to another, he shall gather you hence."

legislator of the Jews also says, "*in thy mouth, in thy heart and in thy hand,*" thereby indicating in a figure, words, thoughts and actions (66-68).

We need to consider not only the manifest but the latent function of this material. On the surface we have an argument that contrasts the virtuous with the empty-headed. Indeed, the contrast fits well the technique of ancient dialectic, which forced the speaker to become clear as to the assumptions upon which his statement was based. One can begin to see that there is an economic reality underpinning this material. The description of the extractive economy given above indicates this. The assumption of a limited goods economy with the accompanying "plundering" characteristic of ancient economic theory is contrasted with another vision of what constitutes the true commonwealth. Philo presents a different vision for genuine living, one that does not demand extraction or diminishing of resources, time, or energy. Instead, the possibility for attaining this envisioned relationship, this access, is *near*. Virtue can be attained by a genuine incorporation of what these words mean. The results can only lead to development both for the individual and for society (69-70). Section 69 gives us a vocabulary of bountiful growth, never ceasing to bear fruit, while section 71 makes the point that this process refers to potentialities within humanity. The hidden possibilities of wisdom like "smoldering sparks" may eventually blaze into a commonwealth of true citizens.

Our investigation shows that the text from Deut 30:11-14 figures within the missionary propaganda of Hellenistic Judaism. Philo's appeal to prospective proselytes is based upon a beneficial or surplus economic vision, quite distinct from what one would call a limited goods economy (Carney: 137-234). Moreover, this vision of virtue was a promise of access to the one patron who could deliver the goods. Indeed, the divine oracles, cited from the written tradition, confirmed the present appeals to repentance and reform. In effect, the citation of Deut 30:11-14 was a utopian exercise, offering a world view that differed from the present social order. A different patron was presented who could effect what the present culture could only hint at. To enter into Philo's interpreted tradition meant that the proselyte not only became a true citizen but was engaged in the construction of the finest commonwealth (πολιτεία).

Perhaps the best example of what I have called a "utopian exercise" is found in *De spec. leg.* 4.160-169. Although Deut 30:11-14 is not directly cited, the Deuteronomic momentum towards realization of utopian vision by the individual is certainly present. We find Philo using both the process of reading aloud and that of writing to reach one of the deepest values of his culture. Here cultural progress and chirographic technique combine to provide the means for a reflective ego. As we shall shortly see, writing allows the reader the occasion to engage in dialectic, whereby questions can be asked of what has been read. The dream of the philosopher-king becomes a reality in the "kingly soul" for Philo.

Beginning with section 160 we have an extended re-writing of Deut 17:18-20. When the royal person writes out in his own hand a summary of the laws, he begins to cement them to his soul. How does this happen? Unlike thoughts that are "swept away" from the mere reader (i.e. listener), what is written down is set fast and can be looked at again. This allows the royal soul to dwell on each point until it securely grasps it (160). He will achieve a constant and unbroken memory of God's ordinances. Such a description is quite in keeping with the establishment of writing as a communication technology. In contrast to an oral technology that exists in the embedded performances of body and tradition, a written technology enables the person to separate from the acoustic crowd and to examine, perhaps for the first time, the grounds for such and such a statement. An autonomous rational personality emerges from the spell of oral memorization. Indeed, Philo illustrates this last point quite graphically as he continues:

> Further when he reads (ἀναγινώσκων) he will reason thus with himself (λογισμὸν ἕξει τοιοῦτον): "I (ἐγώ) have written these words ... I write them in a book in order to rewrite them straightway in my soul, and receive in my mind the imprints of a script more divine and ineffaceable" (163).

From section 163 to 167 Philo presents what might be termed an internal soliloquy on the lips of the "royal soul." Actually it is the embodiment of the dialectic (λογισμὸν) that is brought about through reading (ἀναγινώσκων). What Philo presents in this text is exactly what ancient dialectic in its simplest form was meant to do, namely, to ask a speaker to repeat himself and explain what he meant (Havelock: 208). The individual's rewriting of the "kingly passage" in Deuteronomy causes a literal restatement of meaning, which is theoretically embedded now in the royal soul. Sections 164-167 continue this paraphrase of the psyche. The emergence of the reflective, rational person is indicated by the introduction of the first person singular. A more graphic illustration of the development of the chirographic personality could not be found. It should further be noted that, as the royal ego continues to internalize the meaning of the scroll, connections with the political reality of the world are not left behind. Proper internalization of the summary of the laws will enable one to live a life of equality, balance, and honor and to leave behind an immortal legacy.

What is so singular about this text is that one of the fondest dreams of the ancient world, the philosopher-king, becomes realizable by anyone who would truly read and internalize the Jewish laws. A written tradition is understood as a vehicle of power, conveying the energy and the vision for the culture. As one enters fully into this tradition, writing out the words, a different self emerges, which is free from the constraints of a sensate-bound present. The dialectic within, the internal argument, allows the space for a reasoning ego to appear. We have seen earlier that one who enters into the world of Deut 30:11-14 is a true citizen; now we see further that a literate citizen can become king. For Philo a chirographic culture is not a limiting situation. On the contrary, the written technology advances the oral reading of Jewish Scripture and brings out again the utopian dreams that have been present since Plato. Writing aids and abets the hope for a civilized and pious humanity.

Utopian Sounds

We can now begin to decipher the movements of Philo and Paul. The consideration of Deut 30:11-14 is a canny selection on both their parts. For within a society where there is a decidedly weak sense of active participation (Eisenstadt and Roniger: 206-7), both Philo and Paul take up a tradition that works in the opposite direction. Deut 30:11-14 challenges the listener to an active and immediate response. In a world where the control and labelling of resources are in the hands of a few, both Philo and Paul are declaring that access to power, the most profound and the most extensive, is right before the listener, who has the opportunity to choose to exercise this access.

Yet there is a rather significant difference between Paul's approach to the Deuteronomic material and Philo's. While it must be pointed out that Philo's material would have been read aloud also, it is the case that Philo's material works beyond the protreptic to a dialectic, beyond the utterance and its confirmation of Jewish "oracles" to a reconstruction of the tradition by means of the emerging chirographic personality. For Philo the tradition becomes genuinely realized when the individual utilizes the finest technologies available and establishes a royal self separate from the masses. In so doing the person brings to life the cultural dream of the philosopher-king. At the same time, Philo's position is not so much subversive as it is an attempt to bring about the utopian possibilities of the world in an irenic and gradual manner. He does, of course, maintain a critical stance towards what one could easily term the commonplace economic behavior of the first century. Furthermore, it would seem that Philo considers this vision as possible within the institutionalized (albeit modulated through interpretation) and pluralistic lines of Hellenistic Judaism. In short, it would seem that Philo represents a movement of continuity, employing the best of his culture for the benefit of the world.

Paul, on the other hand, may well represent a counter-cultural position. Certainly his vision of the imminent end would suggest a stance of discontinuity. There is more here to suggest what would be an alternative perspective. Clearly Paul has bought into the universal dreams of the hellenistic world. On the other hand, the way in which these dreams are implemented differs from Philo's position in scope and means. The essential clue in Romans 10 is its fundamental orality. Here orality is not an indication of a social traditionalist. Rather, this orality signals a direction contrary to the basic directions of the established social lines and centers. It is much more a grass roots approach, an attempt at building a popular coalition, which would permit universal access to the source of genuine power—God. The sounds of Romans 10 play off the social possibilities of the relationship (*Dikaiosune*) perceived and felt by the communities. Gifted with the spirit ($\pi\nu\epsilon\hat{u}\mu a$), that is, the capacity or basic resource for access and power, the communities can establish a new pattern of trust and participation. The lines of established patronage and kinship would then be placed seriously into question. In light of this it becomes understandable why Rom 10:1-13 is set within the question of Paul's kinfolk. For Paul is exploring the universal thrust of the Jewish mission while at the same time going beyond the conventional lines of kinship. In short, Paul is engaged in the process of popular coalition-building, transcending the various elitist structures and power conveyances of his day. He has taken up alternative means to the more valued and powerful technologies of his day. Furthermore, the oral performance of Romans 10, with its anticipated interplay between speaker and audience, attempts to effect this alternate social vision and relationship. One does not step back but enters into what actually surrounds the listener. The voice of *Dikaiosune* emerges full-bodied in the corresponding sounds of all who believe. The proof of this is in the actual performance as the people "call upon the name of the Lord."

WORKS CONSULTED

Carney, T. F.
    1975   *The Shape of the Past: Models and Antiquity*. Lawrence, KA: Coronado.

Dewey, Arthur J.
    1982   "Spirit and Letter in Paul." Harvard University Th.D. Dissertation. Forthcoming from Edwin Mellen.
    1987   "Social-historical Observations on Romans (15:23-24)." *Proceedings, Eastern Great Lakes Midwest Biblical Society* 7: 49-57.
    1994   "Εἰς τὴν Σπανίαν: The Future and Paul." Pp.321-49 in *Religious Propaganda and Missionary Competition in the New Testament World*. Ed. Lukas Bormann, Kelly Del Tredici, Angelica Standhartinger. Leiden, New York, Köln: Brill.

Eisenstadt, S. N. and L. Roniger
    1984   *Patrons, Clients and Friends: Interpersonal Relations and the Structure of Trust in Society*. Cambridge: Cambridge University Press.

Georgi, Dieter
    1976   "The 'Divine Man' as a Propagandistic Pattern." Pp. 27-42 in *Aspects of Religious Propaganda in Judaism and Early Christianity*. Ed. Elisabeth Schüssler Fiorenza. Notre Dame: University of Notre Dame Press.
    1986   *The Opponents of Paul in 2 Corinthians*. Philadelphia: Fortress.

Havelock, Eric A.
    1982   *Preface to Plato*. Cambridge: Harvard University Press.

Kelber, Werner
    1983   *The Oral and Written Gospel. The Hermeneutics of Speaking And Writing in the Synoptic Tradition, Mark, Paul, and Q*. Philadelphia: Fortress.

Liddell, H. G. and Robert Scott, rev. H. S. Jones
    1968   *A Greek English Lexicon*. Oxford: Oxford University Press.

Malina, Bruce
    1981   *The New Testament World*. Atlanta: John Knox.

Ong, Walter J.
    1970   *The Presence of the Word*. New York: Simon and Schuster.

Philo
    1967   *Quod Omnis Probus Liber Sit*. Trans. F. H. Colson. LCL. Vol. 7. Cambridge: Harvard University Press.
    1968   *De Confusione Linguarum*. Trans. F. H. Colson, G. H. Whitaker. LCL. Vol. 4. Cambridge: Harvard University Press.
                De Specialibus Legibus. De Virtutibus. Trans. F. H. Colson. LCL. Vol. 8. Cambridge: Harvard University Press.

Performance, Politics, and Power: A Response

Antoinette Clark Wire
San Francisco Theological Seminary

The articles by Richard F. Ward and Arthur J. Dewey are both efforts to recover Paul's letters as performance, but "performance" understood in two very different senses. I want to review the contributions of each approach and press each person to extend his work. Then I will consider some further questions posed for the study of Paul's letters by recent work on orality and literacy.

Richard Ward corrects our modern habit of seeing Paul's letters as books, whether they are read as foundation documents by communities or as sources of inspiration by believers. He sees them rather as scripts for performance by Paul's messengers, who were to dramatize his letters before their intended hearers in the way that Jews at the time would perform their scriptures on proscenium stages of synagogues or outside synagogue doors. Ward sees the messenger serving as proxy for the author's own presence, interpreting not only by reading but by whatever additions or explanations seemed called for. Ward illustrates this mode of performance by citing Quintillian's instructions on the exact hand and body movements proper to oratory, with or without manuscript. Yet these seem wooden compared to what could be expected on Ward's thesis that Paul's colleague arrives in Corinth to give the counter-performance of 2 Cor 10–13 against an earlier performance by those Paul calls false-apostles. And Ward needs to be clearer that we have no way of knowing whether Paul's battle in Corinth was won—unless of course we choose to reorder the fragments of 2 Corinthians to make them end with the Corinthians reconciled to Paul.

There are several directions in which Ward might extend his research on Paul's letters as strategic oral communication. It is widely accepted that Paul's letters were also oral in their dictation, at least up to their closing lines (Rom 16:22; Gal 6:11), and the co-authors mentioned in the first lines of five letters could be scribes. This poses the question whether Paul's delivery was also dramatic, with the letter carrying the speech where Paul could not go. There is no evidence that the letters were intended to be reread, but some were meant to circulate on to other individuals or nearby groups as Paul would have done had he come (1 Thess 5:27; 2 Cor 1:1; cf. Col 4:16). This suggests that the letter as speech–

container was seen to be disposable once heard by everyone, written to have its impact on first hearing and in its given order rather than to hover over the community and be recirculated in whole or part as new situations developed.

Since the letter-carrier does not seem to be the same person as the amanuensis or co-author, the picture is not a simple one of the original hearer of the letter becoming its speaker. Was this because someone else was already travelling and would carry the letter, or did Paul reserve the coveted position of messenger/speaker to persons he was promoting as his agents (Timothy, Titus) or to those whose respect within the community he wanted to foster (Stephanus in 1 Cor 16:15–18, Epaphroditus in Phil 2:25–30 and 4:18, and Onesimus in Phlm 10–21)? Stephanus' authority could be greatly bolstered by being the voice of 1 Corinthians if the letter were accepted. But Paul shows he also knows the risks of a bad reception in his plea not to despise Timothy when he comes but to send him back quickly (1 Cor 16:10–11). Is Paul afraid his associate will not be able to bear the full flood of their oral response to 1 Corinthians? Paul's selections of the letter-carrier and reader of 2 Corinthians may also involve fiscal matters; Titus' heightened profile could help him raise funds (2 Cor 8:6, 12–13).

All of this suggests that the politics are far more complex than to allow Paul to chose his emissaries for voice, stance, and gestures alone. At the same time, the description of Titus' trip to Corinth while Paul waits in Macedonia for news (2 Cor 2:12–13, 7:5–16) supports the most radical extension of Ward's thesis: Paul sometimes chooses not to go when he well could, but to send a proxy with the right letter because his "icon" is more likely to receive welcome than his bow-legged, balding, and difficult self (2 Cor 10:10; Acts of Paul and Thecla 3). If so, Paul's communication strategy is highly flexible and combines oral and written modes in whatever way he expects will work.

This presents a sub-problem: do Paul's letters all intend to gain acceptance or could their rejection in some cases be taken as a fulfillment of strategic communication? There is a long tradition of prophets claiming to be vindicated by their rejection (Isa 6:9–13; Mark 4:12; Luke 7:29–35; 11:29–35, 42–52), and those who represent Paul may need to be seen in light of his view of himself as apostle/ambassador for the Christ who was rejected on arrival. Can we assume that the irony of Paul's fool's speech will communicate itself through a congenial speaker or only through one as difficult to hear as Paul himself? Could the rejection of Paul's argument by hearers in Corinth be a sign, not that they have misunderstood, but that they have understood? If so, everything involved in the letter as strategic communication must work—including its offense—for the performance of the emissary to stand adequately for Paul.

This raises a further problem for modern interpretation of Paul's letters. If the letter was not so much information or even parenesis but counter-performance to a previous performance, or even a provocation geared to offend, it must have been precisely tuned to a particular group at a certain time. This makes the prospect of understanding it in another culture and epoch remote indeed, whether or not it is well performed today. If the reading was not only counter-performance but provocation, not only defense but attack, and in every case in struggle against others who also claimed to represent Christ, our only hope for understanding is to hear the whole debate as argument and weigh the merits of each view to represent the gospel of Jesus Christ. Having no other texts from these communities at this time, we must use Paul's argument as the basis for a reconstruction of both sides of the debate and learn, if you will, to hear with equal respect both the performance to which Paul is reacting and his counter-performance. Only then will we have a chance of seeing that world and its issues before us and be able to consider their relevance, if any, today. This means that the tradition in both literature and biblical studies that privileges the author's meaning as the measure of a text's significance will have to give way to seeking to hear the text as interaction.

Arthur J. Dewey does not gauge the impact of orality on Paul's letters by considering how they were read aloud, though he recognizes that they were. His focus is on the way Paul juxtaposes appeals to the oral and the written in argumentation. Saussure's definition of the word "performance" in contrast to "competence" points in this direction. By this definition the performance does not begin when the messenger starts to read Paul's letter but it occurs the first minute Paul speaks it, not in the sound and breath alone but in every language choice Paul makes. His letter is a single performance of Paul's competence in the Greek language, and more specifically the Hellenistic Jewish and Christian languages, and to understand his performance we have to understand this particular juxtaposition of words, themes, and arguments as an event. Since Dewey does not have in hand the oral speaking or reading but only the written record of Paul's letters, he turns to the text to ask what kind of event a certain letter is and how it activates oral and written aspects of Paul's culture.

Dewey's main point is that the oral and written do not operate as opposing spheres in Paul's letters, as he thinks Werner Kelber argued by setting the oral gospel off against the foil of the literary law. Rather

Dewey sees speech and writing (which is also always spoken) as two different means Paul uses to augment power in the communities he addresses. This is tested in an exegesis of Romans 10. Here Dewey reads Christ not to be "the end of the law" but "the point of the tradition," which is to give all access to righteousness, that is, to the security of being clients of an all-sufficient patron. Though Moses wrote that "everyone doing these things (of the tradition) will live by them," this is countered by the voice of personified righteousness that comes from faith. In the words of Deut 30:11-14 she assures that what they seek is not far but near, "on your lips and in your heart," being "the word of faith" that Paul proclaims and they confess. Two quotations from the prophets echo this oral confession, thus confirming antiphonally from oral experience and written word the universal access without distinction for all who hear. Although Dewey overplays his hand at some points—suggesting, for example, that the citation of Moses can be both a contrasting foil for the voice of righteousness and "a promise that comes to reality" in it—he is certainly correct that Paul is "not preoccupied with linguistic distinctions but with the more substantial problems of power and access" and "has included the written tradition within the orbit of the oral phenomenon."

In a second argument Dewey contests what he takes to be Kelber's implication that Paul as an oral traditionalist is politically reactionary. Dewey argues rather that Paul in this interpretation of Deut 30:11-14 presents a utopian perspective. Dreams of realizing universal harmony recur in Greek and Hellenistic-Jewish thought, and Dewey shows how Philo, in an interpretation of Deuteronomy parallel to Paul's, argues that even non-believers can have access to God by repentance, which is "very near, residing in three parts of our being, mouth, heart and hands." Thus everyone is equipped to be a good citizen, and the literate, through reading and rereading Scripture, are equipped to rule. Dewey sees Paul as yet more radical because he does not defend a literate ruling class. The spirit that alone rules the new communities gives all access to the source of power and through its gifts of mouth and hand builds a kind of grassroots popular coalition where human patronage and kinship systems become redundant.

This thoughtful contextual reading of Romans 10 shows what is possible when Paul's entire argument is taken as the performance to be observed. Yet Paul cannot be declared a social radical on the basis of one text. Kelber draws on 1 Thessalonians and 1 Corinthians to show how Paul can become an advocate of "not going beyond what is written" (1 Cor 4:6; Kelber: 168-77), though Kelber explains this in a traditional way by the churches' excessive "enthusiasm" rather than entertaining Paul's possible weaknesses or genuine conflicts of interest. Perhaps Dewey will now turn to other letters of Paul to carry out such studies of how Paul can mobilize oral and written technologies to limit as well as to extend access to power.

When Dewey contests the idea that Paul is a conservative "oral traditionalist," he raises a broader question about whether the term "oral traditionalist" should be applied to Paul at all. I will close by discussing this question and suggesting some possible steps in further study of orality in Paul.

It is true that Paul draws on certain early Christian oral traditions about Christ's baptism, common meal, and resurrection (Rom 6:3-4; Gal 3:27-28; 1 Cor 11:23-25, 15:3-5), elaborating their mythical narratives for the context in which he writes. And some stories he tells about himself are also by the time of writing at least twice-told tales incorporating traditional forms (Gal 1:11-2:17; 1 Cor 2:1-5; 2 Cor 12:1-10). But the great bulk of his letters are not narrative oral traditions at all but are his own arguments defending or advocating certain conduct in highly provocative ways. He uses accusation and praise, oaths and blessings, instructions and explanations, quoting written even more than oral traditions and in general responding to his own difficult questions with yet more difficult answers. In Christian literature it is not Paul's letters but the gospels that are brimming over with "residual orality," as Ong puts it (14), stretching toward the epic genre in their traditional forms, stock phrases, inner rhythm, mythic themes, dramatic contests, and—except possibly in Mark's case—an outlook in which the eccentric gives way to revelations of regularity and order (Russo). Paul, on the other hand leaves his readers very much in the air because he explicitly and in his own name contests key traditions and figures.

Then what do we call the orality of Paul's letters spoken and delivered in the churches, which is not the orality of a traditional oral literature first shaped among the non-literate? Here I find Havelock's classic *Preface to Plato* suggestive for his contrast between Homer's oral traditional literature and Plato's dialogues. Socrates always appears provoking people orally and the dialogues were certainly read aloud, but the evocation of story in Homer has given way in Plato to the dialectic of question and answer and the critique of so much that is traditional (in spite of some arguments from tradition). This kind of orality speaks for a particular individual and, like Paul's letters, uses a genre allowing a very polemical address with the intent to disrupt and persuade. Such dialogues and speeches are and continue to be oral genres, but in classical practice they become staples of Greek higher education in rhetoric and are often used by literary people to enter the broader public sphere of communication. By writing speeches, dialogues, or letters, one could extend the impact of one's critical thinking through the mouths of others and—if Havelock is right—put in question thereby the rule of traditional stories and customs over the popular mind.

Recent scholars are turning away from such a sharp polarizing of tradition and critical thought, which brought with it exaggerated praise for classical Athens over its archaic past, as if the voweled alphabet led directly to objective thinking and human liberation. For example, Jack Goody, once known for his contrasting of oral and literate societies, more recently in his *The Interface between the Written and the Oral* has focused on connections and overlap between oral and written communication and the relation of both to social structure (see also Waldman; Tambiah). Especially for understanding orality in partially-literate societies such as Paul's, our study must center on the complex interaction of writing and orality and such issues as the extent to which different ways of recording affect how people think and act, the role of literacy in defining and intensifying differences in social power, and the continuing impact of traditional oral narratives in family and group identification.

Both the contrasts and the overlaps in orality and literacy can put new questions to Paul's letters. How does he juxtapose or integrate his critical dialectical thinking and his evoking of Jewish and Christian traditions? Do his often-congenial openings and closings reflect a letter rhetoric that is a mere envelope for his argument, or have they a significant impact when read as a framework of his "speech"? What can we tell about how readers and non-readers are expected to function in the communities to whom Paul writes? How is his own relative influence, in contrast to that of his many opponents within the churches, affected by his skills in the use of the oral letter medium? One would hope to get from such study some clues about how the letter genre became important in parts of early Christianity—and in turn how the narratives of Jesus' and the apostles' lives appeared where conditions in the interface of oral tradition and literacy were different. And in all this study we also need to raise hermeneutical questions about what we are missing of Paul's communication in our chirographic and electronic society.

WORKS CONSULTED

Goody, Jack
    1987   *The Interface between the Written and the Oral*. Cambridge: Cambridge University Press.

Havelock, Eric A.
    1963   *Preface to Plato*. Cambridge: Belknap of Harvard University Press.

Kelber, Werner
    1983   *The Oral and the Written Gospel: The Hermeneutics of Speaking and Writing in the Synoptic Tradition, Mark, Paul, and Q*. Philadelphia: Fortress.

Ong, Walter J.
    1987   "Text as Interpretation: Mark and After." *Semeia* 39:7–26.

Russo, Joseph
    1978   "How, and What Does Homer Communicate? The Medium and the Message of Homeric Verse." Pp. 39–52 in *Communication Arts in the Ancient World*. Ed. Eric A. Havelock and Jackson P. Hershbell. New York: Hastings House.

Tambiah, S. J.
    1968   "Literacy in a Buddhist Village in Northeast Thailand." Pp. 81–131 in *Literacy in Traditional Societies*. Ed. Jack Goody. Cambridge: Cambridge University Press.

Waldman, Marilyn R.
    1985   "Primitive Mind/Modern Mind: New Approaches to an Old Problem Applied to Islam." Pp. 91–105 in *Approaches to Islam in Religious Studies*. Ed. by Richard Martin. Tuscon: University of Arizona Press.

III

RECONSTRUCTING JESUS: UNDERSTANDING MEDIA: THEORETICAL ISSUES

JESUS AND TRADITION: WORDS IN TIME, WORDS IN SPACE

Werner H. Kelber
Rice University

ABSTRACT

This essay reexamines the historical-critical paradigm that has informed our reconstruction of Jesus' message and the ensuing tradition. Whereas the focus of historical criticism has been exclusively on texts, e.g. words committed to chirographic space, the model offered here takes into account both chirographs and speech, e.g. words transacted in space and time, and also the points of interface between the two. The resultant paradigm seeks to revise the logical procedures underlying historical criticism so as to approximate more closely the media realities of late antiquity.

A first part undertakes a detailed analysis of the *modus operandi* used in reconstructing Jesus' authentic sayings. In place of historical criticism's fixation on the singular originality of the *ipsissimum verbum* or the *ipsissima structura*, an oral thesis is developed that features the multi-originality and equiprimordiality of sayings. In oral poetics, each utterance of a saying is time-bound, renewable, alterable, and freshly original.

A second part refocuses attention from tradition perceived as transmissional processes toward the means of communication. In place of historical criticism's emphasis on intertextuality and processes of textual stratification, a model of tradition is developed that highlights the oral and scribal means of communication, the interdependence of media and meaning, conflicting media demands and multiple intersecting causalities. No single schematic illustration can pretend to describe all the discrete features of tradition. It is suggested, however, that biosphere is an appropriately inclusive metaphor for tradition understood as a collective cultural memory, comprised of discourse and chirographs, and shared by speakers and hearers alike.

> What we are wrestling with, it
> would seem, is not just . . .
> "oral" versus "literary," but an
> inadequate theory of verbal art.
>   John M. Foley, *Immanent Art*

> To capture the blend of the fixed and the flexible,
> the interaction of oral and written, the
> inter-dependence of individual "performer"
> and attentive audience within the Gospel
> tradition, in a way which truly represents
> the process of living tradition, is one of
> the great challenges still confronting
> researchers in this field.
>   James D. G. Dunn, *Testing the Foundations*

INTRODUCTION

The current academic discipline of biblical scholarship is in no small degree a product of the interdependent forces of logic and print culture. Logic, as we have come to know it, was formalized with the aid of writing. Apart from the Hindu-Arabic invention of numerals, few events were more closely intertwined with the rise of logic than the alphabetic revolutions. They converted spoken language into artifacts that facilitated the indexing of sound with a limited number of signs. An ingeniously devised economy of symbols effected detachment from and control over the human lifeworld (Havelock 1982:3-149). A triumph of logic itself, the alphabetization of language increasingly came to serve as a catalyst in the formation and implementation of abstract thought. Print further depersonalized words and transformed the manuscript culture, empowering language with a sense of objectification unknown before (Ong 1958). Luther's rejection of the fourfold senses of Scripture, his high opinion regarding the *sensus literalis* to the exclusion of tradition and all non-literal senses are features unthinkable without the invention of letterpress printing. It imparted to the Bible a sense of objective authority that made it possible to think of it as standing on its own, apart from tradition and in conflict with traditional authority. Originating in, but gradually alienated from rhetoric, the status of logic consistently rose in proportion to the processes of the technologizing of language. Both as a contributor to and beneficiary of the media transformations, logic has extended its reach across the threshold period of the sixteenth century, accelerated its pace through the seventeenth and eighteenth centuries, and engendered the scientific and technological revolutions of modernity, which have driven their methods into the high gear of electronic technology.

Print is the medium in which modern biblical scholarship was born and raised, and from which it has acquired its formative methodological habits. Along with the letterpress we inherited a sense of objectivity and rationality that has permeated our sensibilities in dealing with biblical texts. In print culture it stands to reason that exegesis is perceived and practiced as a rule-governed science. In biblical scholarship it seems as if the rationality of reason no longer needs be defended. The rules of logic are sanctioned by their very implementation. It is eminently reasonable, therefore, to conduct the search for the historical Jesus, itself a product of logic's intellectual history, in keeping with the laws of logical consistency and by application of a logically-devised classificatory apparatus. It is likewise consistent with the logic of typographic objectification and linearization to conceptualize tradition largely along the lines of transmissional, evolutionary directionality. And it makes sense in typographic culture to visualize texts as palimpsests, with layer superimposed upon layer, and stratum superseding stratum, building up to layered edifices that, if taken apart by standards of literary, typographic consistency, will take us back to the single root of the evolutionary tree.

Outside of biblical studies there is a growing awareness that standards of linguistic regularity and notions of fixed verbal property are not usable in chirographic culture and inapplicable for oral discourse (Coward; Goody; Goody and Watt; Graham; Stock, 1983, 1990). The reification and neutralization of texts, while highly congenial to the typographic processing of language, has made us forget that ancient chirographs came to life, both from the angle of composition and from the angle of reception, in an environment saturated with oral sensitivities. Precisely because handwritten documents were not perceived to be strictly autonomous entities with strictly impermeable boundaries, they interacted in part and *in toto* with oral discourse. This is exceedingly difficult for us to understand because the methods we deploy in biblical studies have instilled in us the idea of autonomous textual entities, which grew out of texts, linked up directly with other texts, and in turn generated new texts. We have grown accustomed to operating in a scholarly orbit, which, while uncannily depopulated and barren of emotive significance, is crowded with texts that seem to commune only with one another and in the absence of human mediation. And yet, texts never simply traffic in one-to-one relations with texts. The time-space links between texts are filled with dictation and recitation, acts of hearing and remembering, and a universe of vocal values, sensibilities, and actualities. Moreover, we seem to have dismissed from our thought the misunderstandings, hesitations, and silences. Forgotten also is forgetfulness. Tradition, as we see it, moves with smooth perfection and in measurable textual cadences toward truths made perfect in texts. Yet it must be stated that rarely, if ever, are texts simply explicable in reference to other texts. Truths were incarnate in voices no less than in texts. Not only do texts function in multiple degrees of interaction and tension between chirographic and oral drives, but they also implement a rich diversity of phonic, visual, and imagistic values. The "relentless domination of textuality in the scholarly mind" (Ong 1982:10) has caused us to lose touch with human minds and memories, with the processing of language via texts *and* by word of mouth, and the interfacing of all these realities. Once we begin to think of all that has been left unthought, tradition will no longer be reducible to textual transmission, and Jesus no longer comprehensible in terms of the *ipsissimum verbum* or the *ipsissima structura*.

Jesus The Speaker Delivered Unto Print

There is no end in sight to writing lives of the historical Jesus. A phenomenon unknown to ancient and medieval Christian piety, the life of Jesus historically comprehended was a product of the rise of logic and historical consciousness in Western intellectual history. Ever since Hermann Samuel Reimarus inaugurated the first truly historical and critical investigation into the life of Jesus (1778), the search for the "real" Jesus has continued unabated. Believers and agnostics, scholars and novelists alike have found the challenge irresistible. Albert Schweitzer's *Quest* (1906) is symptomatic of the imperative claim that the Jesus of history has laid upon modern consciousness. Although uncommonly astute about the heroic but intrinsically flawed quest of the preceding century and a half, Schweitzer himself could not resist the temptation of adding his own chapter to what he conceded had been "a constant succession of unsuccessful attempts" (6). In our own time, the quest is carried on with undiminished enthusiasm, skill, and inventiveness. Hope for the definitive life of Jesus springs eternal. During the past quarter of a century, a large and growing number of studies on Jesus have appeared in the English-speaking world alone. Among the more prominent authors are S. G. F. Brandon (1967), Morton Smith (1978), Geza Vermes (1981), Bruce Chilton (1984), Harvey Falk (1985), E. P. Sanders (1985), Marcus J. Borg (1987), and John P. Meier (1991). Not unexpectedly, these writers confront us with a stunning plurality of portraits of Jesus. The one element of continuity that spans the history of the quest from past to present is the diversity of Jesus images. Precisely because each author has claimed to have given account of the *historical* Jesus, the situation is nothing short of "an academic embarrassment" (Crossan 1991:xxviii).

When in the following we direct our attention to Crossan's own work on *The Historical Jesus* (1991; 1994), we do so because of all the recent books on Jesus his contribution has attracted the most intense scholarly and popular attention. It has been suggested that Crossan's Jesus is a product of the Enlightenment tradition of the lives of Jesus written by G. E. Lessing, F. Schleiermacher, D. F. Strauss, E. Renan, A. Ritschl, J. Weiss, A. Schweitzer, and J. Klausner (Van Beeck). What is symptomatic of these Enlightenment works is that they all cast Jesus "as the historic proponent of the most attractive humanism imaginable" (Van Beeck: 88). Indeed, Crossan's Jesus, the Jewish rural Cynic, a healer and exorcist who practiced itinerancy and confronted his contemporaries with spiritual and economic egalitarianism, is attractive to many of us. However, Crossan's theological agenda is not the issue of this essay. What is at issue is the methodological design which, it is argued, is solidly rooted in the logic of Enlightenment.

One of the most impressive features about Crossan's work is its systematic design. Few, if any, lives of Jesus have been constructed on so logical and reasonable a methodological basis and executed with such skillful consistency. Broadly viewed, his method rests on three pillars: a macrocosmic approach—which examines from a cross-cultural perspective social and economic revolutions, poverty and freedom, millennialism, magic and magicians, peasant unrest and political violence, food and meals, etc.; a mesocosmic approach—which interprets these same phenomena in the Greco-Roman context of late antiquity; and a microcosmic approach—which studies the sayings of and stories about Jesus in their respective historical settings. In focusing on the third pillar of Crossan's method, the methodological treatment of the Jesus literature, we fail to do justice to the impressive synthesis of his work. Still, Crossan's strategy in dealing with the thesaurus of Jesus materials is fundamental to his reconstructive project. To be sure, individual components of this third approach have been in use for some time, but no one before Crossan has deployed so judicious an apparatus of formal principles in collecting, evaluating, and classifying the available Jesus materials. His taxonomic and methodological competence sets imposing standards for Jesus research.

Along with a vast majority of scholars, Crossan shares the conviction that the gospels are "deliberate theological interpretations" (xxx). His reconstruction, as far as the Jesus materials are concerned, is therefore largely centered on the sayings and stories. The modern historian intent on writing a life of Jesus is thus confronted with "the textual problem of the Jesus tradition" (xxxi), e.g. with materials embedded in various contexts of tradition. Specifically, sayings were either retained in their essential core, adjusted to new circumstances, or newly created. In view of their entanglement in tradition, it is incumbent upon historical scholarship to "search back through those sedimented layers to find what Jesus actually said and did" (xxxi). In order to accomplish this objective, Crossan classified the Jesus materials in terms of multiple, triple, double, and single attestation. Next he compiled a comprehensive inventory of Christian literary sources both inside and outside the canon. Based on chronological priority, he divided the early tradition into four strata, which are dated from 30 to 60, from 60 to 80, from 80 to 120, and from 120 to 150 CE. Finally, he constructed a database that assigned materials of each of the four types of attestation to each stratum in the tradition. For reasons of space, Crossan's evaluation relied almost entirely on the first stratum, and in the interest of maximal objectivity, he disregarded single attestation even in the first stratum. Hence, plurality of independent attestation and chronological priority of strata determine historical reliability of data. "A first-stratum complex having, say, sevenfold independent attestation must be given very, very serious consideration" (xxxii).

In treating multiple attestation in the first stratum, Crossan drew further distinctions between *sources* and *units*, *complex* and *core complex*. A saying, for example, may have four independent *sources* in the Gospel of Thomas, Mark, Matthew, and John, but six *units*, because Matthew and Luke each developed an additional version based on Mark (xxxiii). The compilation and juxtaposition of all the *units* add up to what he called a *complex*. Paying particular attention to the *sources*, i.e. the independent attestations, Crossan then made his final strategic decision. Rather than seeking to obtain a fully articulated wording of the saying, he proceeded to move from *complex* to the "core of the complex" (xxxiii). Meticulous attention to the individual units of the *complex* disclosed certain trends and idiosyncrasies in the tradition. The resultant comparative trajectory of tradition in turn enabled him to make deductions as to the plausibility of the core saying. Once a plausible core was established, additional corroboration was ascertained by way of historical commensurability. The end result is "a common structural plot" (261), or the "single parable," or "the original image" (254). It constitutes the "core of the complex" which lies behind the complex of verifiable units.

Crossan's reconstruction of Jesus is firmly anchored in methodology. This feeds and gratifies our scientific interest in method. His work is all the more persuasive to the modern reader because its method is based on formal logic. It reassures us, citizens of the age of science, in the conviction that method informed by logic produces a high ratio of sustainable results. The logic that drives his method entails efficient orderliness, systematic sharpness, and unambiguous clarity of thought. Crossan's methodological apparatus is a brilliant exercise in organization, categorization, stratification, quantification, tabulation, and prioritization. Ordering, the methodical arrangement of items, is a favorite child of logic. Confronted with a multiplicity and multiformity of phenomena, logic administers the implementation of organizing principles. Words are sequestered and regrouped by virtue of resemblances or successiveness. In order to be arranged systematically, items need first to be indexed. Words must, therefore, be categorized so as to be apportioned to divisions of classification. Stratification is one form of classification. Tradition is thereby divided into strata or layers, which are measured according to chronological gradation. By implication, tradition takes on a linear and layered look. On the premise that each text has a date and belongs to this or that period, all available texts are distributed over all discernible strata. In this way texts are categorized, i.e. appointed a fixed place in their respective strata. Furthermore, the logic of quantification is set into motion; it places a high value on the numerical strength of materials. Accordingly, singular or multiple occurrences are perceived to make a difference. To further enhance analysis, words thus organized, classified, indexed, and numbered must be tabulated. Based on the combined properties of chronology and plurality, i.e. remoteness in time and quantitative strength, words are then entered into a comprehensive list, placed one next to the other and catalogued according to their full indexing values. The very logic of this arrangement of words makes continuous reading or hearing supremely difficult. But the purpose of the entire methodological management of words is not to promote their comprehension or enjoyment. Rather, it is designed to make words serviceable to logical analysis. And the principal agent in ascertaining the one historical sense is the Baconian method of inductive reasoning, a branch of logic that infers from multiple particulars to the one singular. It is logic's most effective strategy, which, in synergistic harmony with all other devices, labors to produce the desired findings.

In Crossan's method we recognize the application of logic that has become our dominant, although not exclusive, mode of thinking. The principal question it raises is whether Jesus, the oral performer, and the early tradition that delivered him unto writing has played by our rules. How did Jesus, speaker of aphorisms and narrator of parables, and those early dictators and scribes perform and retrieve words, constitute and contextualize meaning? Were they committed, as we are, to the ethos of pure formality, linearization of thought, compartmentalization of language, stratigraphic causality, and majority rule? How did they speak, compose manuscripts, and reappropriate these spoken and written words? Are words and groupings of words really apprehensible as distinct and isolable sediments deposited at different layers in tradition? These questions are loaded rhetoric that implies another, rather different, access to ancient language and communication, and one that should be competing for our attention.

We commence by raising an issue with logic on its own terms. By what reasoning does one privilege majority rule to the complete exclusion of singularity of attestation? To take a single instance, Crossan designated the complex on "ask, seek, knock" as authentic (435), because of its first stratum placement and multiple attestation. (Contrary to his own methodology, however, Crossan did not use it in his reconstructive work.) While representative of six independent *sources* (Papyrus Oxyrhynchus = Gospel of Thomas, Gospel of the Hebrews, Q, Mark, Dialogue of the Savior, and Gospel of John), it exists in seventeen *units* altogether (P. Oxy., one; Gos. Thom, three; Gos. Heb., one; Matt and Luke [=Q], two; Mark with parallel in Matt, two; Dial. Sav., three; John, five). Of these seventeen units only two pairs of sayings respectively render identical versions: first, P. Oxy. 654:2 and Gos. Thom. 2 (confirming the scholarly consensus that the papyrus represents a part of the Greek version of the Gospel of Thomas), and second, Matt 7:78 and Luke 11:9-10, verses which represent the sayings source Q. Apart from those two exceptions, no other two versions are exactly the same. Hence, the seventeen units confront the reader with fifteen different renditions. Clearly, the complex proved to be immensely useful in and for tradition. But why must this be an argument for authenticity? In fact, the variability is so pronounced (including single stiches, double stiches, triple stiches, double assertion of triple stiches, and quadruple stiches [Gos. Thom.: seek/find, find/troubled, troubled/astonished, astonished/ruled]) as to cast doubt upon the very idea of core stability. What we find, it seems, is more difference than identity. Can this vast difference be schematized into an evolutionary tree with a single root? The high ratio of independent occurrences, plus the multiple deployment and virtually inexhaustible variability of occurrences are evidence of the serviceability and popularity of these sayings in the tradition. This fact neither confirms nor rules out Jesus' own utterance. But it is inadmissible to posit *as a matter of methodological principle* the iterative and adaptive behavior of tradition as ground for historical authenticity.

The issue is complicated by the fact that multiple attestation cannot be limited to tradition. As will be argued below, reiteration and variation of words and stories must be assumed for Jesus' own proclamation. Multiple, variable renditions, while observable in tradition, are highly plausible in Jesus' own oral performance. Hence, both Jesus and tradition operated on the principle of multiple attestation. Hence, the move from multiple attestation to core complex in the search for the historical Jesus is not quite as compelling as it might appear. What if Jesus himself spoke sayings and stories more than once, at different occasions, and in different versions?

Equally problematic is the exclusion of all instances of single attestation from the reconstruction of Jesus' life. On what grounds do we apply Ockham's razor and excise singularity as a matter of principle? Knowing about the intensity of redactional and revisionist activities in the tradition, should we not attend to singular attestation with a heightened sense of curiosity? To be sure, singularity of utterance neither confirms nor rules out authenticity. But can it, *as a matter of principle*, be excluded from consideration altogether? This exclusion of singular attestation raises a number of difficult questions. Can one lay claim to the historical life of Jesus if its reconstruction essentially relies on Jesus' sayings, however well these are contextualized in macrocosmic and mesocosmic settings? Is there a single modern historian who based her or his composition of the life of a historical personage on an extremely selective group of sayings attributed to that person? How can one lay claim to the historical life of Jesus whose reconstruction rules out singular attestation of sayings if, by Crossan's own count, two-thirds of all complexes have single attestation (xxxiii; 434)? In fact, his inventory has given full account of what he regards to be authentic Jesus materials. Among the fifty-five complexes of single attestation in stratum one, he considers twelve to be authentic instances (441-43). This raises further questions. How does one verify authenticity amidst singularity, and why, if a number of singular attestations are in fact considered authentic, are these not used in the reconstruction of Jesus' message? Can methodological logic deliver on its promises?

By all accounts, Jesus was a *speaker* of aphoristic sayings and parabolic stories. Therefore, the modern historian, persuaded of the literary-theological nature of the gospels and intent on coming to terms with Jesus' message, is confronted with the issue of speech. She or he must first learn that speech, in distinction from writing, is not traceable to external verification. It surrenders itself in the act of speaking. While the voicing of sayings and parables was destined to affect minds and lives of hearers, it left no *externally* visible residues. A text outlasts the act of writing, but spoken words exist only in the act of speaking and in the memories of hearers. It is hard to escape the impression, therefore, that the words of the historical Jesus, if taken on their own terms, are not quantifiable in any form or division, if only because they are not available to us for purposes of retrieval and classification. This is a dismaying truth for those who believe that logic, based on the visual accessibility of language, must perforce yield the words of the historical Jesus.

To say that speech leaves no visible trace is to compare it negatively vis-à-vis writing. But it is a fact from which all our thinking about Jesus' proclamation must proceed. Words spoken have no quantifiable existence. Logic's critical apparatus, on the other hand, utterly depends on the external visualization, hence permanence, of language. Logic's competence to depersonalize and reorganize knowledge grows out of and relies on a long and intense experience with the written, printed word. But if spoken words "cannot be 'broken' and reassembled" (Ong 1967b:323), logic cannot get a hold of the performative poetics of Jesus' proclamation. We are bound to conclude that the oral cast of his words is unknowable through formal thought based on literary and typographic materiality. Reimagining his oral poetics is a task supremely difficult because it goes against deep-set literate inclinations.

When Jesus pronounced a saying at one place, and subsequently chose to deliver it elsewhere, neither he nor his hearers could have perceived this other rendition as a secondhand version of the first one. Each saying was an autonomous speech act. And when the second rendition, delivered before a different audience, was at variance with the first one, neither the speaker nor his hearers would have construed a difference between the literal, original wording and its derivative (Lord 1960:101, 152). No one saying was elevated to the privileged position of *ipsissimum verbum* at the expense of any other saying. Without a trajectory to invite comparative thought, each saying constituted an original act and an authentic intention. When Crossan stated that "Oral sensibility and *ipsissima verba* are . . . contradictions in terms" (1983: 38), he should have used the singular, *ipsissimum verbum*, which is in fact what he meant to say: the search for the single, original, correct saying is pointless in orality. In view of the fact that the quest for the historical Jesus is heavily based on the premise of the retrievability of the single, literal saying, Crossan's renunciation of that very premise merits wider recognition. As questers we tend to regard the concept of the *ipsissimum verbum* as an inescapably logical fact of linguistic life because we find ourselves living in a world of texts, each of which we believe must have originated in or be traceable to an *Urtext*. But when we take serious account of speech and oral performance, we learn to appreciate a poetics that cannot make sense of singular originality in the literary mode of thought. What to scribal sensibility appear to be variables of a single *Ur*-saying, for oral sensibility are a plurality of authentic sayings. But when we acknowledge that orality is trafficking in *ipsissima verba*, we embrace an idea that subverts the very concept of the *ipsissimum verbum*.

When Crossan discarded the concept of the original saying, he did so in favor of the *ipsissima structura*, the core complex underlying multiple versions (1983:38; 1991:xxxiii). *Ipsissima structura* raises the issue of structure versus fluidity, or fixity versus flexibility, an issue central to oral tradition and poetics. Let us first recognize that the picture of relative stability of Jesus' sayings conveyed to us in the Q passages of Matthew and Luke is not the product of oral dynamics. The striking verbal agreements of the relevant Matthean and Lukan versions is only intelligible on the assumption of Q's textual identity (Kloppenborg 1987: 42-51). Q had reached chirographic stability, even though, we shall see, it sought to resist and overcome it. The stability one encounters in oral tradition is not this kind of near-literalness. In oral aesthetics, stability refers to traditional story patterns, themes, and phraseology, or, to use Foley's definition, to "elements and strategies that were in place (long) before the execution of the present version" (8). The bracketing of the word "long" is ours and intended to leave open the issue of the tradition's chronological depth. No oral performer operates without these commonplaces, and Jesus and the tradition were no exception. In the field of orality-literacy studies, commonplace features are conventionally assigned to the tradition. Commonplace stability is perceived to be the work of tradition. Crossan, however, works with a stability that is neither the textual nor the oral kind. Instead, he pruned all existant versions from contextual and compositional variables of tradition and assigned the resultant core complex to historical individuality. The stability Crossan seeks is assumed to give us access to the Jesus of history. For example, the fourfold independent attestation of the saying on "Kingdom and Children" suggests an underlying "central and shocking" metaphor that goes back to Jesus (Crossan 1991:269). The question is whether we can grope our way through tradition to the mind of Jesus by reconstructing a core complex. Must not any such reconstruction necessarily remain speculative? More than that, are not these processes of reconstruction the result of extreme abstraction that runs counter to speech, if only because in speech verbal reality is never totalized, never fully realized? Although Crossan reactualized and individualized the *ipsissima structura* by reinstating it into the historical matrix, the search for the common denominator underlying all existant versions operates neither on oral nor on textual principles of stability, but rather on structuralist premises. What we get is something akin to a universal grammar of the Jesus tradition. Albert Lord's dictum, although arising out of an experience with different materials, is still apropos: ". . . we are deluded by a mirage when we try to construct an ideal form of any given song" (1960:101). To collect and place side by side all written versions of a dominical saying and to trace a trajectory back to the core structure, will give us something that had no existence in oral or textual form. Even if we managed to extract a pattern common to all existing versions of a saying, we would have succeeded merely in conjuring a structuralist stability that by oral, historical standards is a fictional construct.

The search for the *ipsissimum verbum* and the *ipsissima structura* is thus based on the recognition of structural stability, a stability that seeks to transcend the variability of all the differences in tradition. Here we discern one of the deepest desires of logic, namely to conquer the flux of temporality and to secure time-obviating fixedness. But if we are to imagine Jesus as speaker, we must imagine his words being caught up in the drift of time. Sound and sounded words, proclamation and hearing, are inescapably time-bound, and "no other sensory field totally resists a holding action, stabilization, in quite this way" (Ong 1982:32). By itself, structural stability does not get us to oral performance. At the very most, it may give us the instruments on which the music was played. But the music is forever beyond our audition.

The value of redundancy is axiomatic in ancient culture. Precisely what we literate people tend to shy away from, oral practitioners in antiquity and dominantly oral societies regarded as a great virtue (Peabody: 4; Abrahams). Repetition both on the synchronic level and in diachronic contexts found its rationale in the physical circumstances surrounding speakers and audiences (Ong 1982:39-41). From there it permeated oral-derived and oral-dependent texts (Gray). The straight, consecutive course of thought was simply not the way words were attuned to crowds and hearers of texts. Unless words and locutions were restated, and sayings and stories retold, a speaker would not connect with hearers. This need for repetition applies with special force to the charismatic, itinerant speaker whose mission utterly depended on the receptive quality of his message. Redundancy was an essential, rhetorical device. Addressing the same people frequently and different people deliberately, he had no choice but to communicate the message more than once. There is every reason to assume, therefore, that repeated renditions characterized Jesus' speech habits. This point is worth stressing because our search for the *ipsissimum verbum* and the *ipsissima structura* has imprinted upon our minds the model of singular verbal originality.

Oral redundancy bears no resemblance to the idea of duplication inherent in print. The latter takes pride in the uniformity of textual productions modeled on *the* original, while repetition in oral aesthetics involves variation. Repetitions almost always vary, and hence are rarely literal repetitions. In face-to-face communication, the rhetorical doctrine of efficaciousness prevails over standards of exactitude (Ong 1982:57-68), operating on a logic not of sequentiality and sameness, but of reinforcement and multiple effects. It can well be expected, therefore, that repeated renditions of a saying, story, or song were not exactly identical, even if communicated by the same person. Repetition entailed variability. To put the matter differently, transmission and composition converge in oral performance (Lord 1960:5). Although the speaker used traditional materials, she or he was composing while speaking: "each performance is more than a performance, it is a recreation" (101). The idea was not to reproduce what was said previously, but to (re)compose so as to affect the present circumstance. In order to assure a maximum degree of resonance, speech had to adjust to different audiences to varying degrees. Once again, variability in repetition is highly pertinent to the mode of verbalization practiced by the charismatic speaker who is anything but restricted to a single occasion or a single community. When Jesus (re)iterated previously communicated words, ideas, and stories, he was bound, time and again, to (re)phrase his message in the interest of efficaciousness. This warrants our attention because the *ipsissimum verbum* and the *ipsissima structura*, concepts that have defined the course of our discussion, have barred from our minds the oral aesthetics of variability in repetition.

At the heart of oral poetics lies the intermingling of stability with flexibility (Peabody: 96). It is perhaps the most difficult process to grasp and one for which we lack a single name. We have no language capable of expressing the combined features of stability, repetition/variability, and originality—terms already shaped by textual and typographic experiences. The charismatic itinerant did not think of his multiple renditions as variables, let alone inconsistencies, because he could not associate his proclamation with a fixed model. Although traditional patterns assisted him in remembering and (re)phrasing, the idea of making changes to a traditional core that needed to be preserved was entirely foreign to him. It is only writing that exposes different versions and "favors awareness of inconsistency" (Goody and Watt: 49). And it is writing that invites us to abstract from the perceived changes an *ipsissimum verbum*, or an *ipsissima structura*, or a single core complex. "We find it difficult to grasp something that is multiform" (Lord 1960:100), and still more difficult to imagine multiformity in the proclamation of a single person. But if already in the case of the Homeric bards Lord had reason to caution us not to look "for that consistency which has become almost a fetish with literary scholars" (95), how much more does his advice apply to Jesus, whose message was ill-tolerated by the establishment and rapidly mythologized by his followers. He was at once tradition and its knowing recreator. If we can free ourselves from the methodological principle that variability is the work of tradition and core stability typical of Jesus, we can grant him a verbal latitude broad enough to include performancial redundancy and verbal polyphony. His proclamation was irreducible to *ipsissima verba*; it occured in multiformity that was tantamount to multioriginality. A thrice-narrated parable was not comprehensible in terms of a core structure and three variables thereof, but only as three equiprimordial renditions. Each rendition was an original version, and in fact *the original version*.

Tradition: Stratification Versus Biosphere

Tradition is a phenomenon as elementary and riddling as human life itself. In the past, Roman Catholic theology in particular has undertaken systematic efforts to conceptualize tradition and specifically its relation to scripture (Burghardt). In a non-specific sense the term is current coinage in the humanities and social sciences, but rarely ever subject to sustained theoretical reflections. Conventionally, when we speak of tradition and the traditional, we have in mind something that is immutable and resistant to change. Tradition as a state of immobility has received both positive and negative interpretations. Positively, it is perceived as something to fall back on in times of crisis because it prevails in flux, while negatively it is viewed as the dead weight of the past that has little relevance for the present. Both the Reformation and the Enlightenment advanced a sense of the polarity of tradition versus modernity. "With modernity identified with change, and by implication with the positive values associated with progress, tradition automatically came to mean the culturally changeless and historically immobile" (Stock 1990:160).

In the discipline of New Testament studies the concept of tradition has been institutionalized in terms of the transmissional processes that are thought to have preceded the writing of the synoptic gospels and John. Rather than polarizing tradition vi-à-vis modernity, the discipline has adapted tradition to the standards of modernity itself. We have interpreted early Christian processes of tradition through the horizontal time-line of history, as understood by Kant, Fichte, Hegel, Schelling, and much of modern historiography. In *The Oral and the Written Gospel* (henceforth: *OWG*) I questioned the dominant paradigm of the tradition's evolutionary growth and steady incremental expansion toward the narrative gospel (1983:1-43). My criticism of this model was a twofold one. First, the model of the evolutionary growth and near-deterministic thrust of the synoptic tradition is problematic because it has every appearance of a theoretical construct formulated by the logic of hindsight. In fact, the very designation of *synoptic tradition* is problematic because it enforces the impression that all traditions preceding the synoptic gospels were bound to move toward and flow into these narratives. Strictly, one should speak of *presynoptic traditions*, a less restrictive term that frees us from the deterministic model of synoptic directionality. Second, the model of the evolutionary growth is also problematic because its single-minded focus on the processes of transmission fails to take account of the means of communication. Texts are given primacy over speech, and to the degree that speaking is taken into consideration, its behavior is modeled on texts. It is noteworthy that directionality and text-centeredness, the very features that have dominated our work on the early tradition, are closely interrelated phenomena. Typography, more than chirographic culture, encouraged "the habit of assimilating matter in sequences, one item after the other" (Ong 1967a:11). Our task now is to reimagine this encompassing reality that we routinely, but unreflectively, refer to as tradition.

Let us commence not with the processes of transmission, but with orality and scribality, the means of communication. To us the notion of "text" conjures up a schooling system, the privacy of reading, and above all literacy. In antiquity, however, schooling was largely limited to upper class boys and a few slaves from wealthier families; and private reading was a distinct rarity (Botha). As for literacy, it is notoriously difficult to measure it in our own culture and more so in the distant past (Bonner; Harris; Graff; Marrou). Perhaps more importantly, it is a term that easily lends itself to anachronistic assumptions. As a general rule, reading was practiced as a reading aloud to oneself or to audiences, and hence closely allied with recitation and auditory apperception (Achtemeier; Balogh; Saenger). "Reading and hearing" (ἀναγινόσκειν καὶ ἀκούειν or *legere et audire*) became standard phrases for the auditory reading process throughout the ancient world and far into the Middle Ages (Balogh, 207). It is in this context that one must appreciate the words of introduction written by the author of *Revelation*: "blessed is he who reads and those who hear the words of the prophecy" (1:3: μακάριοσ ὁ ἀναγινώσκων καὶ οἱ ἀκούοντες τοὺς λόγους τῆς προφητείας). A writer either followed the dictates of a speaker, or his or her own dictation. Written words, whether read or copied, were likely to be spoken aloud. "Vocalized writing in antiquity was only a version of the conventional form of literary activity: dictation" (Balogh: 218). Therefore, whether dictated or read, texts were transacted in an oral, aural field of communication and sense perception. They "functioned as a subset of a basically oral environment, and that means that, when we turn to interpreting culture and communication of the time [of the first century CE], we need to be continually reminded of . . . [their] orality" (Botha: 206). Literacy, therefore, may not be an adequate term to describe the ancient media realities surrounding texts. For us the term suggests *the combined skills* of reading and writing. In the ancient world, a reader was a speaker or a hearer, and not necessarily a writer at all, while a scribe trained in the art of chirography was not necessarily an interested reader, i.e. dictator or auditor. Instead we should remember that papyri and manuscripts were "connected to the physical presence of people and to living speech to an extent that is consistently underestimated today" (Botha: 207). Thus in thinking about tradition, we should first imagine a world of communications in which speaking had primacy, and both the production and consumption of manuscripts grew out of the living tissue of speech.

In our discipline, tradition is virtually synonymous with textual transmission, and the chain of transmission is almost always explicated along developmental lines. The process of tradition is often assumed to be divisible into clearly identifiable, autonomous textual strata. We imagine a pure textual environment where texts function in relation to other texts under the aegis of a linear, developmental governance. A telling example is the recent work on the transmissional history of the sayings gospel of Q (Kloppenborg 1987; Mack). Commencing with Q as *proto-biography*, Kloppenborg has retraced its history to an underlying redactional stratum comprised of a *chriae collection*, which was characterized by prophetic and apocalyptic announcements, and still further back to a source of *wisdom speeches*, which were paraenetic in nature. Comparing Q and Thomas materials, Koester has postulated an underlying sayings gospel that must have been very primitive in nature and close to Jesus' own voice (1971a:166-87; 1971b). One keeps going backward until one accounts for every layer as an explanation and interpretation of a prior layer. "The cartography stretches from text to text, to the last text in *terra incognita*" (Cartlidge: 404). Or, to take our vantage point from the tradition's *arche*, we watch the unfolding of tradition from single sayings to sayings clusters, and from sayings gospel to proto-biography, which in turn signals the way toward the narrative gospel.

The paradigm of the evolutionary trajectory remains the all-determining, but unexamined philosophical underpinning. It raises a host of historical and linguistic questions. On what grounds can we ascertain Q's generic identity as proto-biography? We can know that at the outset Q situated John in the "circuit of the Jordan," setting the stage, religiously and geopolitically, for Q's message (Kloppenborg 1990:145-60). But John's wilderness locale does not constitute a genre definition. We must also admit that Matthew and Luke saw to it that the incipit, Q's own genre designation, was erased. It is worth remembering, moreover, that it was a fluke of history, namely Matthew's and Luke's simultaneous absorption of Q, that puts us in a position to disentangle Q, or parts thereof. As far as Matthew and Luke were concerned, they intended to bury the genre of Q in their respective narratives.

Are we not operating on modern standards of literary and theological consistency if we use wisdom and apocalyptic as defining criteria for separating strata in the tradition? (Williams: 105; Collins: 152). Horsley's proposal that we learn to think of Q, its composition and social location, in terms of cluster formation comes much closer to ancient compositional realities than do stratification theories (1991). His thesis that the discernment of a sapiental versus an apocalyptic stratum in Q "may be rooted more in the conceptual apparatus of modern New Testament scholarship than in the text of Q" (196) deserves our most serious attention. We must ask, moreover, to what extent has our knowledge of Thomas conditioned the allocation of wisdom materials to a first stratum of Q? Are Thomas and Q traceable to a single, underlying *arche*-type, or are they not rather participants in a polyphonic sayings tradition in which words intersect, replay, reconnect in ways that do not necessarily line up on a single trajectory? After all, we do not find in Thomas and Q the kind of verbal agreements that persuaded us to postulate the textual identity of Q in the background of Matthean and Lukan parallels.

Moreover, the layered concept of tradition raises questions about the adequacy of our theory of the verbal art in antiquity. We presume the compositional practice of successive layering without explicit reflection on matters of ancient scribality and hermeneutics. How is one to imagine, technically and chirographically, the production of a stratified text? Does the behavior of language, both oral and written, match the stratigraphic, evolutionary rationale that shapes our reconstructions of tradition?

Thinking of texts in oral contextuality, rather than in terms of literary consistency, allows us to rediscover the functional quality of ancient chirographs. The ancient world of communications exemplifies the unbound nature of all language. Fundamentally, chirographs were not perceived as having firmly fixed boundaries. Fluidity of texts is "particularly characteristic of sayings collections, where there is no train of thought or causal nexus to stabilize the text from saying to saying" (Robinson 1986:160-61). Standing at the intersection with speech, any textualized saying or, for that matter, any part of a text could be called upon to commune with the life of tradition. In part, tradition kept itself alive precisely by freely appropriating elements of chirographic culture. Nor did chirographs have temporal limitations, which would confine them to this period or that stratum. What served in the past could well be reused for the present. It would be wrong, moreover, to associate ancient texts with private authorship or ownership. For the most part, texts were viewed as constituents of a collective cultural enterprise or of a communal memory. Unrestricted by laws against plagiarism, they were eminently usable, quotable, alterable. All this suggests a behavior quite different from stratigraphic logic, which seeks an exact determination of stages in the tradition. Only typography could persuade us to think in terms of tidy, closely controlled language spaces.

The observation that scribal products are embedded in the soft matrix of speech takes on special significance in the cases of Q and the Gospel of Thomas. In *OWG* I have suggested that Q displays "a fundamentally oral disposition" (1983:201). Underlying many of the criticisms that have been leveled against this proposition lurks the controversial issue of Q's hermeneutical posture. Kloppenborg has emphasized the historicizing frame of Q's final version and the absence of the prophetic formula τάδε λέγει ὁ κύριος (1987:34-37). Manifestly, it is not the Exalted Lord who is speaking in Q. But is the document adequately understood as a proto-biography that gives us the pre-resurrectional past of Jesus? As is well known, Q attributes to Jesus a mixed speaking style comprised both of historicizing and contemporizing introductory formulae (Boring 1982:179-82). To keep the problematic in focus, one should first recall that Lukan and Matthean editing most likely strengthened the historicizing side of the dialectic in the interest of merging Q with their narrative genres. When, therefore, Luke 9:58 reads καὶ εἶπεν αὐτῷ ὁ Ἰησοῦς, and the Matthean parallel 8:20 καὶ λέγει αὐτῷ ὁ Ἰησοῦς, one is well advised to deviate from "Lukan priority" and give preference to Matthew's present tense. It should furthermore be acknowledged that in many instances these formulae elude our reconstructive efforts. Comparing, for example, Luke 13:20 (καὶ πάλιν εἶπεν) with its Matthean parallel 13:33 (ἄλλην παραβολὴν ἐλάλησεν αὐτοῖς), one is compelled to conclude that we are dealing with a Lukan and a Matthean formulation respectively. Kloppenborg suggested that the dialectic tension between contemporizing and historicizing diction had shifted toward the latter in the last stage of the Q redaction with the addition of the temptation story (1987:256-62) which altered the hermeneutical posture of Q as a whole. In Kloppenborg's view, the effect is comparable to the displacement of words of the Risen Lord into a narrative of the pre-resurrectional Jesus (257). However, this is precisely the kind of analogy that skews the hermeneutics of Q.

A prime characteristic of Q, negatively speaking, is the absence of the kerygma of passion and resurrection. On this we can all agree, I believe. It crucially determines the hermeneutical posture of Q in that it distinguishes it both from Mark who projected Jesus into the pre-resurrectional past, and from the other three canonical gospels, which clearly distinguish between a pre-Easter and post-Easter Jesus. Not unlike the Gospel of Thomas, Q does not think in terms of a pre-resurrectional versus post-resurrectional differential at all. Tödt hit the mark in stating that "we cannot help getting the impression that it did not even occur to the members of the community which collected the sayings of Jesus in Q to distinguish between pre-Easter and post-Easter sayings, it being self-evident to them that the earthly and risen Jesus are one and the same" (265). In different words, Jesus as historicized and actualized person claims one and the same authority. The "addition" of the temptation story (if we have to think in terms of redactional stages) cannot be compared with a shift from post-Easter to pre-Easter status, for Easter as a hermeneutical differential is alien to the genre of Q. Thus, far from altering the hermeneutical stance of Q, the story comports entirely with the genre's mixed style. In media perspectives, Q seeks to resist the stabilizing effects of writing by fusing Jesus' past with his present in an effort to "realize the urge to continue to teach what Jesus had been teaching" (Tödt: 265). Therein lies the "fundamentally oral disposition" of Q.

The media disposition of the Gospel of Thomas bespeaks greater complexities. The identification of the speaker with the "living Jesus" in the gospel's incipit accommodates oral interests in a very particular sense. He is unmistakably introduced as a present and presently speaking authority. His present standing is further underscored by the absence of a thoroughgoing narrative syntax with its historicizing effects. It is doubtful whether this Jesus can be equated with the crucified/risen One of the canonical tradition, because the kerygma of death and resurrection is as alien to Thomas as it is to Q. As for Jesus' death, it need not surprise us that none of the 114 sayings of Thomas reveal any interest in the subject matter. For if it is a purpose of Thomas to realize the presence of Jesus as speaker of aphorisms and parables, any reflection on his death would be irrelevant, indeed self-contradictory. A genre that is intent on extending the "living Jesus" into the present cannot at the same time propagate his absence in death. As for Jesus' resurrection, Thomas is not cast into the genre of a revelation discourse of the risen Christ. Sharply to the point is Koester's observation that "there are no features compelling us to understand the work as a secret revelation after the resurrection" (1971a:167). It is therefore inadmissible to seek the rationale for the speaking posture of the "living Jesus" in the resurrection. What we do observe is a Jesus who, while consistently speaking in the past tense, continues to address the present of the Thomas community. Although *de facto* spatialized and in a sense frozen in time, his words are perceived to be living words that transcend spatial boundaries. As in the case of Q, we observe the phenomenon of the past and present Jesus speaking with one and the same authority.

Unlike Q, however, the Gospel of Thomas is further characterized by a certain amount of tension between its chirographic existence and Jesus' speaking posture. Tension first surfaces in the incipit, which identifies "the secret sayings which the living Jesus *spoke*" with those that "Didymos Judas Thomas *wrote.*" What is noticeable about these words is a remarkable self-consciousness concerning the media realities: Jesus' speech acts are available to the readers/hearers as products of writing. As we saw, this is precisely the problem that Thomas seeks to overcome by synchronizing the past of Jesus with his present. Moreover, what distinguishes the words of the "living Jesus" is their oral efficaciousness: they have power to give life. And yet, life is not directly available through speech and hearing, for Thomas's Jesus imposes the arduous task of interpretation (*hermeneia*) upon the hearers of his words. There are still deeper media problematics inscribed in this gospel. Esoteric secrecy is a case in point. Thomas maintains the fictional scenario of Jesus' esoteric instruction to a privileged group of insiders, most of whom appear to be disciples. Among them Simon Peter, Matthew, Thomas, Mary, and Salome are mentioned by name. But this esoteric scene of intimate discourse conflicts with the gospel's written identity, which extends an open invitation to all who can hear what seemed to be intended only for the few. Thus the chirograph compromised the protectionist instincts of esoteric secrecy. Spoken to the few, but written for the many, the gospel is deeply animated by the desire to retain the *viva vox* of the "living Jesus" (Kelber 1989).

Although the tradition is available to us exclusively in texts, not all texts are intelligible on the model of intertextuality and successive layers of literary growth. The genre of the sayings gospel illustrates the tenacity of oral drives and strategies in the tradition. This is not to deny that the genre is unthinkable without the technology of writing. Sayings and parables were divorced from their speaking environment and recontextualized in a scripted arrangement. But in underwriting the validity of the aphoristic and parabolic units of Jesus' speech and in going to great lengths in extending his voice and speaking posture into the present, the genre remains at the service of a basically oral sense and sensibility. Lest we exaggerate the media tensions in Thomas, we need reminding that the Gospels' oral motivation enjoyed the support of a media world in which the boundaries between writing and speech were fluid. Benefiting from the free flow of communication that existed between chirographs and living speech, the genre could induce a sense of presence that sought to prevail over the pastness created by all writing.

Given our growing awareness of the media complexity of presynoptic realities, we cannot assent to models that recreate tradition as exclusively textual processes of production, transmission, and transformation, depersonalized and diagrammatically traceable through space, any more than we can accept a reduction of tradition to discourse and the aesthetics of reception, untouched by literacy and transacted in primal oral purity. Brian Stock's observation that in medieval culture "oral and written traditions normally function in relation to each other" (1990:145), will apply to the Hellenistic era as well. Writing was linked to speech in so many ways that our typographic apperception of textuality will never let us know. Our text-centrism has blinded us to imagining ways in which speech could emanate from chirographs or in turn generate writings. But once we think of tradition as interactive processes, we concede the presence of a dynamic that is other than either orality or literacy, for which we have no name and about which we have little experience.

If we conceive of tradition as a more inclusive and less tangible reality than our literate senses let us know, we must also consider the role of hearers. To be sure, words interiorized, faith engendered, doubts raised, hopes aroused, expectations reversed, and images invoked are intractable features. Vanished forever are the speakers, voices, and listeners. Reader-response criticism deserves credit for having rehabilitated the role of the reader by focusing on the rhetorical directives inscribed in texts. The ensuing shift in orientation from the mimetic to the pragmatic axis has reawakened us to the signal involvement of audiences in the work of tradition (Iser; Fowler). No doubt, interest in receptionist aesthetics "opens the way to a greater sensitivity to the oral and relational dynamics" (Coward: 182) that characterized the transaction of ancient texts. And yet, in order to grasp the fuller implications of hearers' participation (not simply responses!), we will in the end have to overcome our textbound thinking and come to terms with a reality that is not encoded in texts at all. It means that we must learn to think of a large part of tradition as an extratextual phenomenon. What permitted hearers to interiorize the so-called parable of the "Good Samaritan," for example, was a culture shared by speaker and hearers alike. Unless hearers have some experience or knowledge of the role of priests, Levites, and Samaritans in society, or rather of their social construction, this parable will not strike a responsive chord with them. Whether hearers are Samaritans themselves or informed by anti-Samaritan sentiments will make a difference in the way they hear the story. Shared experiences about the dangers of traveling, the role of priests and Levites, and the ethics of charity weave a texture of cultural commonality that makes the story resonate in the hearts and minds of hearers. Tradition in this encompassing sense is a circumambient contextuality or biosphere in which speaker and hearers live. It includes texts and experiences transmitted through or derived from texts. But it is anything but reducible to intertextuality. Tradition in this broadest sense is largely an invisible nexus of references and identities from which people draw sustenance, in which they live, and in relation to which they make sense of their lives. This invisible biosphere is at once the most elusive and the foundational feature of tradition.

The concept of tradition as biosphere suggests that the great divide thesis, which pits oral tradition vis-à-vis gospel text, can in the end not supply the answer to questions concerning tradition and gospel. If the emphasis in *OWG* fell on that division, it was because a novel approach requires a strong thesis. It does not, however, discredit orality studies any more than it outdates examination of the role of scribality in the life of tradition. In fact, we need just such strong theses for revision and reorientation. To grasp the overlaps and interfaces, we have to understand the hermeneutics of speech and writing, even if they rarely, if ever, existed in a pure state.

The issue of the canonical gospels' engagement in tradition, and tradition's relation to these gospels, has thus remained unresolved. One reason for this state of affairs is plainly the inaccessibility of the presynoptic traditions. But we are not entirely locked in ignorance either. There is a broad sense of agreement that the gospels did not grow directly out of orality any more than they originated in the historicity of their subject matter. Albert Lord's ingenious explication of the gospels as oral traditional narratives has met with little approval among biblical scholars (1978). Such are the agreements of wording and sequences of episodes that the hands and voices of chirography cannot entirely be ruled out, especially as regards the relation of Matthew and Luke vis-à-vis Mark. To be sure, the gospels, along with other ancient chirographs, were enmeshed with speech by way of composition, recitation, and reception. But this is not to say that they are autographs of speech, i.e., multiforms of essentially the same oral genre. Writing, no matter how closely allied with oral sensibilities and practices, did make a difference. Mark's parabolic narrative, for example, is clearly designed to be read to and heard by audiences, but it is not simply speech transposed into a text, a rendition of an oral traditional narrative. Those are distinctions worth keeping in mind. While the gospel invites oral performance, it is not the product of oral traditional composition *in the sense of the Homeric epics*.

In addition to literary consistencies among the synoptic gospels, another reason for questioning Lord's thesis is the fact that Mark's gospel provides precious little evidence for seeking to preserve a traditional narrative. Staving off oblivion in the interest of preserving a core tradition does not get us to the heart of its compositional intentionality. We come closer to Mark's purpose if we hear the narrative not as an insurance against forgetfulness, but as a hermeneutically charged transaction. In different words, the gospel is intelligible as a narrative addressing hearers by engaging tradition sundrily and selectively, but not by reappropriating it comprehensively. Crossan has proposed that Mark's gospel came to be written as a result of multiple revisions of *Secret Mark, Papyrus Egerton 2* (1985), and the passion story of the *Gospel of Peter* (1988). Koester has credited Mark's narrative for having united aretological materials with the passion story (1990:292), and he further viewed canonical Mark as "an abbreviated version of the *Secret Gospel of Mark* " (302). Robinson (1970, 1982), Boring (1977; 1982:195-203), and my own work (1983:199-211; 1987:107-33) finally interpreted canonical Mark as a corrective to the genre of the sayings gospel. I remain convinced that of all the traditional features Mark appears to have absorbed and revised, the sayings gospel deserves pride of place (Kelber: 1992:42-58). The relative paucity of dominical sayings, the christological focus on the cross, the withholding of the living Lord from the disciples, the role reversal of the disciples from insiders to outsiders, the rigorously constructed pre-Easter form of the narrative, and the deconstruction of secrecy (Kelber, 1988:1-20) are principal features that run directly counter to the fundamentally oral disposition of the genre of the sayings gospel. What matters here, however, is that the proposals put forth by Crossan, Koester, Robinson, Boring, and myself give us a sense both of the polyphonic nature of the presynoptic tradition and of the diachronic depth and complexity encoded in the narrative gospel. The more complex the picture of the gospel's plural engagements in tradition, the less plausible is the concept of the gospel as uninterpreted fulness of what preceded it. Irrespective of the merit of each of the above proposals, it is increasingly apparent that Mark's gospel abounds in multiple traces, plural echoes, displacement features, and revisionary strategies. No longer imaginable as the culmination of tradition's assumed evolutionary trajectory, it appears both as the beneficiary of tradition and as an interventionist with respect to some of tradition's fundamental drives.

Those who had a hand and voice in composing the gospel absorbed information of different kinds. "But how is one to imagine—technically, psychologically, religiously—Mark's skillful juggling of a number of texts, using them, revising them, deconstructing them, while all along composing an impressively coherent narrative?" I asked a few years ago (1987:120). The more numerous the materials Mark appears to be coping with, the less his gospel is imaginable as the reworking of a single text. But the principle of intertextuality also becomes increasingly implausible, unless we are prepared to locate "Mark" in a well-funded library. In the end, it seems, we cannot think of the gospel narratives' apart from their social habitat, media world, and biosphere. The gospels were products of urban Christian communities. If we adopt Stock's model of "textual communities," one may think of social settings in which certain individuals were responsible for the dictation and writing of these narratives, while the majority of the community were hearers. Considering the proliferation of the Christian movement that had already occurred in the Pauline communities, one can plausibly assume the existence of a plurality of interpretive features, of rival interpretations, of a competing gospel genre even, in those post-War communities that authored and hosted the gospels. Not unlike Paul, Mark had access to plural and rival features of the tradition through chirographs, oral communication derived from and filtered through chirographs, and by word of mouth. On Paul's model, moreover, we can begin to think not of unidirectional intertextuality or pure orality, but rather of human memory, which, while nourished in the tradition's biosphere, was perfectly capable of redescribing parts thereof.

The gospel text once in existence was to be performed orally or celebrated liturgically, either in part or perhaps *in toto*. In either case, it was read aloud and reinterpreted in sermons, thus complicating tradition by a "secondary orality," one derived from and filtered through the medium of a single text. And it may also become the springboard for new texts as other gospels, commentaries, and homilies come to be written. It is in this multimedia sense that we have to imagine the workings of tradition, and in this multimedia environment that we have to place the gospel as the defining center of a community.

Conclusion

This essay has attempted to raise consciousness about the Enlightenment parentage of the modern discipline of biblical scholarship. Throughout, the underlying, nagging question has been whether the scholarly discourse of reason corresponds with the hermeneutical sensibilities of late antiquity. To be sure, serious doubts about the premises of historical criticism have been raised before. From the collapse of the liberal quest, for example, we had to learn the lesson that written language and historical actuality do not relate to each other in a one-to-one relationship. What we have to learn additionally is that our understanding of the hermeneutical status and functioning of language itself is patently culture-bound. Our search for singular originality concealed behind layers of textual encumbrances reveals much about the force of our desire, but falls short of understanding the oral implementation of multioriginality in the present act of speaking. Only on paper do texts appear to relate in a one-to-one relation to other texts. The fixation on authorial intent, on language as self-legitimating discourse, on the reduction of tradition to processes of textual transmission and stratification, and on the perception of ancient chirographs as visualizable, disengaged objects opens a vast conceptual gap that separates our own typographic rationalities from ancient media sensibilities.

In reawakening consciousness about a world of tonal values, oral poetics, and speaking texts, the essay attempted to rehabilitate media sensibilities, including the time-bound nature of speech, that had been part of the biblical tradition throughout the ancient and medieval history. I am persuaded that the integration of issues such as speech and the oral matrix of chirographic life, media interfaces, and the human sensorium—issues that have clearly not been given their due—matters considerably for a more adequate, indeed different, understanding of our religious tradition. If we take into serious account the extensive work done on speech and writing in the last few decades, we can no longer reduce tradition to a history of ideas abstracted from texts and disincarnated from contexts. Instead of focusing singlemindedly on processes of transmission and transformation of meaning, we should include reflection on the constitution of meaning. Furthermore, if we can wean ourselves from the notion that texts constitute the center of gravity in tradition, we may be able to imagine and work with a vastly broader concept of tradition and assign texts their proper place within it. There is a need as well to reexamine the editorial and source critical theories that have informed the work of historical criticism and to scrutinize their validity in light of ancient rhetorical and chirographic realities. There is, lastly, but most importantly, the much neglected sensory dimension in the tradition. Whereas in the logical tradition of the Enlightenment, imagistic, acoustic, and emotive apperception were largely banished from the work of reason, in the ancient tradition perception is a form of imagination. It is standard epistemological experience far into the Middle Ages that word and pictures are conjoined, that sensation interacts with intelligibility, and sight and hearing serve as catalysts of cognition. Instead of pure thought based on textuality, we find the rhetorical deployment of discourse, chirographs soaked in oral contextuality, interfacing media that plug into the cultural matrix of tradition, and all of these features polyphonically appropriating the human sensorium.

WORKS CONSULTED

Abrahams, Roger D.
    1978   "License to Repeat and Be Predictable." *Folklore Reprint Society* (Indiana University) 6:1-13.

Achtemeier, Paul J.
    1990   "OMNE VERBUM SONAT: The New Testament andthe Oral Environment of Late Western Antiquity." *JBL* 109:3-27.

Balogh, Josef
    1926   "Voces Paginarum." *Philologus* 82: 84-109, 202-40.

Bonner, Stanley Frederick
    1977   *Education in Ancient Rome: From the Elder Cato to the Younger Pliny.* Berkeley: University of California Press.

Borg, Marcus J.
   1987   *Jesus A New Vision: Spirit, Culture, and the Life of Discipleship*. San Francisco: Harper & Row.

Boring, M. Eugene
   1977   "The Paucity of Sayings in Mark: A Hypothesis." Pp. 371-77 in *SBL Seminar Papers*. Missoula: Scholars.
   1982   *Sayings of the Risen Jesus: Christian Prophecy in the Synoptic Tradition*. SNTSMS 46. Cambridge: Cambridge University Press.

Botha, Pieter J. J.
   1992   "Greco-Roman Literacy as Setting For New Testament Writings." *Neot* 26:195-215.

Brandon, S. G. F.
   1967   *Jesus and the Zealots: A Study of the Political Factor in Primitive Christianity*. New York: Scribner's.

Burghardt, Walter J.
   1951   "The Catholic Concept of Tradition." *Proceedings of the Sixth Annual Convention of the Catholic Theological Society of America* 6:42-76.

Cartlidge, David R.
   1990   "Combien d'unités avez-vous de trois à quatre ?: What Do We Mean by Intertextuality in Early Church Studies?" Pp. 400-411 in *SBL Seminar Papers*. Atlanta: Scholars.

Chilton, Bruce D.
   1984   *A Galilean Rabbi and His Bible: Jesus' Use of the Interpreted Scripture of His Time*. Wilmington: Glazier.

Collins, Adela Yarbro
   1988   "Narrative, History, and Gospel." *Semeia* 43: 145-53.

Coward, Harold
   1988   *Sacred Word and Sacred Text: Scripture in World Religions*. Maryknoll: Orbis.

Crossan, John Dominic
   1983   *In Fragments: The Aphorisms of Jesus*. San Francisco: Harper & Row.
   1985   *Four Other Gospels: Shadows on the Contours of Canon*. Minneapolis: Seabury/Winston.
   1988   *The Cross That Spoke: The Origins of the Passion Narrative*. San Francisco: Harper & Row.
   1991   *The Historical Jesus: The Life of a Mediterranean Jewish Peasant*. San Francisco: Harper San Francisco.
   1994   *Jesus: A Revolutionary Biography*. San Francisco: Harper San Francisco.

Dunn, James D. G.
   1984   "Testing the Foundations: Current Trends in New Testament Studies." An Inaugural Lecture. University of Durham.

Falk, Harvey
   1985   *Jesus the Pharisee: A New Look at the Jewishness of Jesus*. New York: Paulist.

Foley, John Miles
1991   *Immanent Art: From Structure to Meaning in Traditional Oral Epic.* Bloomington and Indianapolis: Indiana University Press.

Fowler, Robert M.
1991   *Let The Reader Understand: Reader-Response Criticism and the Gospel of Mark.* Minneapolis: Fortress.

Goody, Jack
1977   *The Domestication of the Savage Mind.* Cambridge: Cambridge University Press.

Goody, Jack and Ian Watt
1968   "The Consequences of Literacy." Pp. 27-68 in *Literacy in Traditional Societies.* Ed. Jack Goody. Cambridge: Cambridge University Press.

Graff, H. J.
1987   *The Legacies of Literacy: Continuities and Contradictions in Western Culture and Society.* Bloomington: Indiana University Press.

Graham, William
1987   *Beyond the Written Word: Oral Aspects of Scripture in the History of Religion.* Cambridge: Cambridge University Press.

Gray, Bennison
1971   "Repetition in Oral Literature." *Journal of American Folklore* 84: 289-303.

Harris, William V.
1989   *Ancient Literacy.* Cambridge: Harvard University Press.

Havelock, Eric A.
1982   *The Literate Revolution in Greece and Its Cultural Consequences.* Princeton: Princeton University Press.

Horsley, Richard
1991   "Logoi Propheton? Reflections on the Genre of Q." Pp. 195-209 in *The Future of Early Christianity.* Ed. Birger A. Pearson. Minneapolis: Fortress.

Iser, Wolfgang
1978   *The Act of Reading: A Theory of Aesthetic Response.* Baltimore: Johns Hopkins University Press; German original: *Der Akt des Lesens,* 1976.

Kelber, Werner H.
1983   *The Oral and the Written Gospel: The Hermeneutics of Speaking and Writing in the Synoptic Tradition, Mark, Paul, and Q.* Philadelphia: Fortress.
1987   "Narrative as Interpretation and Interpretation of Narrative: Hermeneutical Reflections on the Gospels." *Semeia* 39:107-33.
1988   "Narrative and Disclosure: Mechanisms of Concealing, Revealing, and Reveiling." *Semeia* 43:1-20.
1989   "Sayings Collection and Sayings Gospel: A Study in the Clustering Management of Knowledge." *Language & Communication* 9: 213-24.
1992   "Die Anfangsprozesse der Verschriftlichung im Frühchristentum." Pp. 3-62 in *ANRW*, Part II, Vol. 26, 1. Ed. Wolfgang Haase and Hildegard Temporini. Berlin/New York: de Gruyter.

Kloppenborg, John S.
1987   *The Formation of Q: Trajectories in Ancient Wisdom Collections.* Studies in Antiquity & Christianity. Philadelphia: Fortress.
1990   "City and Wasteland: Narrative World and the Beginning of the Sayings Gospel (Q)." *Semeia* 52:145-60.

Koester, Helmut
1971a   "One Jesus and Four Primitive Gospels." Pp. 158-204 in *Trajectories through Early Christianity*. Philadelphia: Fortress.
1971b   "The Historical Jesus: Some Comments and Thoughts on Norman Perrin's *Rediscovering the Teaching of Jesus.*" Pp. 123-36 in *Christology and A Modern Pilgrimage: A Discussion with Norman Perrin.* Ed. Hans D. Betz. Claremont: New Testament Colloquium.
1990   *Ancient Christian Gospels: Their History and Development.* Philadelphia: Trinity, and London: SCM.

Lord, Albert Bates
1960   *The Singer of Tales.* Harvard Studies in Comparative Literature 24. Cambridge: Harvard University Press; rpt. New York: Atheneum, 1968.
1978   "The Gospels as Oral Traditional Literature." Pp. 33-91 in *The Relationships Among the Gospels: An Interdisciplinary Dialogue.* Ed. William O. Walker, Jr. San Antonio: Trinity University Press.

Mack, Burton L.
1993   *The Lost Gospel. The Book of Q & Christian Origins.* San Francisco: Harper.

Marrou, Henri-Irénée
1956   *A History of Education in Antiquity.* Trans. George Lamb. New York: Sheed and Ward.

Meier, John P.
1991   *A Marginal Jew: Rethinking the Historical Jesus.* New York: Doubleday.

Ong, Walter J.
1958   *Ramus, Method and the Decay of Dialogue.* Cambridge: Harvard University Press.
1967a   *In the Human Grain: Technological Culture and its Effect on Man, Literature and Religion.* New York: Macmillan.
1967b   *The Presence of the Word: Some Prolegomena for Cultural and Religious History.* New Haven and London: Yale University. Paperback ed., University of Minnesota Press, 1981.
1982   *Orality and Literacy: The Technologizing of the Word.* London and New York: Methuen.

Peabody, Berkeley
1975   *The Winged Word: A Study in the Technique of Ancient Greek Oral Composition as Seen Principally through Hesiod's Works and Days.* Albany: University of New York Press.

Reimarus, Hermann Samuel
1956   "Von dem Zwecke Jesu und seiner Jünger." Pp. 254-376 in *Gotthold Ephraim Lessing, Gesammelte Werke*, 8. Berlin: Aufbau. Eng. trans. Ralph S.

Fraser, pp. 59-269 in *Reimarus: Fragments*. Ed. Charles H. Talbert. Philadelphia: Fortress, 1970.

Robinson, James M.
1970   "On the *Gattung* of Mark (and John)." Pp. 99-129 in *Jesus and Man's Hope*, Vol. I. Ed. Dikran Y. Hadidian. Pittsburgh: Pittsburgh Theological Seminary. Reprinted: pp. 11-39 in *The Problem of History in Mark and Other Marcan Studies*. Philadelphia: Fortress, 1982.
1982   "Gnosticism and the New Testament." Pp. 40-53 in *The Problem of History in Mark and other Marcan Studies*. Philadelphia: Fortress.
1986   "On Bridging the Gulf from Q to the Gospel of Thomas (or vice versa)." Pp. 127-75 in *Nag Hammmadi, Gnosticism & Early Christianity*. Ed. Charles W. Hedrick and Robert Hodgson, Jr. Peabody: Hendrickson.

Saenger, Paul
1982   "Silent Reading: Its Impact on Late Medieval Script and Society." *Viator* 13:367-414.

Sanders, E. P.
1985   *Jesus and Judaism*. Philadelphia: Fortress.

Schweitzer, Albert
1968   *The Quest of the Historical Jesus: A Critical Study of its Progress from Reimarus to Wrede*. New York: Macmillan. First German ed., 1906; second ed., enlarged, *Geschichte der Leben-Jesu Forschung*. Tübingen: Mohr (Siebeck), 1913.

Smith, Morton
1978   *Jesus the Magician*. San Francisco: Harper & Row.

Stock, Brian
1983   *The Implications of Literacy: Written Language and Models of Interpretation in the Eleventh and Twelfth Centuries*. Princeton: Princeton University Press.
1990   *Listening for the Text: On the Uses of the Past*. Baltimore and London: Johns Hopkins University Press.

Tödt, Heinz Eduard
1965   *The Son of Man in the Synoptic Tradition*. Trans. Dorothea M. Barton. Philadelphia: Westminster.

Van Beeck, Frans Jozef
1994   "The Quest of the Historical Jesus: Origins, Achievements, and the Specter of Diminishing Returns." Pp. 83-99 in *Jesus and Faith: A Conversation on the Work of John Dominic Crossan*. Ed. Jeffrey Carlson and Robert A. Ludwig. Maryknoll: Orbis Books.

Vermes, Geza
1981   *Jesus the Jew*. Rev. ed. Philadelphia: Fortress.

Williams, James G.
1988   "Parable and Chreia: From Q to Narrative Gospel." *Semeia* 43:85-114.

WORDS IN TRADITION, WORDS IN TEXT: A RESPONSE

John Miles Foley
University of Missouri—Columbia

In "Jesus and Tradition: Words in Time, Words in Space," Werner Kelber advocates an increased complexity in our concept of oral tradition as applied to the origins, history, and phenomenological reality of the Gospel texts. In calling for a more articulated model for the reception we call interpretation, Kelber is very much in step with the evolution of comparative studies in oral tradition;[1] in fact, in more than one way he is pushing theory well beyond the "cutting edge" in other fields. As with *The Oral and the Written Gospel* (1983) and numerous of his other writings (esp. 1987, 1990), Kelber's remarks force the scholar of oral traditions to elaborate further and even to rethink certain ideas and positions. In this brief response I would like to underline a few of his more telling observations and perhaps provide a comparative context for some of his newer, more revolutionary suggestions.

First, Kelber's recognition that Orality versus Literacy, or Speech versus Writing, constitutes a mastertrope with both brute explicative potential and endemically limited articulative force amounts to a healthy acknowledgment that the so-called Great Divide model of media has outlived its usefulness. He very sensibly and perceptively argues that such a powerful thesis was needed to break ground, to fracture the well-established sinecure of textual-chirographic thinking that reflexively dominated earlier scholarship. But he also indicates, with equal justification, that the initial spade-work has been completed, and it is now time to strive for greater complication and verisimilitude in our characterization of oral traditions and texts with roots in oral tradition.

I shall have more to say on this salient point in a moment when tackling the question of the persistence of oral traditional structures in a written text, but for the present let it simply be observed that studies in a wide variety of language areas—particularly ancient and Byzantine Greek, South Slavic, the medieval vernaculars, and Native American[2]—

---

[1] Cf. the plurality of oral traditions reported in Finnegan (1970, 1977), Foley (1985), and the journal *Oral Tradition*. On the distinctions that must be made on the basis of various traditions (linguistic and stylistic qualities), genres, and performances or documents, see Foley (1990:1-19 and passim).

[2] E.g. on ancient Greek, Edwards (1986, 1988, 1992); on Byzantine Greek, Jeffreys

have echoed this point of view in demonstrating a wide spectrum of oral traditional forms. Even the late Albert Lord, pioneer of the Oral-Formulaic Theory, insisted on a variety of "mergings" of oral tradition and literacy in a pair of articles published in 1986.[3] At this juncture the time seems ripe for a "second growth" in studies in oral tradition, an evolution that will reinstate the textual survivors—as well as those expressive forms that have never been textualized—in the heterogeneity of their original social contexts.

Especially crucial for the comparative field of investigation that I represent are Kelber's radical reflections on that elusive creature "tradition."[4] Lord had pointed out in 1960, in his landmark *The Singer of Tales*, that "after all that has been said about *oral* composition as a technique of line and song construction, it seems that the term of greater significance is *traditional*. Oral tells us 'how,' but traditional tells us 'what,' and even more, 'of what kind' and 'of what force'" (220). Very few have followed out this distinction, however, and the idea of oral tradition has been collapsed in most areas to the simple construct of "orality."[5] But, although this term in the equation may seem to contrast more dramatically with the written or literary model whose hegemony the mastertrope was intended to break, in fact the nearly exclusive recourse to "orality" and its similarly oversimplified cohort "literacy"[6] has denatured Parry's and Lord's original concept of a living, ongoing process. Subtract "tradition" and you are forced to deal with *all* spoken discourse, texted or textless, as an undifferentiated mass of varia. Orality alone is a "distinction" badly in need of deconstruction, a typology that unfairly homogeneizes much more than it can hope to distinguish; it is by itself a false and very misleading category.

---

and Jeffreys; on South Slavic (and medieval Spanish), Miletich; on Old English (in a comparative context), Foley (1990, 1991); on Native American, Swann and Krupat, as well as Toelken (1969, 1987), Toelken and Scott.

[3] For a history of the Oral-Formulaic (or Parry-Lord) Theory, see Foley (1988); for bibliography, Foley (1985), with updates in *Oral Tradition*.

[4] See Ben-Amos on the various connotations of this term; see also Hobsbawm and Ranger on "the invention of tradition."

[5] Note that Parry himself began this movement when he charted a course that led from the discovery of *tradition* in Homer (his 1928 French theses) to what he considered a necessarily consequent *orality* (the 1930 and 1932 articles in *Harvard Studies in Classical Philology*); for all of these writings, see Parry (1971). Once the leap from tradition to orality was made, however, "unwrittenness" caught the imagination of many subsequent scholars to such a degree that it supervened the more fundamental quality of tradition and led to such pursuits as mathematically analyzing a text for (written) formulaic evidence of orality (e.g. Magoun for Old English, Duggan for Old French).

[6] On the problematization of the concept of "literacy," see esp. Boyarin; O'Keeffe; Doane; Foley (1995: ch. 3).

For this very reason Kelber's brilliant metaphor of the "biosphere" for *tradition* is particularly welcome. By this metaphor he designates "a collective cultural memory, comprised of discourse and chirographs, and shared by speakers and hearers alike." Within this biosphere, in other words, no event—no matter how singular it may appear at the time—ever really occurs out of context; each work of verbal art is nourished by an ever-impinging set of unspoken but implicitly articulated assumptions shared among the discourse community. To remove the event from the biosphere of tradition is therefore to sap its cognitive lifeblood, to deprive it of very obvious potential for conveying meaning, to silence the echoes that reverberate through it (and its fellow performances or works) under the aegis of its immanent context.[7] It is not difficult to see how such interpretive malfeasance could—in fact must—result in misunderstandings and misreadings traceable directly to the act of denaturing the communicative act. If a work is handicapped by stripping away the traditional context on which it depends for a great deal of its meaning, by forcing it to exist outside its naturally sustaining biosphere, then by definition its reception will also be denatured. In Receptionalist terminology, the necessary indeterminacy that is part of any work of art will be increased beyond an acceptable level, and the reader's or audience's construal of the work will be founded on too meager—and too superficial—a skeleton of signals.[8]

Are originative oral traditions still important to oral-derived and traditional works that survive only in written form? Any worthwhile answer to this troublesome question should be undertaken in concert with what Kelber suggests about the complexity of the model—in particular, the inadequacy of the linear or stratigraphic model. In respect to texts that emerge from oral traditions and that draw structurally from the oral traditional idiom,[9] it will be a mistake to suppose that the curtain falls with the advent of literacy and texts, that the performative meaning of the idiom is immediately and irreversibly rendered textually tacit. What will be required for perception of the idiom's special connotations is, of course, an informed *audience* alive to their illocutionary force, that is,

---

[7] I have taken up this nourishing, associative aspect of tradition at some length in *Immanent Art* (1991), with particular reference to the ancient Greek, medieval English, and modern South Slavic traditions.

[8] For a Receptionalist view of oral tradition, see Foley, 1991:38-60. Cf. Renoir's related notion of "oral-formulaic context" for medieval Germanic poetry.

[9] I prefer to construe this dynamic as the *rhetorical persistence of traditional forms* (see esp. Foley 1992; 1995: ch. 3). Whatever the particular shape or nature of the traditional inheritance, which of course will vary from one tradition and one genre to the next, certain signals can and do persist in the textual medium, issuing to the reader the kind of hermeneutical challenge described by Kelber.

readers or auditors who can invest the entexted utterance with its due heritage of performative meaning. Without that experience and ability no reader or auditor can construe the map of textual signals in traditional context. We may further observe that once such an audience has been "written out of existence" by decades of exclusively textual discourse, there is no possibility of simply reintroducing the original resonance of the work. From that point on it is left to scholars to reestablish analytically—and, it must be admitted, artificially—what we can of the lost context of oral tradition. Such a latter-day salvage operation can never simulate the receptive capabilities of the audience for whom the work emerged in context as a fact of social life, but that obvious and inescapable problem does not excuse us from doing what we can in this regard; any movement toward more faithful reception will be a finite improvement.[10]

The widespread phenomenon of texts with oral traditional roots offers one illustration of the thesis that the blanket concept of "orality" subverts more than it distinguishes: exclusive focus on the false typology of orality versus literacy will disenfranchise those works that, while surviving only in writing, still depend fundamentally on a pre-textual traditional dynamics and, as I have argued, on a traditional idiom that to an extent persists in the textual arena.

Since I join Kelber in advocating a realistic complexity in the discussion, let me add a related consideration to help chart more carefully the topography we have too long treated as a Great Divide. This would be the sociolinguistic category of "registers," as employed for example by the anthopologist Dell Hymes, who defines them as follows: "major speech styles associated with social groups can be termed *variants*, and major speech styles associated with recurrent types of situations can be termed *registers*" (1989:400; see also Foley 1992, 1995). What the concept of register offers is a way of characterizing the specialized idiom dedicated to a particular kind of speech-act, with the understanding that every individual within a given society controls numerous registers of discourse, each of which he or she deploys according to the social context and each of which carries with it a more or less dedicated set of associations that are invoked merely by its appropriate usage or performance. I would argue that the persistence of the oral traditional idiom in texts—for example, in medieval vernacular poetry—is one striking case of the integrity of a register withstanding what we might imagine its immediate death-blow, the advent of writing and texts. Of course, no register will survive intact indefinitely under such conditions,

---

[10] On the limited but still appreciable progress that can be made in the reception of ancient Greek and medieval English traditional documents, see Foley (1991:135-242, and 1995:chs. 5-6).

and, while there are myriad (heretofore troubling) instances of narrowly focused oral traditional registers long outliving the inscription of other registers, still there comes a time when literate noetics, in Walter Ong's sense (1982:31-77), becomes so general as to sentence most traditional genres to a predominantly textual incarceration.[11]

Here, then, lies the challenge of how to respond to Kelber's hermeneutic of "words in time, words in space," which I would translate to "words in tradition, words in text," and the yet greater challenge of how to reconcile our increasingly complex grasp of oral traditions and texts with the facts of the New Testament situation. The first and most fundamental problem in this regard is the nature of the presynoptic tradition itself. As Kelber reminds us, our knowledge of that tradition is in a very uncertain (though not at all hopeless) state. To an outsider like myself, the forbidding mélange of extant, reported, and hypothesized texts and collections—the synoptic gospels themselves, the Gospel of Thomas, Q, the sayings gospel (genre), and the Nag Hammadi remains—begs but does not answer the question of what tradition lies behind or beneath or alongside the four canonical texts. To have a sense of the ecology of the biosphere, I need from my colleagues in biblical studies some clearer idea of the flora and fauna that constitute it. *Traditions* earn their identity by being continuous over time, at least to some degree; and their special ability to convey extratextual meaning economically and metonymically depends in no small measure on their ongoingness. What expressive forms were there or might there have been in the early Christian and Jewish communities where the gospel texts were written? Can we assemble an ethnography of speaking for these communities,[12] some overall notion of the contemporary repertoire of dominant idioms or discourses? If we are to move beyond the mastertrope of orality/literacy as an oversimplified first approximation, we need to know more about the stuff of tradition.

What follows, then, is a response to Kelber's forward-looking remarks not from the microscopic analytic perspective of the biblical scholar, a vantage point well beyond my reach, but rather from the macroscopic, interdisciplinary viewpoint of comparative studies in oral tradition.

In the oral traditions with which I am familiar—the ancient Greek, Anglo-Saxon, and South Slavic narrative and lyric poetries—the idiom of

---

[11] There are of course numerous exceptions: the international ballad tradition, which has existed in oral and written form for centuries, is a salient one; see e.g. Harris; McCarthy.

[12] On the approach through the ethnography of speaking, see esp. Bauman 1977; Bauman and Sherzer. Foley (1995) attempts to dovetail this approach with the Oral-Formulaic Theory, particularly as extended to Immanent Art (see also Foley 1991, 1992).

presentation adumbrates special instructions for decoding the linguistic integers it contains. This is true of oral traditions whose actual performance can be directly experienced (so that paralinguistic and nonlinguistic cues can also be weighed and interpreted) and of works with roots in oral tradition, where certain features persist from performance into textual rhetoric.[13] Classicists who have worried overmuch about the literal (textual) meaning of phraseology in such works, for example, have not seldom been forced into either impossibly clever explications of apparently nonsensical lines or into the no longer popular judgment that "Homer nodded." What such literalists or textualists have missed, and what the Parry-Lord Oral Theory in its nascent form also missed, is the possibility that these nominal linguistic integers deferred primarily to extratextual signifieds, that through metonymic reference to the biosphere of tradition, they institutionally implied or indexed much more than their denotative values. Such value-added meaning contributes to what I have elsewhere called a work's "immanent art," with the concrete spoken or written part standing *pars pro toto* for the unutterable or uninscribable implied whole (see Tyler). For this reason, I have argued, the South Slavic epic singer or *guslar* feels no contradiction in referring formulaically to his beloved hero Marko's birthplace as *kleti Markovac*, "damned Markovac"; when queried about what for us seems a contradiction, he simply replied that "it has to be said like that" (Foley 1991:244-46). Many moments in Homer illustrate the same principle, none more clearly than the *pykinon epos* (intimate word) that so economically marks "a message or communication of great importance, one that if properly delivered and received would change the present course of events profoundly" (Foley 1991:155); it is the full traditional, immanent force of this phrase that Andromache feels in Book 24 as she mourns the permanent loss of the possibility of exchanging a last *pykinon epos* with Hektor.

In this brief response I cannot pause to illustrate the importance of immanent meaning at the narrative levels of typical scene and story-pattern (see Foley 1991:61-189). Suffice it to say that both the scene-to-scene texture and the tale-type as a whole have crucial connotative

---

[13] As Hymes puts it, "especially in an oral tradition performance is a mode of existence and realization that is partly *constitutive* of what the tradition is" (1981:86). Bauman similarly observes that "performance represents a transformation of the basic referential . . . uses of language. In other words, in artistic performance of this kind, there is something going on in the communicative interchange which says to the auditor 'interpret what I say in some special sense; do not take it to mean what the words alone, taken literally, would convey'" (1977:9). As will be suggested below, the "keying" of performance can be accomplished rhetorically in a textual medium; there will of course be differences, but the pre-textual and textual do not in and of themselves constitute a Great Divide.

contributions to make to the negotiation of meaning. The oral traditional register provides ready, indeed institutionalized, reference to the world of tradition that both dwarfs and gives life to each instance of formulaic phrase, typical scene, and story-pattern. To summarize the specialized import of the oral traditional register, I would borrow an interpretive proverb from my forthcoming book: "performance is the enabling event, tradition the enabling referent" (1995).

Let us now apply these observations to the subject at hand. If the presynoptic tradition, or traditions, were wholly continuous with the received texts of the canonical Gospels, then I would expect each gospel— and each traditional unit within each gospel—to reflect the wholeness of the life of Jesus by synecdoche. That is, the four evangelists' documents, written though they be, would to a degree still necessarily draw their meaning from the biosphere within which they were conceived, to which they continued to defer, and without which they would constitute at best partial visions of a lost wholeness. Given the paucity of surviving records and our great temporal and cultural distance from that biosphere, we might or might not be able to recover the metonymic implications of this or that passage, but it would be incumbent upon us at least to try to fill out the interpretive map by recourse to extratextual or extrasituational resources.

As I understand the probable history of the process, however, the written narratives of the synoptic Gospels are, *from the point of view of linguistic register*, discontinuous in major ways with the precedent tradition(s). While the Gospels may refer to the same "content," the idiom through which that content is conveyed differs significantly from what went before. From the perspective of the outsider and comparatist, it is this disparity in sociolinguistically defined registers—and therefore in the endemic metonymic properties of the sign vehicles—that certifies Kelber's assertion that the writing of the gospel narrative engages tradition selectively, not comprehensively. It is, in short, not the canonical Gospels' mere writtenness but rather their modulation in linguistic register and therefore in capacity for generating meaning that creates distance from the implied tradition and causes the synoptic Gospels to resonate on their own terms, *both* textually *and* traditionally. The rules of the composition/ reception game have changed because the signifying idiom that supports that game has changed.

And yet they have not changed completely. A realistically complex perspective is achieved, as Kelber argues, only when we "hear the [Markan] narrative not as an insurance against forgetfulness, but as a hermeneutically charged transaction." The same may be said, to varying degrees and in various ways, for virtually any work that derives in some way from oral tradition: whether we are speaking of Homer's primordial poetry or modern African novels,[14] communication proceeds via the nourishing biosphere of traditional implication, without which the significative landscape may seem sterile or even nonsensical. And yet textuality is a contributor as well—once again, as Kelber stresses, according to the dialectic of discourse in force in that time and place for that expressive act.

As a way to visualize the complications involved, Kelber adopts the "textual community" model invented by Brian Stock (1983, 1990) to elaborate the complexity of the diglossic later Middle Ages. This model has a number of strengths: it provides a realistic and suitably articulated account of the ongoing encounter among individuals, oral traditions, texts, and communities, and it places discourse where it belongs in social context (rather than isolating it—textually—in a rite of supposed purification). With reference to immanent meaning and performance, the physics of communication in the medieval situation depended not only on the literate individual who crafted the community text but also on the sealed-off interpretive community that could reify ideas and crystallize a unique expression of those ideas apart from the multiformity of the otherwise ever-impinging tradition. When the audience and individual, who in an ongoing oral tradition are united in the event of performance by institutionalized reference to the untextualizable tradition, come to respond to the objectified and explicit rather than the unobjectifiable and implicit, then the text can and does become central to the community hermeneutic. Let me leave the judgment to those more qualified than I, but this situation sounds like a promising parallel to the context within which the gospel texts arose and flourished.

To recapitulate, then, Werner Kelber's "Jesus and Tradition: Words in Time, Words in Space" has much to offer the "interpretive community" of studies in oral tradition. In addition to deconstructing the mastertrope of orality versus literacy, historically a first approximation that has brought us this far but which we must now discard, he advocates a fresh assessment of the media of oral tradition, writing, and print as full and interactive partners in communicative dynamics. In his concern with understanding such media as more than inert containers of data (see also Bakker), and again in his critique of simplistic notions of "tradition," Kelber's remarks dovetail with current theoretical proposals in oral tradition and folklore, most notably in Ethnopoetics, the Ethnography of Speaking, and Immanent Art (Foley 1992, 1995; Bauman 1977; Hymes

---

[14] Cf. esp. Obiechina's concept of embedded oral stories as "narrative proverbs" that provide a traditional context for (nontraditional) moments and figures in African novels.

1981; Tedlock). Finally, I have tried to mesh Kelber's vision of text and tradition with certain insights on metonymic referentiality, sociolinguistic register, and the shift of audience reception necessarily entailed in a radical shift of idiom. In this last respect I have suggested, on the basis of comparative evidence, that it may not have been the mere writing of the synoptic Gospels, but rather the apparent fact of their being written in a disparate register that foreordained the eventual and permanent apotheosis of the synoptic texts.

WORKS CONSULTED

Bakker, Egbert
 1993 "Activation and Preservation: The Interdependence of Text and Performance in an Oral Tradition." *Oral Tradition* 8:5-20.

Bauman, Richard
 1977 *Verbal Art as Performance.* Rpt. Prospect Heights, IL: Waveland Press, 1984.
 1986 *Story, Performance, and Event: Contextual Studies of Oral Narrative.* Cambridge: Cambridge University Press.

Bauman, Richard and Joel Sherzer, eds.
 1989 *Explorations in the Ethnography of Speaking.* 2nd ed. Cambridge: Cambridge University Press.

Ben-Amos, Dan
 1984 "The Seven Strands of *Tradition*: Varieties in Its Meaning in American Folklore Studies." *Journal of Folklore Research* 21:97-131.

Boyarin, Jonathan, ed.
 1993 *The Ethnography of Reading.* Berkeley: University of California Press.

Doane, A. N.
 1991 "Oral Texts, Intertexts, and Intratexts: Editing Old English." Pp. 75-113 in *Influence and Intertextuality in Literary History.* Ed. Jay Clayton and Eric Rothstein. Madison: University of Wisconsin Press.

Duggan, Joseph J.
 1973 *The Song of Roland: Formulaic Style and Poetic Craft.* Berkeley: University of California Press.

Edwards, Mark W.
 1986 "Homer and Oral Tradition: The Formula, Part I." *Oral Tradition* 1:171-230.
 1988 "Homer and Oral Tradition: The Formula, Part II." *Oral Tradition* 3:11-60.
 1992 "Homer and Oral Tradition: The Type-Scene." *Oral Tradition* 7:284-330.

Finnegan, Ruth
    1970   *Oral Literature in Africa*. Oxford: Clarendon.
    1977   *Oral Poetry: Its Nature, Significance, and Social Context*. Cambridge: Cambridge University Press.

Foley, John Miles
    1985   *Oral-Formulaic Theory and Research*. New York: Garland.
    1988   *The Theory of Oral Composition: History and Methodology*. Bloomington: Indiana University Press. Rpt. 1992.
    1990   *Traditional Oral Epic: The Odyssey, Beowulf, and the Serbo-Croatian Return Song*. Berkeley: University of California Press. Rpt. 1993.
    1991   *Immanent Art: From Structure to Meaning in Traditional Oral Epic*. Bloomington: Indiana University Press.
    1992   "Word-Power, Performance, and Tradition." *Journal of American Folklore* 105:275-301.
    1995   *The Singer of Tales in Performance*. Bloomington: Indiana University Press.

Harris, Joseph, ed.
    1991   *The Ballad and Oral Tradition*. Cambridge: Harvard University Press.

Hobsbawm, Eric and Terence Ranger, eds.
    1983   *The Invention of Tradition*. Cambridge: Cambridge University Press.

Hymes, Dell
    1981   *'In Vain I Tried to Tell You': Essays in Native American Ethnopoetics*. Philadelphia: University of Pennsylvania Press.
    1989   "Ways of Speaking." Pp. 433-51, 473-74 in Bauman and Sherzer.

Jeffreys, Elizabeth M. and Michael J. Jeffreys
    1983   *Popular Literature in Late Byzantium*. London: Variorum.

Kelber, Werner H.
    1983   *The Oral and the Written Gospel: The Hermeneutics of Speaking and Writing in the Synoptic Tradition, Mark, Paul, and Q*. Philadelphia: Fortress. Rpt. Bloomington: Indiana University Press, 1995.
    1987   "The Authority of the Word in St. John's Gospel: Charismatic Speech, Narrative Text, Logocentric Metaphysics." *Oral Tradition* 2:108-31.
    1990   "In the Beginning Were the Words: The Apotheosis and Narrative Displacement of the Logos." *JAAR* 58:501-30.

Lord, Albert B.
    1960   *The Singer of Tales*. Cambridge: Harvard University Press. Rpt. New York: Atheneum, 1968 et seq.
    1986a   "Perspectives on Recent Work on the Oral Traditional Formula." *Oral Tradition* 1:467-503.
    1986b   "The Merging of Two Worlds: Oral and Written Poetry as Carriers of Ancient Values." Pp. 19-64 in *Oral Tradition in Literature: Interpretation in Context*. Ed. John Miles Foley. Columbia: University of Missouri Press.

Magoun, Francis P., Jr.
    1953   "The Oral-Formulaic Character of Anglo-Saxon Narrative Poetry." *Speculum* 28:446-67.

McCarthy, William B.
1990 *The Ballad Matrix: Personality, Milieu, and the Oral Tradition*. Bloomington: Indiana University Press.

Miletich, John S.
1981 "Oral Literature and 'Pučka književnost': Toward a Generic Description of Medieval Spanish and Other Narrative Traditions." Pp. 155-66 in *Folklore and Oral Communication*. Ed. Maja Bošković-Stulli (a special issue of *Narodna umjetnost*).

Obiechina, Emmanuel
1992 "Narrative Proverbs in the African Novel." *Oral Tradition* 7:197-230.

O'Keeffe, Katherine O'Brien
1990 *Visible Song: Transitional Literacy in Old English Verse*. Cambridge: Cambridge University Press.

Ong, Walter J.
1982 *Orality and Literacy: The Technologizing of the Word*. London: Methuen.

Parry, Milman
1971 *The Making of Homeric Verse: The Collected Papers of Milman Parry*. Oxford: Clarendon.

Renoir, Alain
1988 *A Key to Old Poems: The Oral-Formulaic Approach to the Interpretation of West-Germanic Verse*. University Park: Pennsylvania State University Press.

Stock, Brian
1983 *The Implications of Literacy: Written Language and Models of Interpretation in the Eleventh and Twelfth Centuries*. Princeton: Princeton University Press.
1990 *Listening for the Text: On the Uses of the Past*. Baltimore: Johns Hopkins University Press.

Swann, Brian and Arnold Krupat, eds.
1987 *Recovering the Word: Essays on Native American Literature*. Berkeley: University of California Press.

Tedlock, Dennis
1983 *The Spoken Word and the Work of Interpretation*. Philadelphia: University of Pennsylvania Press.

Toelken, J. Barre
1969 "The 'Pretty Language' of Yellowman: Genre, Mode, and Texture in Navaho Coyote Performances." *Genre* 2:211-35.
1987 "Life and Death in the Navaho Coyote Tales." Pp. 388-401 in *Recovering the Word: Essays on Native American Literature*. Ed. Brian Swann and Arnold Krupat. Berkeley: University of California Press.

Toelken, J. Barre and Tacheeni Scott
1981 "Poetic Retranslation and the 'Pretty Languages' of Yellowman." Pp. 65-116 in *Traditional Literatures of the American Indian: Texts and Interpretations*. Ed. Karl Kroeber. Lincoln: University of Nebraska Press.

Tyler, Stephen A.
   1987   *The Unspeakable: Discourse, Dialogue, and Rhetoric in the Postmodern World.* Madison: University of Wisconsin Press.

BLOWING IN THE WIND: A RESPONSE

Bernard Brandon Scott
Phillips Graduate Seminary

When Paul healed the cripple at Lystra, the people cried out, "The gods have come down to us in the likeness of men!" They identified Barnabas with Zeus and Paul—because he was the spokesperson—with Hermes. The Lycaonians correctly identified as religious the type of event they had witnessed, but in Paul's judgment they applied the wrong model. Even after he had explained the affair to them, he could barely restrain the people from continuing their sacrifice (Acts 14:1-18). Perhaps this story from Acts can furnish an icon for the problem confronting Werner Kelber in his essay "Jesus and Tradition: Words in Time, Words in Space." The habits of tradition are hard to abandon without conclusive evidence that they are inadequate.

Kelber begins his "Conclusion" by stating his purpose, "to raise consciousness about the post-Enlightenment parentage of the modern discipline of biblical scholarship." To raise consciousness requires creating cognitive dissonance, since people do not shift from one paradigm to another without a revolution. Kelber seeks to restore to New Testament scholarship a sense of the importance of tradition, which he metaphorically terms a biosphere, while he attempts to replace the tradition in which the modern scholar operates. It is not enough to offer alternative explanations. As Kuhn has argued about scientific revolutions, the new paradigm must explain anomalies that the old paradigm cannot explain or perhaps even perceive.

Kelber explicitly attacks two of the most powerful traditions of modern science: typography (or, as I would prefer, the printing press) and the idea of evolutionary development. The two, of course, are interrelated, and the first is a condition for the second. These are powerful intellectual traditions in which we live. Charles Darwin, the father of evolutionary biology, bequeathed the idea of evolutionary development as part of his unintentional legacy. The model of historical development borrows by analogy from the model of biological evolution. This idea has proven so fecund that biblical criticism regularly employs the model of archaeology, using historical tools to expose the strata of both the text and early Christianity. So arranged, the evolutionary model identifies the earliest layers as "primitive" or "original," and later levels as "developed" or "secondary." Ironically, evolution's early conflict with religion makes it a powerful alternative explanation of religious realities. Thus the use of an evolutionary model to understand religion certifies the hermeneutics as "modern," because Darwin's revolution is at the core of what it means to be a modern scientific person.

Yet there is a scientific alternative to Darwin. At the turn of the century Ferdinand de Saussure began a quieter revolution, a revolution that has now triumphed in the intellectual world. Saussure rejected the explanatory power of the diachronic to explain the particular, and instituted the science of the synchronic, which examines the particular as part of a system. For Saussure we understand the particular not by knowing where it comes from, but by knowing how it functions within its current context. Kelber does not name an alternative to the evolutionary model, but what he proposes is a synchronic method.

The printing press, the other tradition that Kelber questions, is an even more primary constituent of the consciousness that Kelber seeks to raise. The culture created by the printing press affects our way of proceeding, one might even say of our way of being-in-the-world. This is by far a more intractable issue than the evolutionary model, since in this case one cannot simply choose an alternative explanatory theory. Typographic culture is a true biosphere that goes to the heart of the way our consciousness as moderns is formed. Elizabeth Eisenstein's aphorism highlights the permeating effect of the printing press. "Learning to read is different from reading to learn" (Eisenstein: 1:65). For her this remark signals the primary difference between a chirograhic or manuscript culture and a print culture. Printing does not mark the difference so much as does the way reading changes in a print culture. In a manuscript culture, the production of the manuscript demands a major effort. It is estimated that "a manuscript of the New Testament represented a small fortune" (Aland and Aland: 77) . The richly illuminated manuscript, while beautiful to look at, is not easy to read. The iconography's real function is to key *memoria*. In a pre-print world, learning for the most part took place outside of or apart from reading, in apprenticeships or in the debates of the rabbis or the scholastics. In a print culture, learning takes place primarily in the act of reading, so that one is taught to read in order to be able to learn from reading books. In a manuscript culture, one reads (*lectio*) to refresh memory, the storehouse (*thesaurus*) of knowledge. This shift signals a move from the public to the private. Ancient texts functioned in a public, rhetorical forum, and were not self-existent realities, but part of a web of human voices. As Kelber says, "The linking *time-spaces* between texts are filled with dictation and recitation, acts of hearing and remembering, and a universe of vocal values, sensibilities, and actualities." But since silent reading makes the text an interior, private affair, it becomes an independent, individual, experience. Texts are self-existent, circumscribed realities that can be arranged into an evolutionary chain of development. They are no longer voices in an unending conversation linked together by memory.

The main problem with Kelber's proposal comes not at the level of theory but at the level of pragmatics. As he notes, "the tradition is available to us exclusively in texts." Once spoken, an oral performance goes out of existence. Its fleeting existence, its impermanence, pales before the blackness of a written text and threatens to turn to quicksand in the critic's hands. We much prefer textual methods because they provide us with something solid, a textual reality that fits with our own typographic world. For this reason, both literary criticism and the social sciences have made much progress because they do not challenge as directly the basic textual assumptions of scholarship.

Kelber uses as a touchstone John Dominic Crossan's The *Historical Jesus: The Life of a Mediterranean Jewish Peasant*. He does not say why he singles out Crossan's work, which is not the most obvious offender. Helmut Koester, for example, in his brilliant *Ancient Christian Gospels* never refers to the issue of orality and literacy. Even though Crossan's method is very interdisciplinary and open, it makes a good test case in that it is dominated by an evolutionary, typographic model. "The principal question it raises is whether Jesus, the oral performer, and the early tradition that delivered him unto writing, has played by our rules." The answer is clearly no, but I am not convinced that at the level of pragmatics Crossan is as guilty as Kelber has argued or that Kelber has a clearly worked-out alternative.

Kelber questions Crossan's privileging *"as a matter of methodological principle* the iterative and adaptive behavior of tradition as ground for historical authenticity" and his refusal to use sayings with only single attestation. Crossan privileges complexes that have both early and multiple attestation because he is seeking a sure foundation on which to build his reconstruction of the historical Jesus. He is not arguing that singular attestations do not derive from Jesus, only that he will not build his case upon them (Crossan: xxxiii). Crossan assumes that the early and multiple attestations indicate that the complex is authentic because it is both widespread and deep within the tradition. Crossan does not automatically accept all complexes that are early and widespread, but argues each case (243-47; see also Scott 1994: 26). In dealing with oral and memorial societies, such a privileging seems to me valid. As Ong argues, in an oral culture one must think memorable thoughts (Ong: 34). The more memorable a cluster, the more likely it will be performed repeatedly and the more variation will be encountered. Crossan deals with the variability in the cluster by means of an evolutionary model; he seeks to explain the variation by the varying circumstances of early Christianity.

Kelber's rejection of Crossan's methods is based on formal grounds, but Kelber seems to picture the first century as a purely oral culture. Vernon Robbins has more correctly characterized it as a rhetorical culture:

> Performing oral and scribal activity in this way creates a rhetorical culture—one in which speech is influenced by writing and writing is influenced by speaking. Recitation, then, is the base of a rhetorical culture. People know that certain traditions exist in writing. They also know that all traditions, whether oral or written, need to be composed anew to meet the needs of the day. Each day as they spoke, they were interacting with written traditions: whenever they wrote, they were interacting with oral traditions. This interaction characterized their thinking, their speaking, and their writing" (113).

In a rhetorical culture, even the speaker interacts with textuality. Thus, for example, while Jesus does not quote the scripture in his parables, he does refer to and reinterpret its symbols, as for example in the parables of the Leaven and the Mustard Seed (Scott 1989: 324-27; 384-86). Given this interaction between orality and textuality in a rhetorical culture and the textual interrelations and developments in early Christianity, Crossan's method is on the right track, although it needs a great deal of refinement.

Fundamentally, I believe that Kelber's understanding of orality makes the quest for the historical Jesus impossible. Kelber argues that Jesus' speech acts "left no externally visible residues." "A text outlasts the act of writing, but spoken words exist only in the act of speaking." Now Kelber draws his conclusion, "It is hard to escape the impression, therefore, that the words of the historical Jesus, if taken on their own terms, are not quantifiable in any form or division, if only because they are not available to us for purposes of retrieval and classification." Yet it seems to me that this is precisely where Kelber has overstated his argument. Memory does make available to us the Jesus *tradition*.

Perhaps I can best continue my conversation with Kelber by reflecting on the problems I faced in writing my own work on the parables of Jesus, *Hear Then the Parable*, rather than defending or explaining Crossan. When I began to work seriously at my volume on the parables I had reached conclusions very similar to those of Kelber, first under the influence of Walter Ong and then of Kelber's own work. I began with a very conscious effort to study the *oral* parables of Jesus and their various performances in the tradition. Initially this meant coming to terms with the dominant tradition as represented by Joachim Jeremias. Jeremias sought to reconstruct the *ipsissima verba* Jesu and the *Sitz im Leben* of the parable.

Since speech leaves no external *visible* residues, there can be no one original version. As a consequence, Kelber dismisses the effort to reconstruct the *ipsissima verba* and *ipsissima structura*. For Kelber, each performance constitutes "an original." He concludes, "A thrice rendered proclamation of a parable is not comprehensible in terms of one original and two variables thereof, but only as three equiprimordial renditions." I extended the argument to attack the second pole of Jeremias' method, *Sitz im Leben*. If there is no one single original, if we must imagine multiple performances of a parable, then there can be no single life situation that defines the meaning of the parable. Kelber's discussion of redundancy indicates that he would agree with this extension of the argument.

If there is no single original, external, visual artifact, and no single *Sitz im Leben*, what is there for the critic to examine? Can we not move behind the text, except to say that there once was a whisper? Kelber would seem now to answer that we cannot, a more radical position than he espoused in *The Oral and the Written Gospel*. He now argues that even if a critic were able to collect all written versions of a saying "and to trace a trajectory back to the core structure, [it would] give us something which never existed in oral, historical reality. Even if we managed to extract a pattern common to all existing versions, we would have succeeded merely in conjuring a structuralist stability which by oral standards is a fictional construct." This seeking after stability is precisely what Kelber sees as the deepest seduction of logic, "to conquer the flux of temporality and to prove time-obviating fixedness." I am reminded of Franz Kafka's "Imperial Message:"

> [A]nd if at last he should burst through the outermost gate—but never, never can that happen—the imperial capital would lie before him, the center of the world, crammed to bursting with its own sediment. Nobody could fight his way through here even with a message from a dead man (5).

One must admit with Kelber that there is no textual visual residue to orality and "structural stability does not get us to oral performance." In fact the oral performance is forever irretrievable. Yet the oral performance was not without effect, so that there is a residue in memory. What we possess in the corpus of Jesus' parables is the memory residue preserved in textual performances.

If this is the case, the interpreter faces a twofold methodological task: 1) an assessment of the textual performance; 2) an analysis of the memory residue as the result of an oral performance. In assessing a textual performance or performances of a parable I identified four elements to be considered:

1. *Shift to Textuality*. Every medium has its own ideology. One must be alert to the effects of scribalism on a parable. Here Jülicher made the

correct methodological step in his rejection of allegory, however flawed his interpretative strategy may have been. Allegory is an infallible guide to the presence of scribalism. The hierarchical, textual nature of chirography, as opposed to the concrete immediacy of orality, tends consistently toward the allegorical reading. An example from a rabbinic parable clearly illustrates the situation.

Parable

There was once a poor woman who dwelt in the neighborhood of a landowner. Her two sons went out to gather gleanings, but the landowner did not let them take any. Their mother kept saying, "When will my sons come back from the field; perhaps I shall find that they have brought something to eat." And they kept saying: "When shall we go back to our mother; perhaps we shall discover that she has found something to eat." She found that they had nothing and they found that she had nothing to eat. So they laid their heads on their mother's lap and the three of them died in one day.

Commentary

Said the Holy One, blessed be He: "Their very existence you take away from them! By your life! I shall make you, too, pay for it with your very existence!"

And so indeed it says, Rob not the weak, because he is weak, neither crush the poor in the gate; for the Lord will plead their cause, and despoil of life those that despoil them (Prov 22:22-3). (*The Fathers according to Rabbi Nathan*: 158)

In the parable itself a peasant voice protests against the abuses of the wealthy. It registers a strong protest against life's inequality. Perhaps the voice is female, that of a mother appealing to the compassion of other mothers. The tale's tragic plot is driven by the landowner's failure to allow for gleanings contra Leviticus: "And when you reap the harvest of your land, you shall not reap your field to its very border, nor shall you gather the gleanings after your harvest; you shall leave them for the poor and for the stranger: I am the LORD your God" (Lev 23:22; see also 19:9). The parable achieves its effect implicitly. It depends on the situation's innate tragedy and the hearer's pathos for mother and sons. Its condemnation is likewise implicit; it never refers to the landowner's failure to follow Torah's demands. In Robbins's terms, it is an oral phenomenon interacting with a textual one, but in an oral fashion.

When the story was written down, the epistemology changed and scribes began to comment on the story. First, the voice shifted, "*you* take away from them." The scribe who added this comment assumed that the reader/hearer and the landowner shared the same social position and so the tale became a warning for the social elite. Scribe, landowner, and reader belong to a social elite. At the same time God entered, threatening future judgment. Unlike the parable, which employed protest, sympathy, and solidarity, an elite accustomed to power assumes that some Power will set things aright. So the scribe invoked the apocalyptic myth. When chaos threatens to overwhelm order, God will respond. The solution is in the future; the solution is power. Finally, that scribe or another made a second addition to the tale, offering a proof from scripture (a writing) by quoting Proverbs 22:22-3. Writing, not human experience, proves the point. In parable, the story's concreteness proves its truth, its insight; in a scribal culture, texts prove truth: it is written.

2. *Fictional Context*. All parables are now part of a fictional narrative context and in most cases that context is part of the parable's meaning effect as received tradition. Often in historical criticism, this fictional context has provided the so-called historical context. The tyranny of this fictional context on the meaning effect of the parable must be rigorously resisted. This is especially difficult because it is one of the most subtle effects of textuality. Scholarship has gradually come to see that Luke has framed the parable From Jerusalem to Jericho (10:30-35) in terms of the question, who is my neighbor. One can see the Lucan construction, but exorcising its interpretative, hermeneutic effect is much more difficult. For example, Marcus Borg sees the Lucan situating of the parable, but never the less *locates the point* in the attack on the purity system and advocacy of compassion (Borg: 55). This is only the good neighbor under a different disguise.

3. *Stylistic Characteristics*. Each author who performs a parable has his or her own distinct stylistic characteristics. These must be assessed for their effect on the performance. In my judgment these are not always as problematic for the meaning effect as the previous two factors.

4. *Ideology*. More important is the ideology of the primary narrative and narrator of the fictional context of the parable. The understanding of a gospel's ideological stance is very important in making a final assessment of the textual performance of a parable.

My aim in this process was not to strip away the layers of redaction to reveal a pure parable, but to assess the characteristics of the textual performance on the meaning effect of the parable. I assume that there is an originating structure of the parable that the author is performing in a textual situation. By way of analogy, when we repeat a joke, we are performing an originating structure even though each performance will have its idiosyncratic characteristics, i.e., audience, style, etc. For me the memory residue of a parable is this originating structure. This is what the singer, rhetor, or author performs, to which audiences for centuries have responded, and which now a critic seeks to analyze as a parable of Jesus. This presents two major problems. First, we do not have access to an oral performance of the parable by Jesus, and second, this originating structure exists at the level of *langue* and not *parole*; i.e., it exists at the level of structure and not performance. Thus I agree with Kelber's critique of Crossan and suggest that Kelber would have similar problems with my analysis. Yet we must be clear about what is being claimed. I do not claim to have recovered an oral performance or an original parable. Admittedly such are chimera. Nor am I attempting to construct "an ideal form of any given song" (Kelber quoting Lord). Rather, having taken the extant performances into consideration, I have tried to listen for the voice that they believed they were remembering, something I identified as the originating structure, what the ancients termed *memoria ad res* (Carruthers: 86-91). I also grant that this never existed at the level of *parole* but is hypothetical. My method is a literate attempt to understand orality.

This brings to a head my disagreement with Kelber. (1) While agreeing that we cannot reconstruct the *oral* performance (original parable, etc.), Kelber seems to argue that nothing (no externally visible residue) remains. I maintain that the effects of memory (*memoria ad res*) are an analyzable residue. (2) Kelber implies that method should take up the position of an oral poetics. By this he seems to mean more than just reconstructing and describing such an oral poetics. He apparently wants the critic to take up the position of participant in orality. I do not believe that is possible. We can only analyse the residue of orality (memory) from a literate perspective.

To analyse this originating structure, I attempted to construct a methodological web that responded to the oral nature of the parables:

1. *Root Metaphor.* The normal way to organize a discussion of the parables is by theme, but all such efforts simply reflect the literate assumptions of the interpreter. Most often such a scheme is based on an abstract theological pattern. Instead, I organized the parables on the basis of the social situation that furnished the root metaphor (*res*) for the development of the parabolic narrative. Representing the horizontal dimension of social organization were those parables dealing with the family and the village; the vertical axis of power was exploited in those parables based on the patron/client model (Masters and Servants); and finally those parables that employed the everyday artifacts of life (Home and Farm). These provide a metaphorical system (Lakoff and Johnson: 112) for narrative elaboration. The kingdom is like a family; like a master and servant; like a farm . . ." Thus the organization comes from the concrete situation of everyday peasant life and not from an abstract pattern.

2. *Narratology.* I consciously employed a literary, narrative methodology because the parables are narratives, and because I was fighting

what I considered the deleterious effects of the focus on *Sitz im Leben* in the history of modern interpretation. Narratives have a freedom and independence from their context (Bauman: 7-14). This is especially true of repeated, oral narratives. Kelber stresses the necessity of repetition as a rhetorical strategy in orality, but then fails to see that such is the justification for recovering an originating structure. We can thus distinguish two types of meaning in a parable: situational meaning derives from the particular situation; but the literary meaning derives from the narrative itself. "[T]his second level supports and is the condition for the first, for it provides the possibility of both multiple and specific application in the situation of Jesus and the narrative of the Gospels and in subsequent readings" (Scott: 1989: 75). It is this second level of meaning to which we have access in the memory of Jesus' oral performances, not the repeated and varied situational meanings, which are no longer available.

3. *Surface Structure.* Oral memory should leave oral clues in the organization of the surface structure. "The surface structure can be spotted in the mnemonic features of oral language, the use of formulas, chiasmus, wordplays, and so forth" (74). This presents a conundrum to the analysis of an oral phenomenon when all we have concretely are textual clues. Since pure structure is not available, one inevitably deals with an investment of the structure. Searching for signs of orality is problematic since a rhetorical culture has a very high degree of orality. The analysis of the sound character of biblical text is a major unfinished task (Scott and Dean).

4. *Hearer Response Criticism.* With an eye toward the issue of narrative method, I sought to construct a method that could assess the performance characteristics of the parable, and so I adapted a reader-response method to an oral situation. It is at the level of literary method and hearer response criticism that I feel most vulnerable, since in both cases they were adapted from textual, literate methods.

5. *Corpus.* Finally, I tried to keep in mind the corpus of the parables as a control on idiosyncratic interpretation. If I could show a consistency of technique understood in its broadest sense across the corpus, then I considered the method validated.

What I was listening for was the voice inherent in the parable, the distinctive voice that I identified as singing in a minor key, which one reviewer correctly noted was not the best metaphor and which I might now change to "off-key". Nevertheless, that voice is not the historical Jesus who spoke the parables, but a construct, the implied voice of the parabolic corpus. It might be a fictional construct of the historical Jesus.

Kelber too employs a musical metaphor. "At the very most, it [structural stability] may give us the instruments on which the music was played. But the music is forever beyond our audition." Kelber is surely right. Yet to have recovered the instruments and some of the memory of the music is enough.

WORKS CONSULTED

1955   *The Fathers according to Rabbi Nathan*. Trans. Judah Goldin. Yale Judaica Series. New Haven: Yale University Press.

Aland, Kurt and Barbara Aland
1987   *The Text of the New Testament: An Introduction to the Critical Editions and to the Theory and Practice of Modern Textual Criticism*. Trans. Erroll F. Rhodes. Grand Rapids: Eerdmans.

Bauman, Richard
1977   *Verbal Art as Performance*. Rowley, MA: Newbury House.

Borg, Marcus J.
1994   *Meeting Jesus Again for the First Time: The Historical Jesus and the Heart of Contemporary Faith*. San Francisco: HarperSanFrancisco.

Carruthers, Mary J.
1990   *The Book of Memory*. Cambridge Studies in Medieval Literature. Cambridge and NY: Cambridge University Press, .

Crossan, John Dominic
1991   *The Historical Jesus: The Life of a Mediterranean Jewish Peasant*. San Francisco: HarperSanFrancisco.

Eisenstein, Elizabeth L.
1979   *The Printing Press as an Agent of Change: Communications and Cultural Transformations in Early Modern Europe*, 2 vols. New York: Cambridge University Press.

Kafka, Franz
1976   *The Complete Stories*. Trans. Nahum N. Glatzer. New York: Schocken Books.

Kelber, Werner H.
1983   *The Oral and the Written Gospel: The Hemeneutics of Speaking and Writing in the Synoptic Tradition, Mark, Paul and Q*. Philadelphia: Fortress.

Koester, Helmut
1990   *Ancient Christian Gospels*. Philadelphia: Trinity Press International.

Lakoff, George and Mark Johnson
1980   *Metaphors We Live By*. Chicago: University of Chicago Press.

Ong, Walter J.
   1982   *Orality and Literacy: The Technologizing of the Word.* London and New York: Methuen.

Robbins, Vernon
   1993   "Progymnastic Rhetorical Composition and Pre-Gospel Traditions: A New Approach." Pp. 111-47 in *The Synoptic Gospels: Source Criticism and the New Literary Criticism.* Ed. Camille Focant. BETL 110. Leuven: Leuven University Press.

Scott, Bernard Brandon
   1989   *Hear Then the Parable: A Commentary on the Parables of Jesus.* Minneapolis: Fortress.
   1994   "to impose is not / To Discover: Methodology in John Dominic Crossan's *The Historical Jesus.*" Pp. 22-30 in *Jesus and Faith: A Conversation on the Work of John Dominic Crossan.* Eds. Jeffrey Carlson and Robert A. Ludwig. New York: Orbis .

Scott, Bernard Brandon and Margaret E. Dean
   1993   "A Sound Map of the Sermon on the Mount." Pp. 672-725 in *SBL Seminar Papers 1993.* Ed. Eugene H. Lovering, Jr. Atlanta: Scholars.

MODALITIES OF COMMUNICATION, COGNITION, AND PHYSIOLOGY OF PERCEPTION: ORALITY, RHETORIC, SCRIBALITY

Werner H. Kelber
Rice University

ABSTRACT

Broadly viewed, the premise of this essay is that in the ancient world, modes of communication were intertwined with cognitive and sensory perception. Rarely was reasoning conceived of as pure thought. Rather, language, mind, and body were synergistic forces that negotiated knowledge and perception.

The particular focus of this essay is three modes of communication in antiquity: orality, rhetoric, and scribality. Rather than dwelling on language as grammar and syntax, as sign and structure, or on theories of mimesis and correspondence, this study calls attention to the art of oral, traditional composition and performance, to rhetorical practice and theory, and to the impact of scribality on the oral, rhetorical culture. Each of these conventions of verbal art entailed a cultural apparatus of communication, remembering, and traditioning, and each mode of discourse engaged the human sensorium, mobilizing diverse combinations of auditory and visual perception. Homeric culture was the product of oral performers and oral traditional composing-in-performance. Rhetoric, which began with the Presocratics in the fifth century BCE, deployed writing to make oral culture conscious of itself. It advanced the oral medium to the status of a principal academic discipline, and in the process it helped shape the intellectual tools that came to undermine the ancient culture of Homeric orality.

> . . . the "rediscovery" of oral tradition and oral traditional works is a relatively recent phenomenon, the issue, ironically enough, of a post-Gutenberg mentality that has had to strive mightily to reimagine its distant oral origins.
> Foley, *Immanent Art*

> The "art" of rhetoric, though concerned with oral speech, was, like other "arts," the product of writing.
> Ong, *Orality and Literacy*

> It seems to be the case that there was a greater sensitivity in the ancient world to the symbolic significance of sensory metaphors and models.
> Chidester, *Word and Light*

> The works of Greek literature after the Homeric transcription occurred are composed in an increasing tension between the genius of oral and the genius of written composition.
> Havelock, *The Literate Revolution in Greece*

INTRODUCTION

Despite our long-standing preoccupation with language and communication, we have only recently begun to view speech, writing, print, and the new electronic devices as mastertropes that help illuminate aspects of Western thought and culture. In part our fascination with these modes of communication, is attributable to our current experience with the electronic medium, for the global changes which the electronic revolution is generating have sharpened our retrospective faculties. Standing at the threshold of the electronic age, we have become accustomed to discern the differences between orality and rhetoric, between primary and secondary orality, between chirographic culture and the information age, between the alphabetic revolution and the explosive invention of the letterpress, between the typographical organization of language and the behavior of computer programs; and we have learned to appreciate these phenomena as modalities and transformations of the word.

The history of the modes of communication from primary orality to the present is largely a history of transformational processes. By definition, medium/media is a "negotiative concept" (Gronbeck: 12). There are, therefore, historical and linguistic reasons not to reify the media into measurable entities. In actuality, the modes of communication rarely ever present themselves in essentialist purity or as robot imperatives. "Has a purely oral culture, uncontaminated by any sign system, ever existed?" (King: 32). Separating one modality of communication as a distinct entity from every other is likely to distort linguistic realities. It is more advisable to attend to phenomena such as residual oral traces or orality filtered through textuality, transformation of voice and the rhetorical outreach of texts, cooperation and tension between oral and textual drives, the engagement of oral and visual, or audio-visual aids in the work of perception, the tangled interfaces of speech with writing, the gradual dominance of one medium over other media, and the reabsorption of a prior heritage into a culture shaped by new media technologies.

There are also philosophical and hermeneutical reasons that caution us against media reification. We tend to discover each medium in distinction from successive media developments. Orality, for example, can be viewed as the difference writing invented to legitimate its own existence. If for the purpose of analysis the media are perceived as ideal types, their existence is by the same token subject to nominalist skepticism. We need to be mindful of the hermeneutical dimension entailed in media studies. There is a sense in which orality, rhetoric, scribality (as well as print and electronics) are categories of interpretation that tell us as much about our cultural, intellectual, and technological history, as they do about our ability to imagine them.

But even if we recognize that in the "ordinary" life of language, orality, rhetoric, and scribality run together, we need these mastertropes in order to understand their interminglings, mutual reabsorptions and deconstructions. Even if we concede degrees of fictionality concerning the distinctions we make between orality and rhetoric, and the polarity we predicate between speech and writing, we still have to develop a sense of the attributes intrinsic to and privileged by orality, rhetoric, and scribality, so as to come to terms with the dynamics of their interplay.

Thinking about language in terms of media is a world apart from philosophical and theological idealism. The thematization of media modalities has grown out of our experience of the technologizing of language with its momentous impact on culture and society. It recognizes an intimate partnership between oral, chirographic, typographic, and electronic modes of communication on the one hand and meaning-making processes on the other. Logic, for example, is not a given of human cognition. It has a history that evolved, in part at least, in interaction with the history of the permutations of the word. Media favor certain modes of knowing; they structure thought, individual and social identities. To the extent that our humanistic legacy has shown a preference for unmediated notions of meaning, sense, idea, proclamation, and even information, it is ill-disposed to concede any cultural force to the increasingly material means of mediation. As long as one is inclined to treat religious, philosophical, and intellectual developments strictly as a history of ideas, it is difficult to accept "the premise that in general the means of communication tends to condition the content of what is communicated" (Havelock 1978:2). Hermeneutics, for example, which examine the central problematic of understanding, have yet to undertake a sustained epistemological reflection on the role of the media, past and present. The concept of the physiology of perception, moreover, seeks to overcome an often aridly textual, ideational comprehension of our classical and biblical heritage. In taking account of the ancient truism that all our thought is variously linked to the sensorium, we call into question the notion of pure thought. For it was a widely acknowledged fact of ancient epistemology that seeing, hearing, feeling, and remembering interacted with the reasoning processes. And insofar as modes of communication favored certain modes of knowing, they also showed a propensity for engaging certain senses.

From Oral Compositional Theory To Receptionist Aesthetics

In 1795 the academic world was formally introduced to the idea of Homeric orality. In that year Friedrich August Wolf published his *Prolegomena ad Homerum*, which characterized Homer as an oral poet. A nonliterate, oral storyteller, Homer was perceived to have narrated the *Iliad* and *Odyssey*, which after numerous subsequent alterations eventually came to be written down. Then as now, the idea of Homeric orality was greeted with skepticism. Then as now, it seemed preposterous to think of orality—the medium we are apt to forget—as having played a key role in the formative stage of Western civilization. Through the nineteenth century it was not Wolf, but the unitarians and the analysts who dominated the academic debate (Lloyd-Jones: 52). The unitarians attributed the two epics to an individual act of poetic craftsmanship. They were inclined to explain and appreciate Homer as a sterling authorial personality, a veritable genius of a poetic writer. Theirs was a theory predicated on modernity's lofty estimation of the individual and his (but rarely her) literary authorial creativity. The analysts viewed the epics as the result of successive stages of literary growth. They assumed a series of editorial processes, involving revisions, interpolations, and redactions. If the first theory was an expression of the Romantic bent in Homeric scholarship, the second marked the apotheosis of higher criticism.

When in the early twentieth century Milman Parry revived the theory of Homeric orality, it was met with considerably more enthusiasm, especially in the United States and Canada (1930, 1932, 1933). However, it must be stated at the outset that there are few hard-core Parryists around anymore. Parry's work, although grounded in strictly philological principles, fell short of resolving the Homeric question. But his approach to the Homeric texts has introduced a way of thinking that transcends Homeric issues and scholarship, and indeed "supersedes customary notions about the nature of literary language" (Foley 1985:18). Divesting himself of the preconceptions formed both by the unitarians and the analysts, Parry approached the Homeric texts as oral literature, contributing thereby to the creation of the new discipline of orality and literacy studies, or oral literature research.

What intrigued Parry and his successor Albert Lord was something that had baffled generations of scholars before them: how can one account for the *Iliad* and the *Odyssey*, these two massive epics that stand like

Stonehenge monuments at the dawn of Greek civilization? In its most general sense, Parry's thesis of the oral compositional nature of the Homeric texts rests on the observation of a highly patterned, frequently repetitive diction. Homer's language is made up of epithets associated with key characters, formulae (regularly employed groups of words), themes (standardized story patterns), and whole sequences of similar and/or identical lines. Parry concluded that these epithetic, formulaic, thematic, and metric conventionalities on which Homer drew must have come about through the pressures of oral performance. The poet and his language had found a new explanation. Homer was not a sterling literary intellect, but a bard who relied on centuries of orally composed and mediated verse-making. The predictability and commonplace nature of the epics were the result of traditional, oral composition, and had nothing to do with textual overlays. Without ever fully conceptualizing it, Parry discovered oral tradition as the indispensable force in the making of the Homeric epics, and the medium of formulaic, repetitive phraseology as a defining attribute of oral tradition.

Following the early death of Parry, it fell upon Lord to explicate further the nature and consequences of oral compositional processes. A major stimulus, initiated by Parry himself, came from field work in the Balkan countries. In this still predominantly oral culture of Serbo-Croatian traditions, Lord found models of epic singing that allowed him to address the Homeric question by way of a contemporary, living analogy (1960, 1991). Drawing comparisons between the oral traditions of Serbo-Croatian singers and the Homeric epics, he recognized their traditional character. In other words, the comparative work demonstrated that narrative patterns and individual themes were developed in the Greek tradition long before they came to be applied to the Homeric heroes. "Our *Iliad* and *Odyssey* were many centuries in the making" (1960:151).

Oral tradition, as Lord came to expound it, is a modality of communication—singing, composing-performing, and hearing—that knows neither an unalterably fixed text, nor the idea of memorization. Essentially, oral singers operate by absorbing, transmuting, and recombining a repertoire of thematic and formulaic commonplaces. Learning in this tradition is habitual, and performance tantamount to recomposing on established patterns: "the singer is composing as he sings" (17). Learning, composing, performing, and transmitting all merge into one process for which we have no single name. There is a sense, therefore, in which the singers/poets have inherited the questions and the answers from the informing tradition all around them (32). They actualize the legacy of tale-telling with a consistently conservative urge to preserve essential themes and story patterns. On the face of it, stability arises from the pragmatics of communication as it seeks to serve the performers' needs and to accommodate their audiences (53-54). But it is not reducible to utilitarian principles. The tenacity with which tradition holds on to building blocks and thematic complexes springs from that deeper conviction that the story provides "the very means of attaining life and happiness" (220). Stability in this sense, however, is not the same as the modern preoccupation with literal fixity and logical consistency. Oral performers are bound by tradition, but not as something sacrosanct; no single feature of the tradition is frozen in position. Lord's theory of oral composition allows for ceaseless fluctuations, which entail "saying the same thing in fewer or more lines," "expansion of ornamentation," "changes of order in a sequence," "addition of material," "omission of material," and "substitution of one theme for another" (123). To such a degree is variation practiced in oral tradition that no two singers can be said to use the traditional repertoire in exactly the same way (79).

To us stability and flexibility seem mysteriously intertwined in oral tradition. Equipped with modern recording devices, and consciously or unconsciously operating on the premise of a fixed form or performance, we are able to register demonstrable changes in wording, thematization, and structure. But this is not the way oral composing and traditioning appears to the performers themselves. To them changes are not deviations from given models, but the expected mode of retelling priceless lore. In the absence of a single text, variability lies in the best interest of tradition. Strictly speaking, stability and flexibility are not discernible alternatives, and narrative conservatism in no way precludes compositional mobility. Tradition is a "pliable protean substance" (152), the property of all and hence immune to charges of plagiarism. From this perspective, the performing bards are neither reproducers nor repeaters, but co-creators of the tradition. The individual singer is "at once the tradition and an individual creator" (4).

The scholarship inaugurated by Parry and Lord has been of seminal importance for the humanities. Granted that the Homeric situation is not directly transferable to biblical and other classical texts, the rediscovery of the power of the oral medium and its artistic performers in shaping a whole culture has nonetheless challenged us to reexamine concepts we thought we had known for certain. In light of Parry and Lord, received notions of authorship and composition, originality and imagination, reading and writing, text and narrative, memory and cognition, and above all tradition betray their literate predisposition. In its most critical sense, oral literature research as initiated by Parry and Lord can sensitize us to the literate bias in classical, biblical, and medieval studies, and stir thought about an oral civilization and its modes of storing, remembering, and reciting knowledge.

Its impressive explanatory powers notwithstanding, the thesis advanced by Parry and Lord is not without its problems. Media rarely present themselves in essentialist purity. If it is claimed that the Homeric epics were composed without the aid of writing, what impact did dictation and writing have on this oral, traditional civilization? Are the *Iliad* and *Odyssey* conceivable simply as graphs of what the bards had recited? What caused these narratives to be wrenched from a history of centuries of oral compositional performances and transposed into textuality? Lord declared this question to be unanswerable: "We are in the dark about why the poems were written down" (152). Eric Havelock, however, while emphatically expounding the oral compositional patterns of Homer's epics, conceded that "it seems improbable that his poems have not benefited from some reorganisation made possible by alphabetic transcription" (1963:46). He was convinced that the epic language of the *Iliad* and *Odyssey* was "built on acoustic principles, which exploit the technique of the echo as a mnemonic device" (128), but he also suspected links between the epics' textualization and the invention of the Greek alphabet around 700 BCE. In fact, the two epic monuments had to be understood as "the alphabet's first gift to the Greeks as to ourselves" (1982:120). And if one credited the alphabet with "introducing a new state of mind—the alphabetic mind" (7)—would alphabetic script, this "piece of explosive technology" (6), have operated as a mere recording device? Considerations of this kind compelled Havelock to adopt the dual thesis of gradualism and interfacing: the Homeric epics were transcribed by "bits and pieces" (1982:180) from oral verse, with the transcriptions representing a partnership between the oral and the written, whereby the ear was increasingly seduced into collaboration with the eye (13, 179-83).

Of all those who took up the challenge of Parry and Lord, John Foley (1985, 1990, 1991) has offered a singularly imaginative contribution. The shift he inaugurated in Homeric scholarship is from the art of composition to receptionist aesthetics, and from oral traditional theory to "traditional referentiality" (1991:6-8). Proceeding from the understanding that Homeric orality, as developed by Parry and Lord, must remain conjectural, Foley assigned to the ancient Greek epics the designation of "oral-derived texts" (9). Even if the *Iliad* and *Odyssey* were not unambiguously oral, they clearly were not fully literary products either. Their metrical, idiomatic, and scenic repertoire classified them as tradition-dependent literature (1990:1-10, 1991:136). Consistent with the aesthetics of oral-derived texts, Foley argued, traditional phraseology, such as the well-known Homeric epithets, operated not simply in response to the demands of performance, say as metrical solutions to problems caused by verse structure, but as connotative phrases aimed at prompting imaginative recall in the Homeric audience. Reaching beyond their textual situation, these epithets plugged into the larger pool of tradition that they shared with their audience and from which they derived meanings that exceeded their function in the text. The construction of meaning in oral-derived texts, therefore, "includes an extratextual dimension" (1991:7). When, for example, Homer repeatedly invoked the "swift-footed Achilles" in the *Iliad*, he was calling to the hearers' minds not simply this one attribute of the hero. In oral traditional hermeneutics, stock phrases resonated with multiple other features and moments in the hero's life, encoding a reality larger than any single narrative moment. On the metonymic principle of *pars pro toto*, Achilles' "swift-footedness" summoned in the hearers an identity "that comprises the innumerable separate moments of that character's existence in oral traditional story" (141). In moving Homeric studies away from strictly formalist, literary, and compositional theories toward the level of aesthetic function, Foley rediscovered metonymic referentiality, or the ancient hermeneutical principle of associative hermeneutics. Associative relations differ from syntagmatic ones. Whereas a text acquires syntagmatic validation through the interior relation of its words, it negotiates meaning associatively through relations to a world outside the text. In Homeric civilization, Foley suggested, traditional signification was negotiated not primarily inside texts, as we literary folk are inclined to think, but ultimately by the collective memory. This was in fact how these oral-derived texts functioned orally.

RHETORIC AND THE SENSORIUM

Rhetoric is the outgrowth of a media world rooted in and dominated by speaking. This needs to be emphasized because our literate, textual presumptions tend to minimize or distort rhetoric's oral disposition in favor of its literary reflectiveness and close proximity to dialectic (Kennedy 1980:109). All discussions of rhetoric should commence with its oral underpinnings and oratorical aspirations. Rhetorical verbalization, "one of the most consequential and serious of all academic subjects and of all human activities" (Ong 1983:1), was closely linked with the primacy of speech. Even if we grant a rapidly developing scribality and gradations of writing and reading competence in antiquity, rhetorical structures firmly retained their grip on knowledge management. From antiquity through the Middle Ages and up to the seventeenth century, rhetoric played a central role in mediating information and learning, and in engaging the senses. To say that processes of knowing and perceiving were rhetorically shaped suggests at root an interactive concept of language. In keeping with ancient oral epistemology, rhetoric transacted language as if it were of a piece with life situations. Even in its most abstract and theoretical instances, rhetoric was no more inclined to retreat into a world of disengaged letters than to elevate verbalization to extrapersonal status. It clearly understood that language was power, orally processed and operative in relation to hearers. To this end, rhetoric's principal mission was to discover and cultivate the argumentative, persuasive, and sensory potential of words (Aristotle: 1.2, 135b) or, to use Plato's diction, to implant conviction into human souls (*Phaedr.* 270e-272b).

One may think of rhetoric as orality deliberately enlisted into the service of civic life (*rhetorica utens*). Public address was the central focus of rhetoric, and the training of speakers rhetoric's pragmatic concern. Rhetorical language grew in public spaces and remained firmly linked to public reception (Aristotle 1.2,136a). Notwithstanding a considerable fascination among the ancients with the pathology of rhetoric, namely its manipulative and seductive powers, the "art of public speaking," to use Plato's phrase (*Statesm.* 304d), was ideally understood as a means to nourish the *vita activa* and to foster the values of freedom and civic life. To be sure, "when it is a question about the building of walls or equipment of harbors or dockyards, we consult, not the rhetoricians, but the master builders" (*Gorg.* 455b). And yet, Gorgias reminds us, we have let ourselves be persuaded partly by Themistocles, and partly by Pericles, to undertake these building projects in the first place (*Gorg.* 455e). Rhetoric, it seems, is omnipresent in civic life, and one may think of it as possessing "almost superhuman importance" (*Gorg.* 456a). There was, in the words of Isocrates, "no institution devised by man which the power of speech has not helped us to establish" (*Anti.* 254-55). Law and politics, funerals and banquets, festivities and assemblies, medicine and science, epistolography and proselytizing—all were sustained by rhetoric's embracing skills and ambitions.

In the context of communications history, rhetoric was orality grown conscious of itself (*rhetorica docens*). After rhetors had molded and governed ancient culture for centuries, rhetoricians from the fifth century onward brought to consciousness aspects that had been implicit in oral, traditional communication all along. As the oral medium advanced to the rank of a rhetorical discipline, it became the subject of sustained examinations and often pedantic categorizations. Rhetoric as the central educational discipline conceptualized language's didactic and persuasive facilities. There was no end in showing the pliability of oral discourse that appealed to thought and senses, tapped memory, produced conviction, secured assent, reinforced behavior, influenced decision-making processes, aroused emotions, and engaged the imagination. Central to these theoretical reflections were issues such as the modes of argumentation and reasoning, the style of delivery, the nature of composition, the selection of topics, and the types of proof. Handbooks, practical manuals, letters, and treatises of various kinds relentlessly explored the premises on which arguments were based (*inventio*), the arrangement of speech materials into an oration (*dispositio*), the matching of words with speakers, topics, audience, and occasion (*elocutio*), modes of oral delivery and inducement of emotional states (*pronuntiatio*), the lodging, retaining, and summoning of ideas in the mind (*memoria*), and a myriad of other issues. In the absence of literary criticism, which "was slow to develop in antiquity and was never fully conceptualized" (Kennedy: 111), the *rhetorica docens*, alongside dialectic, grammar and poetics, assumed the role of practical and critical theory. As a consequence, rhetoric was harnessed into the gear of logic. In his *Ars Rhetorica*, "one of the driest works in the world" (Jebb: 234), Aristotle organized his material on the basis of a taxonomy of figures, a psychology of human nature, and a systematization of discourse. In short, writing "not as an experienced rhetorician, but as a logician" (Crem: 52), the philosopher presented rhetoric as a scientific discipline. Under his influence, the oral investment in truth and power tilted toward the rhetorical commitment to truth and method.

Whether rhetoric was practiced or systematized, it was always expected to engage the human sensorium and to play the sensory register in the interest of persuasion. Current studies on media, thought, and sense perception widely agree that orality and rhetoric chiefly appealed to the aural, auditory sense, whereas scribality and print technology increasingly inclined toward visualism. Moreover, both hearing and seeing were intimately tied to processes of knowing and perception. Ong's phenomenology of culture and consciousness, for example, links voice with presence, simultaneity, interiority, and unity. Sound represents the world of dynamism and being-in-time; it is "the process sense par excellence" (1977:136). Sight and vision, by contrast, depersonalize relations, dissect the world, present viewers with surfaces, and situate them in sequentiality. When thought is thus bound up with vision, "it becomes pretty exclusively a matter of explanation or explication, a laying out on a surface, perhaps in chartlike form, or an unfolding, to present maximum exteriority" (122-23). Based on the premise that sound personalizes while sight objectifies, Western cultural history is thus macrocosmically imaginable as "moving from a culture in significant ways favoring auditory syntheses to a culture in significant ways favoring visual syntheses" (126). Visualism, serving as an analogue of knowing, steadily enhanced its reach, developed into modern hypervisualism, which contributed toward ever more refined abstraction and formalization of thought. This broad-based model harbors immense explanatory powers, but it also conceals the complexities and tangled interfaces that characterize the history of media, thought, and sense perception on the microcosmic level.

David Chidester has presented selected case studies of perceptual orientations that run counter to the cognitive and symbolic associations traditionally attending sound and sight, and that suggest rather different partnerships between oral and scribal drives (1992). In religious discourse especially, sound can be associated with sequentiality and absence of full reality, while sight exhibits simultaneity and presence. Philo, for example, regarded hearing as an inadequate vehicle for knowledge and truth. In a hierarchy of values he placed seeing above hearing. The ears were inactive organs, sluggish and, as he would have it, "more womanish" (*De Abra.* 150: *thelytera*) than the eyes. Hearing "is proved to lag far behind sight and is brimful of vanity" (*De Con.* 141). It was a sense, therefore, "on which no certain reliance can be placed" (*De Abra.* 60). Sight, on the other hand, was the perfect means for apprehension and contemplation. The swiftest of senses and the one capable of bonding subject with object, it was "more trustworthy than the ears" (*De Ebr.* 82). In the experience of the sacred, however, voice and visual faculties entered into a curious relationship. The theophany at Sinai, for instance, illuminated "a voice which, strange paradox, was visible (φωνῆς—τὸ παραδοξότατον—ὁρατῆς) and aroused the eyes rather than the ears of the bystanders" (*De Vita Mos.* II.213). Using Exod 20:22 as prooftext, Philo symbolized the perception of divinity as a synthetic fusion of voice and light. The people saw the voice of God (Chidester: 30-43).

Augustine, Chidester further reminds us, was keenly aware of intractable problems associated with words (53-72). In *De Magistro*, verbal communication is generally held in low esteem. Words, while making noise, do not in themselves have communicative powers. "By means of words, therefore, we learn only words or rather the sound and vibration of words" (XI,36: *verbis igitur nisi verba non discimus, immo sonitum strepitumque verborum*). Moreover, Augustine's signs theory, developed in *De Doctrina Christiana* and *De Magistro*, articulated a hermeneutics of signification that privileged the transverbal *res* over the verbal *signum*. The real efficacy of the words of Scripture was to remind us of the transverbal realities, and Scripture's final objective was the vision of God that brings forth peace and tranquility (*De Doc.* II,7). Words, on that theory, have referential, but never presentational powers, while sight, the eye of the mind, accesses reality and facilitates union between the believer and God. In similar manner, Augustine's ruminations on memory are dominated by visual metaphors (*Con.* 10; *De Trin.* 11). Serving as the depository of both images and imageless experiences, memory, the "stomach of the soul" (*Con.* X, 14, 25: *memoria quasi venter est animi*), transacts all our conscious and unconscious processes. Remembering is primarily constituted by the act of finding and bringing together the items dispersed in the vastness of memory's deep space. In collecting hidden images or lost traces, one re-collects them, i.e. brings them to consciousness. As Augustine himself explains, "bringing together" corresponds to "thinking" (X,11,25: *nam cogo et cogito sic est*) so that the act of collecting memory's treasures deserves to be called thinking (X,11,25: *quod in animo colligitur, id est cogitur, cogitari proprie iam dicatur*). This intellectual process of gathering and actualizing memory's stored treasures is carried out by visual powers, which, at the instruction of the will, undertake the search for lost items. Memory's images make themselves present to the inner eye (X,16,25: *intuere praesentes*) and even imageless experiences are visually apprehensible (X,12,19: *intus agnovit*). Vision and intellect are here brought together not in dissecting the world or presenting viewers with surfaces, but in a unifying consciousness.

It is tempting to contend that both Philo and Augustine have moved over to the new medium of scribality that helped promote the apotheosis of sight as the *sensus maxime cognoscitivus*. Yet, this is only partially true. Clearly, Philo's depreciation of hearing betrays a mind for which voice, verbalization, and sound had lost their primary cognitive significance. Similarly, Augustine's meditation on the signs character of language was born under the pressure of literate sensibilities. Sign, a visually based metaphor, fails to capture the attributes of spoken words. Homeric orality, far from thinking of words as signs, spoke of the "winged words," a phrase that suggests movement, freedom, and evanescence (Ong 1982:77). But there is more here than meets the eye. For Philo, as for Augustine, the highest potential of sight was fulfilled in the contemplation of God. What they have in mind is not *external visualism* of "the world of ocularly construed 'evidence'" (Ong 1977:125), but *internal visualization*. Furthermore, Augustine's theory of memory and intellection is exclusively concerned with the production, retention, and recall of internal images. This interior visualization, the forming of images from what is heard, is deeply rooted in orality and conceptualized by rhetoric. For Cicero (*De Oratore* II, ixxxvi 351-60), for the anonymous author *ad Herennium* (III, xvi 28-xxiv 40), for Quintilian (*Institutio Oratoria* XI ii 1-51) and many others, memory is the treasure-house of rhetoric, which is filled with the furniture of *imagines* and *loci*. Hence, neither Philo nor Augustine are fully comprehensible as converts to the new medium of scribality, for Philo's seeing of the voice and Augustine's concept of thought as a visual re-collection are concepts still rooted in the old world of rhetoric.

To date, the most plausible case against rhetoric as an exclusive aesthetic of orality, and on behalf of a rhetorical phenomenology of mental imaging, has been made by Nathalia King (1991). Extending a thesis introduced by Francis Yates (1966), King's study, which ranges widely over classical rhetoric up to and including Augustine's *Confessio*, adduces ample evidence of what was a fundamental strategy of the ancient art of persuasion: to bring auditors to see what was being said, so that the images they visualized were vivid to the point of being indistinguishable from actuality. In rhetorical theory, strategies of visualization went by the names of *enargeia* and *ekphrasis* (King: 110-30). *Enargeia*, which was particularly appropriate in the part of oratory known as *narratio*, took pains to display before one's eyes narrative features such as persons, scenes, actions, and so forth. *Ekphrasis* refers especially to works of art, such as, for example, Achilles' shield and the narrative description of the dramatic scenes forged upon it (*Iliad*: 18: 475-605). Both *enargeia* and *ekphrasis* aspired to imaginary visual presence by verbal techniques of animation. We should therefore be on our guard against the assumption that rhetorically informed and oral-derived texts were in all instances following the call of verbal, acoustic principles. Rhetoric entailed a "visual semiotics" (King: 105) that contributed to the organization and presentation of ancient speech, thought, and writing. These visual sensibilities may seem bizarre to us, but they warrant closer attention. More than a quarter of a century ago Yates recognized the validity of the issue: "The influence of the art of memory on literature is a practically untouched subject" (312).

The work of the *rhetorica docens* is unthinkable without the technology of writing. It was scribality, the very medium that subtly undermined orality's commitment to the inseparability of words from life, that defined rhetoric as a cultural factor in its own right. Writing made a difference. It produced the distance requisite for facilitating a conceptual grasp of the artful discipline of speaking. There is a sense, therefore, in which rhetoric as a product of writing not only raised consciousness about the art and method of speaking, but reinvented the oral-rhetorical way with words by representing it through the medium of scribality. And therein lies one of the paradoxes of medium history, or rather of our perception of it. Rhetoricians could not grasp the distinctiveness of speech without writing about it, but writing about it in terms of rhetoric decontextualized speech and pulled it into the orbit of literary, analytical categories. Orality was transformed, indeed undermined, as it was brought to consciousness through rhetorical, scribal reflection (Tyler: 131-37).

LEXIS EIROMENE AND MEDIA ANXIETY

Growing sensitivity to the dominantly oral culture of antiquity has in some quarters encouraged a reassessment of the composition, nature, and reception of ancient texts. Achtemeier, echoing the views of others, has reminded us that ancient texts were composed by dictation and with the aim of catching the attention of the ear (1990). There is impressive evidence that dictation, whether to oneself or to others, was the preeminent mode of writing. It may be assumed, therefore, that ancient texts, originating in speech and lacking in visual codes of punctuation, were perforce organized in conformity with a phenomenology of sound rather than of sight. So pervasive was the oral environment, Achtemeier states, that "*no* writing occurred that was not vocalized" (15). Indeed, not only drama and poetry, but historical writings as well, were reactivated in public readings (Graham: 35). Throughout antiquity and far into the Middle Ages, silent reading (*tacite legere*) was considered an abnormality (Balogh; Saenger). Since both writing and reading were vocal exercises, every ancient text must be treated as an oral reality and listened to as *lexis eiromene*. There were no such things as silent words, and Achtemeier boldly reiterates the Augustinian dictum: "*omne verbum sonat* !" (27, n. 156).

Achtemeier's invocation of the oral environment of ancient Western civilization adds one more voice to a growing chorus of discontent with our print-oriented reification of ancient textuality. His challenge, which has benefited from the seminal studies of Balogh, Parry, Lord, Goody, Ong, Havelock and others, merits close attention. If taken seriously, his call for a reassessment of many of our scholarly suppositions should make us look at the medium status of texts, the use of sources, and the organization of thought negotiated in ancient texts, with renewed attention to oral proclivities. But more is involved here than an oral investment in ancient texts. What is at stake in speech and writing are domains of culture that entail broad issues of self and community, tradition and creativity, authorship and readership, vocalization and visualism, sense perception and the "sensual dimension" of textual history (Graham: 6-7). One may well agree with Ong's statement that in consequence of our awareness of the role of media "our entire understanding of classical culture now has to be revised—and with it our understanding of later cultures up to our own time" (1967:18).

For all its persuasiveness, there are elements in Achtemeier's essay that must give us pause. Dictation, for example, even if taken by writers skilled in shorthand, was bound to slow down speech and to affect thought processes. Although it operated in the medium of speech and often sought to approximate speech-like products, it was nonetheless discourse adjusted to the writing process. Textual compositions, moreover, could be so complex as to defy the very designation of dictation. In one of his later dialogues, Plato narrates how Euclides went about committing to writing a conversation with Socrates (*Theaet.* 143a-c). First, Socrates' interlocutor took notes as soon as he arrived at home. At a second stage, Euclides wrote out in extended form what he could recall in leisure. Thirdly, he questioned Socrates every time he went to Athens, checking his memory against Socrates'. Upon return from Athens, finally, he inserted the corrections into his writings and produced what amounted to a final version. Whether this procedure accurately characterizes Plato's own mode of composition or not, it does describe oral, textual, memorial interactions of significant media complexity. Neither dictation nor any other single term comes close to describing this mode of composition.

A question must also be raised about Achtemeier's singular insistence on the aspect of textual vocalization. Ancient texts, he seems to be saying, are oral to the core. Does this provide us with a sufficiently nuanced sense of speech, reading, and writing in the ancient West? Oblivious to a wealth of visual strategies encoded in texts, he has focused entirely on the acoustic production of meaning. But not everything in rhetoric dwells in the world of sound. Interior visualization, we claimed, engaged the production and reception of texts as well. There was an awareness, even among rhetoricians, that the aesthetics and pragmatics of reading texts needed to be differentiated from those of hearing utterances. Quintilian, for example, gratefully acknowledged the benefit of indefinite reiteration in the process of reading: "we can re-read a passage again and again if we are in doubt about it or wish to fix it in memory" (*Inst. Ora.* 10.1.19). One wonders also whether greater differentiation is not required in attributing oral, rhetorical structuring to ancient texts. Did Herodotus, Thucydides or Josephus, exponents of the developing genre of historiography, compose with the same clarity of voice and under the same audience control as poets of the likes of Hesiod, Sappho, or Pindar? Surely, we can assume that verse and prose, epics and tragedies, letters and *hypomnemata*, dialogues and oracular apophthegms grew out of different media environments and represented varying interfaces between oral and written communication.

In principle, writing never reproduces orality. Textuality always arrests, absorbs, and to varying degrees overtakes speech as it inaugurates its own scribal codes. This is not an anachronistic projection of modernity upon antiquity. That writing could and did make a difference is an experience not merely reserved for modern, media-conscious people, but a topic well-attested in ancient Western culture. There was an awareness among many intellectuals in the ancient world that writing made a difference, and written words could not take the place of spoken words. Alcidamas, for example, affirmed that writing slowed down thought and "places the soul in chains" (*Peri ton*: 16-17). Isocrates noted that he was well aware of the great difference that existed between "discourses which are spoken and those which are to be read;" for when "a discourse is robbed of the prestige of the speaker, the tone of his voice, the variations which are made in the delivery," it makes little impression upon hearers (*Phil.* 25-26). Plato felt that people who relied on written words "call[ed] things to remembrance no longer from within themselves, but by means of external marks" (*Phaedr.* 275a-b). Paul the apostle presumed that the *pneuma* nourished life, while the *gramma* inflicted death (2 Cor 3:6). This deep-felt distrust toward the written word must be viewed as an expression of media anxiety. A culture with millenial roots in oral, rhetorical communication suspected verbal arts that were no longer free to adapt themselves to the needs of the occasion. As a rule, those who shared this view did not shun writing, let alone hearer-friendly writing. But they were ambiguous about the effects of their scribal productions. While availing themselves of the new technology, they were concerned about the mental, verbal inertia it brought to words, and about the inescapable disengagement of the letter from what was widely perceived to be the natural, oral environment of words. Those who felt uneasy about the nature and effects of writing can hardly be expected to have confirmed the medium reality of *omne verbum sonat*. The reality was that written words had lost their vocal identity. The issue, in their view, was not the unlimited vocal potency of words, but the silencing of voice as a result of writing.

Plato exhibited in exemplary fashion the tension of conflicting media forces and a bi-focal approach to the oral/scribal dilemma. In the *Phaedrus*, we saw, he bemoaned the destructive effects of writing and pitied those possessed of the idea that "writing will provide something reliable and permanent" (*Phaedr.* 275c). The art of writing will undermine memory, and along with it a whole culture based on the exercise of memory and the interiorization of language. Writing was "unable to defend and help itself" (*Phaedr.* 275e), he stated categorically, invoking the old world of oral, rhetorical verbalization. In the *Republic*, however, the spirit and tenor of Plato's argument is different. In constructing the ideal state, he felt compelled to challenge the poetic hegemony of Homer, Hesiod, and the like. As Havelock has shown, it is a polemic that was informed by an undercurrent of anti-oralist sentiments (1963). Poetry was a kind of "social encyclopedia" (31) that served as an instrument of cultural education. Equipped with immense powers of memorization, the bards absorbed and repeated what they had been taught. One problem Plato saw in the mimetic art was that it produced phantoms far removed from truth and reality (*Rep.* X, 598-99). Homer, he complained, had practiced "the art of imitation;" he did not possess "real knowledge" (*Rep.* X, 600c). Most likely, Plato's indictment was aimed at the traditional mode of oral composition and performance. A related problem was that the "imitators" made their audiences relive the poeticized legacy of the past, inducing them to "identify almost pathologically and certainly sympathetically with the content of what . . . [they were] saying" (Havelock, 1963: 45). In winning the favors of the multitude, the poets appealed to the inferior part of the soul, and "by strengthening it [tended] to destroy the rational part" (*Rep.* X, 605b). Philosophy was superior to both the poetic and the rhetorical arts because it approached life analytically, distanced itself from the emotions, pursued "pure and unadulterated thought" (*Phaedo* 66a), and refrained from contentiousness—all virtues promoted by the art of writing. In sum, Plato's criticism of the poetic imitators, of poeticized language and its effects on hearers was tantamount to a repudiation of the oral state of mind characteristic of Homeric culture and the oral apparatus of the Greek educational system. His demand that one break with the tribal encyclopedia in the interest of dialectics, that one cultivate the rational part of the soul and the autonomous psyche, operated under the ordering, individualizing impact of the scribal art. In lamenting the defects of writing—which implied nostalgia for oral purity—and in attacking the oral imagination grounded in preserved communication—which relied upon writing—he represented "the cultural schizophrenia common to his time on the oral/literate dilemma" (King: 46, n. 82).

Conclusion

A culture such as ours, which until recently was dominated by the typographic medium, finds it difficult, and perhaps psychologically threatening, to remember that we humans have been speaking creatures for the longest part of our history. While *homo sapiens* has been in existence for roughly 50,000 years, the earliest scripts date from only about 6,000 years ago (Ong 1982:2). With our attention fixed on texts and increasingly on computerized hypertexts and hypermedia, we have to struggle mightily to understand a culture—our own Western legacy—that did not live under the spell of literate and high technological standards of communication. To reimagine the Homeric culture demands that we divest ourselves of preconceptions that are based on our page-turning experiences with written/printed words. Communication in Homer's time was constituted neither by chirographic/typographic signs nor by electronic light, but predominantly by verbalized sound. The Homeric epics, our first records of Greek literary activity, made their appearance in metered language of stunning perfection. This metrical organization of the hexameter, along with formulae and formulaic expressions, alliterations and assonances, redundancies, epithets, and paratactic syntax, attests oral processes operating in conformity with sounded language. A whole cultural apparatus of oral performers and oral composition, remembering, and recitation shares responsibility for enacting the epic tradition. Thought in this tradition was processed in the form of narrative, albeit a narrative that proceeded less along sequential lines and more by associational webs and cumulative effects, and also by persistent ties to tradition's referential matrix. Built on metrical rhythms, the epic narratives also followed thematic conventions. Heroic figures were preferred types, while action was assigned mnemonic advantage over reflection, and warfare over peace. The curators of the Homeric tradition preserved the tradition by enacting it. Theirs was a "cold" culture that shied away from creative departures. This was precisely a point to which Plato raised implacable objections.

Availing itself of the chirographic medium, the *rhetorica docens* began taking stock of the medium of orality, with a view toward rendering assistance to the *rhetorica utens*. Discourse on language was alive and well in ancient rhetoric. Deliberations on the qualification of speakers, the nature of speech, and the art of speaking were every bit as intense and sophisticated as our contemporary discussions on literary theory. In reviewing and revising the ancient oral legacy, the *rhetorica docens* exhibited scrupulous exactness in making distinctions and in focusing on linguistic minutiae. It was driven by an ardent, not to say excessive, devotion to definitional clarity. Speech was divided into deliberative, judicial, and epideictic types, or classified as political, funeral, ceremonial, ambassadorial, and many other kinds of discourse. As to the issues raised, there simply seemed no end to them. What was the relation between virtue and oratory? Can an evil man be a good orator? How did the organization of words affect the implementation of power? What were the differences and proper uses of *encomium*, hymn, and complimentary address? How were individual talent and artistic skill balanced in the writing of good literature? What were the nuances of emotions that caused audiences to change their minds? Was rhetorical style appropriately characterized by balance and symmetry, or by swiftness and impetuousness, or a mixture of both? How did control of breath, modulation of voice, and rhythmical cadences collaborate in the production of persuasive speech? If there was one premise underlying rhetoric's critical theory it was the Ciceronian dictum that the standards of nature were different from those of art (*De Ora.* 3.182). There was little benefit to be derived from words themselves unless they were scrupulously selected and arranged, carefully sounded and enunciated, with a view always toward their efficaciousness.

Rhetoric deeply reflected on the human sensorium and the relation between speech, thought, and the senses. In this regard, our preferred concept of orality and rhetoric as an aesthetic of aurality, uniquely based on the qualities of sound, is in need of revision. While the oral phenomenology of sound, speech, and hearing is not in question, seeing and imaging are essential to oral, rhetorical aesthetics as well. As regards the visual semiotics, a distinction is in order between external visualism and internal visualization. Visualism relies on and benefits from the chirographic presence of language. Visually projected language, while initially operating in an oral field of apperception, will increasingly banish the *interiority of sound* and promote the virtues of readerly silence and reflectiveness. Visualization, it is clearly shown in rhetoric, was inherent in ancient orality. Speech was the medium that also enabled the *interiority of sight* of realities once exterior to the mind. There is a vast body of ancient rhetorical literature dealing with the relation between imaging and cognition (King). To be sure, there is a distinct philosophical proclivity in Plato to disembody thought from all sense perception, hearing and seeing alike. But the rhetorical tradition consistently promoted the refinement and expansion of our sensibilities toward the wider range of a physiology of perception. A large part of ancient language embodied not only principles of oral efficaciousness, but strategies of visualization as well. To no small degree, understanding words, oral and written alike, was mediated by the formation and (re)collection of internal images. It was a way of gaining "insight" into actuality.

The concept of *sola scriptura* whereby (biblical) chirographs could be thought of as standing self-referentially on their own is unthinkable in the ancient world. Nor is ancient hermeneutics overtly friendly toward the historical creed that each text has a date and belongs to this or that period. These are developments that presume and thrive on what Hugh Kenner has referred to as the "stunned neutrality of print" (44). In antiquity, dictation, writing, and reading/hearing took place as interactive transfer of words in a pliable semantic environment. This is why texts unapologetically partook of other writings, and not only writings, but of allusions, faint echoes, and subliminal recollections as well. In producing manuscripts, dictators of texts also plugged into their memories, these interior storehouses, which processed words, images, textual echoes, and emotions alike.

In the fluid semantic environment of antiquity, media interfaces, transits, and tensions are the rule. From the perspective of media studies, a focus on these interactive forces promises to be one of the more productive modes of reading ancient texts. Philo and Augustine served as examples of an aesthetic of perception that, while conditioned in depth by chirographic proclivities, has retained discernible oral, rhetorical sensibilities. There exist countless interdependencies of oral-scribal dynamics and countless combinatory possibilities of visual and oral sensations. More often than not, these are dynamics not readily accessible on the surface of texts. Discernment of media constructions, perceptual orientations, and competing symbolizations of cognition will require strenuously focused attention. In some instances, the media preferences or anxieties are plainly on the surface, be it in terms of advocacy of oral values, the subversion of oral authorities, or lamentation over the detrimental effects of writing. In all instances, attention to the modalities of communication and physiology of perception will be a rewarding task that can liberate us from our historical, ideational reading that has banished the senses from cognition.

Thinking about orality, rhetoric, and scribality in ancient Western culture, we discern language in the flux of communications history, proving itself adaptable to new cultural and technological demands, and capable of sustaining mutations in form and in function. It is from this perspective increasingly difficult to ontologize language with a single sense of theological ultimacy or to arrest its movement in an assumed originary meaning.

Works Consulted

Ancient Works

Alcidamas
    fl. ca. 425 BCE
        "Concerning Those Who Write Speeches" (*Peri ton tous graptous logous graphonton*). Pp. 38-42 in *Readings from Classical Rhetoric*. Ed. Patricia P. Matsen, Philip Rollinson, and Marion Sousa. Carbondale and Edwardsville: Southern Illinois University Press, 1990.

Anonymous
        Ad Herennium. Trans. H. Caplan. LCL. Cambridge: Harvard University Press, 1954.

Aristotle
    fl. 384-322 BCE
        The Art of Rhetoric. Trans. H. C. Lawson-Tancred. London: Penguin Books, 1991.

Augustine
    ca. 389 CE
        S. Aureli Augustini Confessionum. Ed. Martin Skutella. Stuttgart: Teubner, 1981.
    ca. 401 CE
        De Magistro. Pp. 157-203 in *Corpus Christianorum, Series Latina* XXIX, Pars II, 2. Tvrnholti: Typographi Brepols Editores Pontificii, 1970.
    ca. 400-416 CE
        The Trinity (*De Trinitate*). Trans. Stephen McKenna. FC 45. Washington: Catholic University Press, 1962.
    ca. 426 CE
        On Christian Doctrine (*De Doctrina Christiana*). Trans. D. W. Robertson, Jr. The Library of Liberal Arts. New York and London: Macmillan, 1958.

Cicero
    ca. 55 BCE
        De Oratore. Books I, II. Trans. E .W. Sutton. Cambridge: Harvard University Press, 1977. *De Oratore*. Book III. Trans. H. Rackham. Cambridge: Harvard University Press, 1977.

Homer
    fl. 8th century BCE
        The Iliad of Homer. Trans. Richmond Lattimore. Chicago and London: University of Chicago Press, 1951.

Isocrates
    ca. 436-338 BCE

"Antidosis." Pp. 47-57 in *Readings from Classical Rhetoric*. Ed. Patricia P. Matsen, Philip Rollinson, and Marion Sousa. Carbondale and Edwardsville: Southern Illinois University Press, 1990.

"To Philip." Pp. 246-339 in LCL, Vol. I. Trans. George Norlin. London: Heinemann/New York: Putnam's, 1928.

Philo
   born ca. 20 BCE

On Drunkenness (De Ebrietate). Pp. 318-435 in LCL, Vol. III. Trans. F. H. Colson and G. H. Whitaker. London: Heinemann/New York: Putnam's, 1930.

On the Confusion of Tongues (De Confusione Linguarum). Pp. 8-119 in LCL, Vol. IV. Trans. F. H. Colson and G. H. Whitaker. London: Heinemann/New York: Putnam's, 1932.

On Abraham (De Abrahamo). Pp. 4-135 in LCL, Vol. VI. Trans. F. H. Colson. London: Heinemann/New York: Putnam's, 1935.

On Moses (De Vita Mosis). Pp. 276-595 in LCL, Vol. VI. Trans. F. H. Colson. London: Heinemann/New York: Putnam's, 1935.

Plato
   fl. 427-347 BCE

The Collected Dialogues. Trans. Edith Hamilton and Huntington Cairns. Bollingen Series LXXI. Princeton: Princeton University Press, 1961.

Quintilianus, Marcus Fabius
   fl. ca. 35-95 CE

"Institutio Oratoria." Pp. 210-36 in *Readings from Classical Rhetoric* . Ed. Patricia P. Matsen, Philip Rollinson, and Marion Sousa. Carbondale and Edwardsville: Southern Illinois University Press, 1990.

Contemporary Works

Achtemeier, Paul J.
   1990   "*Omne verbum sonat*: The New Testament and the Oral Environment of Late Western Antiquity." *JBL* 109: 3-27.

Balogh, Josef
   1926   "Voces Paginarum." *Philologus* 82: 84-109, 202-40.

Blum, Herwig
   1969   *Die antike Mnemotechnik*. Hildesheim: Georg Olms.

Chidester, David
   1992   *Word and Light: Seeing, Hearing, and Religious Discourse*. Urbana and Chicago: University of Illinois Press.

Cole, Thomas
   1991   *The Origins of Rhetoric in Ancient Greece*. Baltimore and London: Johns Hopkins University Press.

Crem, Theresa M.
1974   "The Definition of Rhetoric According to Aristotle." Pp. 52-71 in *Aristotle: The Classical Heritage*. Ed. Keith V. Erickson. Metuchen: Scarecrow.

Foley, John Miles, ed.
1985   *Comparative Research On Oral Traditions: A Memorial for Milman Parry*. Columbus: Slavica.

Foley, John Miles
1990   *Traditional Oral Epic: The Odyssey, Beowulf, and the Serbo-Croatian Return Song*. Berkeley: University of California Press.
1991   *Immanent Art: From Structure to Meaning in Traditional Oral Epic*. Bloomington and Indianapolis: Indiana University Press.

Goody, Jack
1977   *The Domestication of the Savage Mind*. Cambridge: Cambridge University Press.

Graham, William A.
1987   *Beyond the Written Word: Oral Aspects of Scripture in the History of Religion*. Cambridge: Cambridge University Press.

Green, William Chase
1951   "The Spoken and the Written Word." *Harvard Studies in Classical Philology* 60: 23-60.

Gronbeck, Bruce E.
1991   "The Rhetorical Studies Tradition and Walter J. Ong: Oral-Literacy Theories of Mediation, Culture, and Consciousness." Pp. 5-24 in *Media, Consciousness, and Culture: Explorations of Walter Ong's Thought*. Ed. Bruce E. Gronbeck, Thomas J. Farrell, Paul A. Soukup. Newbury Park: Sage.

Havelock, Eric A.
1963   *Preface to Plato*. Cambridge: Harvard University Press.
1978   *The Greek Concept of Justice: From Its Shadow in Homer to Its Substance in Plato*. Cambridge: Harvard University Press.
1982   *The Literate Revolution in Greece and Its Cultural Consequences*. Princeton: Princeton University Press.

Jebb, Richard Claverhouse
1911   "Rhetoric." *Encyclopaedia Britannica*, 11th ed, Vol. 23: 233-37.

Kennedy, George A.
1980   *Classical Rhetoric and Its Christian and Secular Tradition from Ancient to Modern Times*. Chapel Hill: University of North Carolina Press.

Kenner, Hugh
1962   *Flaubert, Joyce, and Beckett: The Stoic Comedians*. Boston: Beacon.

King, Nathalia
1991   "The Mind's Eye and the Forms of Thought: Classical Rhetoric and the Composition of Augustine's *Confessions*." Ph. D. diss. New York University.

Lloyd-Jones, Hugh
- 1992 "Becoming Homer." *The New York Review of Books* XXXIX, 5: 52-56.

Lord, Albert Bates
- 1960 *The Singer of Tales. Harvard Studies in Comparative Literature*, 24. Cambridge: Harvard University Press; rpt. New York: Atheneum, 1968.
- 1991 *Epic Singers and Oral Tradition*. Ithaca and London: Cornell University Press.

Ong, Walter J.
- 1967 *The Presence of the Word: Some Prolegomena for Cultural and Religious History*. New Haven and London: Yale University; rpt. Minneapolis: University of Minnesota Press, 1981.
- 1977 *Interfaces of the Word: Studies in the Evolution of Consciousness and Culture*. Ithaca and London: Cornell University Press.
- 1982 *Orality and Literacy: The Technologizing of the Word*. London and New York: Methuen.
- 1983 "Foreword." Pp. 1-9 in *The Present State of Scholarship in Historical and Contemporary Rhetoric*. Ed. Winifred Bryan Horner. Columbia and London: University of Missouri Press.

Padel, Ruth
- 1991 *In and Out of the Mind: Greek Images of the Tragic Self*. Princeton: Princeton University Press.

Parry, Milman
- 1930 "Studies in the Epic Technique of Oral Verse-Making. I. Homer and Homeric Style." *Harvard Studies in Classical Philology* 41: 73-147.
- 1932 "Studies in the Epic Technique of Oral Verse-Making. II. The Homeric Language as the Language of an Oral Poetry." *Harvard Studies in Classical Philology* 43: 1-50.
- 1933 "Whole Formulaic Verses in Greek and Southslavic Heroic Songs." *Transactions of the American Philological Association* 64: 179-97.

Saenger, Paul
- 1982 "Silent Reading: Its Impact on Late Medieval Script and Society." *Viator* 13: 367-414.

Sloane, Thomas O.
- 1987 "Rhetoric." *The New Encyclopaedia Britannica*, 15th ed, Vol. 26: 803-8.

Tyler, Stephen A.
- 1986 "On Being Out of Words." *Cultural Anthropology* 1:131-37.

Vickers, Brian
- 1988 *In Defense of Rhetoric*. Oxford: Clarendon.

Wolf, Friedrich August
- 1985 *Prolegomena to Homer*. Trans. A. Grafton, G. W. Most, and J. E. G. Zetzel. Princeton: Princeton University Press; original publication date: 1795.

Yates, Frances A.
- 1966 *The Art of Memory*. Chicago: University of Chicago Press.

www.ingramcontent.com/pod-product-compliance
Lightning Source LLC
Chambersburg PA
CBHW032251150426
43195CB00008BA/410